Paranormal Media

The paranormal has gone mainstream.

Beliefs are on the rise, with almost half of the British population, and two-thirds of Americans, claiming to believe in extrasensory perceptions and hauntings. Psychic magazines like *Spirit and Destiny*, television shows such as *Fringe*, *Ghost Whisperer* and *Most Haunted*, ghost-cams and e-poltergeists, bestselling books on mind, body and spirit, and magicians like Derren Brown have moved from the outer limits to the centre of popular culture, turning paranormal beliefs and scepticism into revenue streams.

Paranormal Media offers a unique, timely exploration of the extraordinary, unexplained and supernatural in popular culture, looking in unusual places in order to understand this phenomenon. Early spirit forms such as magic lantern shows or the spirit photograph are re-imagined as a search for extraordinary experiences in reality TV, ghost tourism, and live shows. Through a popular cultural ethnography, and critical analysis in social and cultural theory, this ground-breaking book by Annette Hill presents an original and rigorous examination of people's experiences of spirits and magic. In popular culture, people are players in an orchestral movement about what happens to us when we die. In a very real sense the audience is the show. This book is the story of audiences and their participation in a show about matters of life and death.

Paranormal Media will be a highly interesting read for undergraduate and postgraduate students, as well as academics, on a wide range of television, media, cultural studies, and sociology courses.

Annette Hill is Professor of Media at the Communication and Media Research Institute, University of Westminster, UK. She has authored numerous books and articles on television and popular culture, including *Restyling Factual Television* (2007) and *Reality TV* (2005).

Paranormal Media

Audiences, spirits and magic in
popular culture

Annette Hill

Routledge
Taylor & Francis Group

LONDON AND NEW YORK

First published 2011
by Routledge
2 Park Square, Milton Park, Abingdon, Oxon OX14 4RN

Simultaneously published in the USA and Canada
by Routledge
270 Madison Ave, New York, NY 10016

Routledge is an imprint of the Taylor & Francis Group, an informa business

© 2011 Annette Hill

The right of Annette Hill to be identified as author of this work has been
asserted by her in accordance with sections 77 and 78 of the Copyright,
Designs and Patents Act 1988.

Typeset in Galliard by
Taylor & Francis Books
Printed and bound in Great Britain by
CPI Antony Rowe, Chippenham, Wiltshire

British Library Cataloguing in Publication Data
A catalogue record for this book is available from the British Library

Library of Congress Cataloging in Publication Data
A catalog record for this book has been requested

ISBN10: 0-415-54462-9 (hbk)
ISBN10: 0-415-54463-7 (pbk)
ISBN10: 0-203-83639-1 (ebk)

ISBN13: 978-0-415-54462-7 (hbk)
ISBN13: 978-0-415-54463-4 (pbk)
ISBN13: 978-0-203-83639-2 (ebk)

For my husband Peter, an angel sent from heaven.

And to my family and friends, an angel choir which fills my heart with happiness.

Contents

Figures

Acknowledgements

The idea for this research on the paranormal in popular culture came from watching *Most Haunted Live* at Halloween, and so I must thank Richard Woolfe for commissioning the series and for speaking to me about it with such insight. Over the course of the project and completion of the book colleagues and friends have helped me with ideas and suggestions. My special thanks to Ian Calcutt, Gary Carter, John Ellis, Steve Griffiths, Julie Donovan and Richard Wiseman, for chatting with me about the topic. Much appreciation to Etzel Cardeña, Peter Dahlgren, Chris French, David Gauntlett, David Hendy, Peter Lamont, Peter Lunt, and Peter Ullgren for taking the time to read draft chapters and offering excellent suggestions for improving the manuscript. Above all, John Corner offered incisive comments on the whole manuscript and I owe him a great big thank you. Special thanks also to Gareth Ellis Thomas, Pauline Hill and Marian Jones for helping me with the photographs and appearing in them. The team at Routledge, and in particular Natalie Foster and Emily Laughton, have done a great job in seeing this book to publication.

For the research itself, my first thanks go to colleagues in CAMRI at the University of Westminster, in particular Sally Feldman, Colin Sparks and Peter Goodwin, for supporting my research and giving me a sabbatical to complete the book. I also thank colleagues at the media department at Lund University for all their encouragement during my Visiting Professorship with them. My two research assistants Dr Lizzie Jackson and Dr Koko Kondo were invaluable. I could not have done the work without their help in the recruitment, organisation and transcription of the fieldwork data. Thank you very much for all your hard work and great ideas. Those people who agreed to be interviewed about their views on paranormal matters in groups and on their own inspired me to understand this subject from as many perspectives as possible. Many thanks to the editor of One Eye Grey for their insights into folklore in London, to P.I.G.S. for inviting us to be a part of their investigations, and to the participants at the event at Pevesney Castle. London Paranormal gave us a warm welcome and were so open to this research that special thanks must go to the team and the participants on events. Ian Shillito in particular made a positive impact on my understanding of paranormal matters. Thank you so much for all your help.

Annette Hill
June 2010

Picture acknowledgements

Figure 2.1: Engraving 'Pelardekorationen vid Ulrika Eleanoras' reproduced in Sigurd Wallin *Kyrkoinredning för Herremän*, Aktiebolaget Sloglunds Bokförlag (Stockholm, 1948).

Figure 5.1: Advertisement for London Paranormal, used with permission of Ian Shillito.

Figure 7.1: Stage show advertisement *An Evening of Wonders*, poster designed by Kerry Donovan and reproduced with kind permission by Michael Vine Associates and the photographer, Gary Moyes.

Figure 8.1: 'An Audience with Derren Brown', photograph courtesy of Derren Brown.

Figure 9.1: Photograph of London Dungeon, courtesy of the photographer, Lizzie Jackson.

All other photographs by the author.

Chapter 1

Ordinary and extraordinary

'It's a phenomenon we don't understand.'

On a freezing cold day in January I bought two psychic magazines. *Spirit and Destiny* 'for women who want the best possible future' and *Soul and Spirit* with special offer 'angel advice cards'. I was shopping with my sisters at a supermarket in a small town in Wales. There on the rack alongside *Cosmopolitan* were magazines with psychic predictions, spiritual makeovers, interviews with celebrity mediums, articles by mystics and witches, offering 'words of wisdom from our leading gurus.' There next to the TV, celebrity gossip and puzzle books were *Take a Break* and its sister magazine *Fate and Fortune*, 'Britain's best loved mystic magazine.' Not long ago these magazines, with their free pagan wall charts, crystals, and affirmation cards, would have been available in occult bookstores, or alternative therapy centres. Now, the paranormal is mainstream – you can buy it with your milk, bread and eggs.

There is a paranormal turn in popular culture. Beliefs are on the rise in contemporary Western societies. Almost half of the British population, and two-thirds of American people, claim to believe in some form of the paranormal, such as extrasensory perception, hauntings and witchcraft. Entertainment, leisure and tourism industries have turned paranormal beliefs into revenue streams. From television drama series such as *Fringe*, reality TV *Most Haunted*, to ghost tourism, paranormal ideas offer new twists on 'things that go bump in the night.' The paranormal in popular culture is distinct from research into the scientifically inexplicable. It is paranormal matters purposely shaped within an entertainment and communication environment. There is a historical tradition to spirit forms, such as magic lantern shows, phantasmagoria, the spirit telegraph and photograph. Fascination with the dead, a desire to see the unique, and a search for unusual experiences, suggest a strong narrative of spirits and magic in society. Paranormal matters show culture is both ordinary and extraordinary.

A sociology of the paranormal in popular culture suggests how people create extraordinary entertainment and communication experiences. One ghost hunting events organiser said ninety nine per cent of what happens on an all night ghost

Figure 1.1 Psychic shopping

hunt is not paranormal at all. And yet many people are searching for a 'disquieting experience' about death and the terror of death. They are looking for experiences that provide evidence of paranormal and afterlife beliefs. As one person put it 'people produce beliefs.' The paranormal as it is experienced within popular culture involves seeing an audience not as spectators or viewers but as participants. People co-perform and co-produce their individual and collective experiences. In a very real sense the audience is the show. Without them there would be no paranormal turn in popular culture. This book is the story of audiences and their participation in a show about matters of life and death.

Paranormal in popular culture

In an interview in *People* magazine Tom Murdic explained how he lived with ghosts. His haunted house is built on the site of a Confederate army camp. It is common for him to see a child spirit walk across the kitchen and disappear into the dishwasher. 'As long as he doesn't run up the electric bill', said Murdic, 'the little guy can stay.'[1] According to Murdic, spirits are 'those anomalies that we just don't quite understand.' Spirits are part of paranormal phenomena, a term commonly used by people to encompass a variety of extraordinary experiences or events, such as hauntings and telepathy, angels and aliens. One person in this study described the paranormal as 'things we don't know, or can't explain' (37-year-old

Figure 1.2 Ordinary and extraordinary

female administrator). It is a word that means the inexplicable: 'I don't want to say this is what it is because I don't know' (25-year-old male student). When people describe paranormal phenomena they say 'you have to feel it to know it':

> You know, when you sense things are going to happen to you. Like you are driving a car and you stop, and you don't know why you stopped until you realise you could have been killed.
>
> (32-year-old male carpenter)

Paranormal matters are when something extraordinary happens in what we like to think of as our ordinary lives: 'it's everyday experience. I always say something different happens everyday ... that's how I look at anyway. You just live it everyday' (45-year-old female care worker).

The phrase 'something different happens everyday' encapsulates the irreducible complexity of the paranormal in popular culture. For Raymond Williams, culture is ordinary (1958, reprint 2001). He writes about culture as 'the ordinary processes of human societies and human minds.' The nature of a culture 'is always both traditional and creative; that it is both ordinary common meanings and the finest individual meanings' (11). This book is about how culture is both ordinary and extraordinary. The nature of the paranormal in popular culture is to be both at the same time, however strange that maybe. How can we know what is ordinary without understanding the extraordinary? What is normal in culture if we have no sense of the paranormal? In her novel *Beyond Black* about a medium working in the broken communities of Britain Hilary Mantel writes: 'there are things you need to know about the dead ... Things you really ought to know' (2006: 193). In this book the voices of people populate the research at every stage, helping us understand the things we really ought to know. Their experiences suggest there are things we need to know about ordinary common meanings and the finest of individual meanings of paranormal beliefs and ideas. There are no easy explanations, only the voices of people and their search for understanding the truth of life and death as they see it. This book follows the process of people's experiences rather than end results. It asks the reader to be a part of this process: 'you start out, you start talking, you don't know what you are going to say. You don't even know your way to the end of the sentence. Then suddenly you do know' (Mantel 2006: 262).

Different definitions of the paranormal within research indicate a problem of clarity and agreed understanding about this phenomenon. Paranormal beliefs can mean 'phenomena that are scientifically inexplicable' (Irwin 2009: 14). These are beliefs 'generated within the non scientific community and extensively endorsed by people who might normally be expected by their society to be capable of rational thought and reality testing' (2009: 16). Goode defines the paranormal as 'the non scientific approach to a scientifically implausible event believed to be literally true' (1999: 31). The Parapsychological Association uses the term psi to refer to experiences that:

> seem to challenge contemporary conceptions of human nature and of the physical world. They appear to involve the transfer of information and the influence of physical systems independently of time and space, via mechanisms we cannot currently explain.[2]

Psi includes experiences such as telepathy, clairvoyance, remote viewing, psychokinesis, psychic healing, and precognition.

In psychology the term anomalous experience means 'an uncommon experience, or one that, although it may be experienced by a substantial amount of the population is believed to deviate from ordinary experience, or from the usually accepted explanations of reality' (Cardeña et al 2000: 4). It is this understanding that is closest to what participants in this study believe to be paranormal. Self-definition has its own problems in audience research because what participants know as paranormal is both a product of their own internal understanding and shaped by external factors in media, culture and society. An extraordinary experience, as understood by participants, is also culturally specific to a Western context where notions of the self, identity and personality are understood as separate entities. Etzel Cardeña (2010: 6) argues 'because cultures determine the ideal and normative definitions of the self' definitions of anomalous experiences are partly predicated on how unusual that experience is perceived to be.

Most participants understand their experiences and those of others within a dominant narrative of selfhood in Western culture. Paranormal ideas, writings and practices offer alternative narratives which include the existence of life after death, other entities, and metaphysical matters. As Cardeña (2010: 20) notes 'cultures and subcultures provide ideologies and techniques to attempt to explain and bring into control gaps and inconsistencies in experience.' Dreams, dance music, hypnotic suggestion, carnivals, role playing and participation in rituals are just some examples of uncommon experiences within everyday life.

As this is a study of the paranormal in popular culture what is understood as an extraordinary experience is framed by a narrative of performance and production, entertainment and information. Indeed, what is understood as paranormal is open to debate. Media representations and cultural practices associated with paranormal beliefs and ideas change the meaning of the term as it is articulated in an entertainment and communication context. In this way, practices in Western societies attempt to explain and bring into control gaps and inconsistencies in cultural and media experiences as much as uncommon experiences in everyday life. When audiences engage with paranormal matters they are aware of the cultural and social context within which their experiences take place. Performance and participation are part of their narratives. The frames of reference change from a psychological understanding of anomalous experience to sociological and cultural contexts.

Patrick McGrath wrote about the experience of living in New York City in *Ghost Town: Tales of Manhattan Then and Now* (2005). Three stories are set in the past and present of a city marked by violence, war and trauma. 'The Year of the Gibbet' tells the tale of a man living during the American War of Independence and the occupation of New York by British troops. He is haunted by memories of his revolutionary mother and his inadvertent role as a young boy in her death by hanging. His story starts during a contagion: 'I have been in the town, a disquieting experience, for New York has become a place not so much of death as the terror of death' (2005: 1). In the third tale, a psychiatrist treats a patient after the attacks on the World Trade Centre, unable to see her own damaged self. She walks through the destruction of Ground Zero: 'as I thread my way along narrow streets that once lay obscured in the shadow of the towers, new perspectives are suddenly apparent' (239). A 'disquieting experience' in the shadow of death can be a process that leads to 'new perspectives.' For McGrath, these perspectives are multilayered, with psychological, social, emotional, physical, spatial meanings: the 'gothic remnant of the south tower' stands 'five stories high' and 'beyond it, from high pipes, water pours ceaselessly into the ruins, where subterranean fires still burn, and smoke lazily drifts up among the tilting cranes into a cloudless October sky' (ibid).

The idea of a disquieting experience is explored in the research throughout the book. There are a number of ways the paranormal in popular culture offers people a disquieting experience. There are spirit forms from the past re-imagined in contemporary contexts. Fears of death and dying are re-interpreted as positive hopes for life after death and relationships with the dead. Paranormal activities are re-invented as reality formats, films and events that ask a never-ending series of questions about evidence. In magazines and books the paranormal becomes a feature of personal empowerment and lifestyle choices. A resurgence in scepticism questions paranormal claims and encourages rational thinking. The popularity of magic as psychological entertainment suggests ambiguous associations with reality and illusion. Aesthetic forms open up debate about paranormal ideas. One woman described paranormal media as 'opening doors.' Paranormal ideas are part of a broader series of questions about identities, feelings and beliefs.

Disquieting experiences change the terms of reference from anomalous experiences in psychology to cultural experiences in media. It relates to the things 'you really ought to know' about death and the terror of death which can only come from the process of experience – 'then suddenly you do know' (Mantel 2006). Disquieting experiences are about being in the moment and then reflecting on your perspective of the world. People can play out their feelings, emotions, sensations, working through what they know and don't know, in a relatively safe environment. These are cultural practices about death that make people feel very much alive. Disquieting experiences are also purposely shaped within media environments. People's questions, curiosities, and beliefs are turned into revenue streams for cultural industries. As audiences, consumers and users, people know they have a role to play in this process. These are disquieting experiences in a media age.

Social and cultural trends

According to anomalous psychologist Chris French 'the truth is most people do believe in the paranormal and a sizeable minority claim to have direct personal experience' (Waterhouse 2008: 8). Watt and Wiseman write:

> Paranormal beliefs are widely held in the population: around the world surveys consistently show that about fifty per cent of people hold one or more paranormal beliefs, and of these, about fifty per cent believe they have had a genuinely paranormal experience. Regardless of whether these beliefs and experiences are 'correct', they are clearly an important part of what it is to be human.
>
> (2009: viii)

Surveys refer to a range of beliefs, from extrasensory perception, or the power of prayer, to survival of the soul after death, or intelligent alien life forms (Watt and Wiseman 2009: vii). Sometimes these beliefs cluster together around a set of specific attitudes and practices related to extrasensory perception, or the existence of afterlife. Other times these beliefs are at odds with each other, so someone can be sceptical of the survival of the soul after death, but believe in intelligent alien life forms. When people believe in the paranormal this does not mean to say they believe in the same paranormal phenomena.

The Gallup survey (June 2005) found three in four Americans to believe in the paranormal.[3] They asked people about their belief in ten paranormal claims, such as extrasensory perception (top of the list at 41 per cent), haunted houses (coming in second at 37 per cent), to reincarnation (20 per cent). Seventy-three per cent of Americans believed in at least one paranormal claim. This figure was similar to a survey conducted by Gallup in 2001. Fifty-five per cent claimed they believed in 'psychic or spiritual healing, or the power of the human mind to heal the body'.[4] The National Science Foundation reported around 40 per cent of Americans used alternative therapies in the 1990s, showing a 50 per cent increase over five years in expenditures totalling $27 billion.[5] A study by the World Values Survey (2008), an organisation which has been compiling data from 350,000 people in 97 countries since 1981, found belief in life after death on the rise worldwide. Eight-one per cent of American respondents and 58 per cent of British respondents believed in some form of afterlife.[6]

Resurgence in paranormal beliefs gives momentum to representations of ghosts, supernaturalism, angels, and fringe science, across multimedia environments. Ghostly drama and TV psychics are part of daily programming. *People* magazine wrote: 'what is it with the dearly departed? Seems they're everywhere lately. Ghosts, ghouls and spirits are invading prime time (*Medium*, *Ghost Whisperer*, *Supernatural*) and buying second yachts for pop psychics like John Edward.'[7] These American dramas are selling well worldwide both in TV/DVD form, and also as webisodes, role playing games and comic books. A related trend is television drama about altered states and fringe science, such as extrasensory perception, or time travel. Top ten TV shows on American networks include characters with paranormal powers, such as *Heroes* (NBC, USA) about extra-ordinary people, or *Flash Forward* (ABC, USA) about a group of people who collectively experience a glimpse of their future while they are unconscious. *Fringe* is created by J J Abrams who also produced supernatural drama *Lost* (Fox Network, USA) and follows a special FBI team and their investigations into phenomena outside of mainstream science, such as telepathy or altered states of consciousness.

USA Today claimed the oddest trend of 2008 was dating the dead: 'from the chaste non-coupling of *Pushing Daisies* to the down-and-dirty sexiness of *True Blood* ... love with the living-challenged is a hot topic ... [8] Paranormal romance is in the bestseller charts with vampire TV and book series *True Blood* (Charlaine Harris, HBO, USA), or the *Twilight* saga. Stephanie Meyers' *Twilight* novels have sold 85 million copies worldwide to date. Her books have spent over 200 days on the *New York Times* bestseller lists; the first movie of the series made $350 million in 2008. The town where the novels are based is a tourist destination for *Twilight* fans, with vampire-themed restaurants, jewellery, and local tours. Not since J K Rowling's *Harry Potter* series has an author attracted such worldwide interest for children's books that cross over into an adult market.

Meyers' editor Megan Tingley at Little, Brown commented on the *Twilight* phenomena: 'we were outside Philly at a suburban Barnes & Noble. The kids had been cutting school to get these tickets and waiting in line forever. When Stephanie came out, these girls next to me started trembling and crying and grabbing each other. It was crazy ... it was like the newsreels of the Beatles or Elvis.'[9]

The revival of Victorian gothic is part of this fascination with the dead. In Catherine Spooner's cultural analysis of contemporary gothic, from music, art and literature, to film and fashion, she argues this gothic revival is self-referential, a mock gothic for metropolitan audiences (2006). As a case study she refers to the Body Worlds exhibition, a modern take on the early waxworks exhibitions after the French Revolution which used death masks to fashion lifelike waxen figures. In von Hagen's Body Worlds modern techniques allow for the use of real bodies and this spectacle of the dead has attracted 17 million tourists to date (Sassoon 2006: 1366). Spooner also sees the return of the gothic as a reflection on the trauma of 9/11. The film *Batman Begins* (Christopher Nolan 2005) is a gothic action movie which blurs the boundaries between heroism and terrorism. In 2008, *The Dark Knight* (the second film by Christopher Nolan in his Batman series) also could be seen as a social critique on violence and a memorial to the dead. Tragically, the film was the last actor Heath Ledger made before his death – he played the character of The Joker. The film had the biggest opening day of all time, grossing over $67 million. Alleged reports of his ghost appearing to people started soon after his death. In an interview with *People* magazine, spirit communicator James Van Praagh claimed: 'I was shaving and all of a sudden I see his face in the back of my mirror ... A thought comes from him immediately: "I f—up." Then he thought about his daughter. Then he was gone.'[10]

The *Observer* newspaper commented: 'everybody believes in ghosts these days. Well, everybody who owns a production company anyway.'[11] Reality ghost hunting TV such as *Most Haunted* (Living, UK) has spawned many other shows, including *Ghost Hunters* (Sci Fi Channel, USA), *Paranormal State* (A&E, USA), *Psychic Detectives* (Court TV, Canada), *Haunting Evidence* (Court TV, USA), *Living with the Dead* (Living, UK), *Psychic Investigators* (ABC, Australian), *The One: The Search for Australia's Most Gifted Psychic* (Channel Seven), and celebrity *Ghost Hunting With ...* (ITV, UK), all of which are successful in the international marketplace. The film *Paranormal Activity* (2007, Oren Peli) is a dramatised account of the director's personal experience of a haunting, shot with hand held digital cameras. It echoes *Blair Witch Project* (1999, Daniel Myrick and Eduardo Sánchez) which was a mock documentary about a group of young people searching for evidence of a witch legend. This previous film used hand held cameras, and night vision shots, to give the appearance of an on scene, as it happens investigation. The film was one of the highest grossing of all time, given its cheap budget. *Paranormal Activity* has had similar box office success, making it the most profitable independent film to date. It relies on the appearance of 'found footage' and night time digital recordings which attempt to capture evidence of haunting phenomena. '*Guardian* critic Peter Bradshaw hailed it as "ingenious and genuinely frightening". He added: "There were moments when I thought I would not just need to change my trousers, but have them professionally incinerated by a biohazard disposal team."'[12] The *Observer* film critic commented on an obsession with visual evidence of paranormal activities, suggesting 'as a document of a generation's refusal to believe anything unless it's on film, it's truly troubling.'[13]

According to *Business Week*, the ghost hunter kit is a 'lucrative business end of the paranormal.'[14] 'Onestopparanormalshop' sells starter ghost hunting kits (electro-magnetic field readers, motion sensors, night vision cameras, electronic voice listening devices). Web content regularly features examples of ghost investigations, often conducted by paranormal societies or amateur groups. 'Paranormal Database' contains thousands of online entries documenting hotspots. The International Ghost Hunters Society has members in 90 countries, and the Worldwide Paranormal Reporting Centre has hundreds of registered online groups. The online ghost hunting community 'ghostsamongus' hosts live ghostcams. You Tube offers tens of thousands of home made paranormal videos and Apple iTunes lists over one thousand paranormal podcasts. Other sites include a package of amateur footage, reports, blogs, and live chatting. 'Ghostvillage' has around 80,000 visitors each month (double that at Halloween), and 'I am haunted' has around 30,000 monthly visitors.[15]

An article in the *Guardian* newspaper on 'how Britain became a nation of ghost hunters' looked at 'a growing number of paranormal-themed experiences springing up around the country.'[16] There are around 2500 ghost hunting groups in Britain, compared to 150 a decade ago. Ghost walks, all night ghost hunting, weekend breaks in haunted places, these are just some of the experiences on offer to tourists. Businesses and communities compete for the title of 'most haunted', with lists for the most haunted pub, hotel, castle, village and city. Europe's Most Haunted city of York attracts four million annual visitors, with haunted historical buildings such as Theatre Royal and regular ghost walks.[17] The city of London thrives on ghost walks, talks and hunts. For example there is the London Ghost Festival where during Halloween people can visit 'London's most famous and infamous ghostly locations' and experience '100 per cent ghosts ... just plain old ghosts, ghosts and more ghosts.'[18] Or, there is London Ghost Week described as 'the event that Londoners have been dieing for.' Highlights from this 'include an all-night vigil in a Victorian school, séances at the sites of Ripper victims and an X-factor-style show to find London's Best Medium.'[19]

Marketing Week claims the paranormal can be one way of dealing with a credit crunch:

> Consumers will increasingly crave perspective and security from a widening range of sources; spiritualism, 'evidence' or astrology ... The search for more fundamental answers, which counterbalance materialist envy, is likely to be

heightened through the impending period of doubts and uncertainties ... Living TV, with its popular *Most Haunted* series and programmes featuring psychics, and Paul McKenna's rocketing book sales are perhaps tiny symptoms of a thirst for making sense of it all.[20]

Bel Mooney reviewed three books before Christmas 2008 on the credit crisis, including Hay House authors psychic Sylvia Browne and motivational speaker Wayne Dyer. Hay House was founded by self-help guru Louise Hay, author of the 1988 bestseller *You Can Heal Yourself* which has sold over 35 million copies worldwide. She asked: 'self-help books have been the publishing phenomenon of the past decade, but can all the power of me-centred, positive thought help us if the end of the world is nigh? ... It's certainly true that when people feel under threat they are more likely to crave "spiritual" solutions to all ills.'[21]

There is also a resurgence in scepticism. High-profile sceptics include the American magician James Randi who runs a foundation for investigating pseudo science. The Paranormal Challenge offers a million dollars to anyone who can prove their paranormal claims – no one has won the prize so far. The British magician Derren Brown specialises in mentalism, a form of magic that has the appearance of psychic powers. For example, his television event 'The Séance' (31 May 2004, Channel Four, UK) demonstrated how séance phenomena could be produced by people through the power of suggestion. Ben Goldacre's *Bad Science* (2008), and related newspaper column and website, critiques the reporting of science in the media. He offers tools for rational thinking and assessments of scientific claims in health and alternative medicine. The website badpsychics. com specialises in exposing the commercialisation and exploitation of paranormal beliefs. There are thousands of commercial websites and companies for professional services that offer premium rate chat lines, email and mobile text psychic consultations, tarot readings, and dream interpretations. Psychicrevenue.com promises 'millions of surfers are checking horoscopes, getting tarot readings and consulting with psychics on a daily basis. It's a PSYCHIC REVOLUTION! PROFIT now from this outstanding opportunity.' According to the Office of Fair Trading in Britain, research in 2007 'into the impact of mass marketed scams indicated that more that 170,000 consumers fell victim to clairvoyant scams every year, losing around £40 million.'[22]

Historical contexts

In *The Haunted: a Social History of Ghosts*, Owen Davies (2007) notes the continuance of ghost belief is a remarkable story over the last 500 years:

> Modern science's attempt to exorcise them has foundered, just like Reformation theology, Enlightenment philosophy and Victorian mass education in previous centuries. Whichever way you look at it, sociologically, psychologically, culturally, as long as people believe in ghosts they will continue

to exist. Neither science nor religion can exorcise beliefs generated by personal experience, and to be haunted by the dead would seem to be a part of the human condition.

(249)

A longstanding cultural fascination with representations of ghosts and phantasmagoria shows how paranormal issues are deeply embedded in the histories of entertainment and communication. Media technologies have been incorporated into the generation and maintenance of paranormal beliefs and stories from the early magic lantern shows, and phantasmagoria, to the invention of the telegraph and the spirit telegraph, the photograph and spirit photograph, the internet and e-poltergeists. The meaning of a medium, as Raymond Williams (1977) argues, is in its structural and relational properties in society and culture. The meaning of a medium, as Deborah Blum (2007) argues, is in its connection between spirits and the world of the living. It is no coincidence that both definitions of the word medium came into popular use in the nineteenth century within a context of a revolution in communications and the birth of modern spiritualism (Sconce 2000). What John Durham Peters (1999) calls the dark side of communication is also a story about how the sharing of ghost beliefs and stories appears to be part of the human condition.

The early histories of spirits in popular culture are similar to other marginal, subversive, or politically troubling entertainment practices. Robert C Allen in *Horrible Prettiness* (1991) examined the history of burlesque, and themes of inversion and sexuality in vaudeville and theatre. As burlesque operated at the margins of culture it was subversive, dominated by female entrepreneurs, and inverted normative assumptions about gender and identity through the playful performance of female/male sexuality. The 'spectacular female performer' raised troubling questions about female actors, the representation of femininity, and women in society (1991: 21). The history of burlesque points to the movement from show to show business. As burlesque became more mainstream it devolved to illicit sexual representations for the working classes, mainly managed by men. Allen argues the history of burlesque is one of irreducible complexity, where 'we can glimpse something of the larger complexities of the ways we construct meaning and pleasure from our engagements with cultural forms, and in the process, are constructed by them' (289).

In the early stages of the Victorian spiritualist movement in Britain and America psychics and mediums mainly worked in their homes, spiritualist churches, or private salons. Mediumship was the domain of women, with a few notable exceptions such as the first psychic Daniel Dunglas Home (Lamont 2006). Marina Warner notes:

> As sitters, monitors, stage managers, as well as mediums, women were ... highly imaginative in new methods of contacting spirits and achieving their own desires, for the most part unconsciously and in good faith.

These obviously included self expression and consolation, especially in social milieux of constriction and muteness … it seems that women who were themselves spirited were strongly attracted to Spiritualism, trance and telepathy: individuals at odds with Victorian domestic ideals.

(2006: 234)

As the movement grew, there were more opportunities for women from different social backgrounds and education to explore individuality 'outside prescribed borders' (ibid). The Boston housewife Mrs Piper was a subject of books and journal articles by the Society for Psychical Research. The Italian medium Eusaphia Palladino was a celebrity, touring Europe and America, creating controversy with her public séances and allegations of fraud (Blum 2007). Writers, artists, influential society women, were exploring the possibilities of spiritualism. As 'the quest for spirit spread into the high streets and public studios' (Warner 2006: 234), the borders between spiritualism, personal psychic practices, and professional products and services became increasingly blurred. The move from show to show business that characterised the industrialisation of theatre, photography and film, also occurred in the psychic professions. The job ghost showman was a legitimate title during this period, reflecting the numbers of traveling performers and theatre shows about ghosts. High-profile cases of fraud, such as the Mumler trial, indicated spiritualist practices were part of a growing business in spirit photography, mediumship, and ghost shows (Kaplan 2008). Trick ghost films made fun of ghost beliefs (Davies 2007).

The move from the margins to mainstream in paranormal beliefs and ideas in popular culture highlights the irreducible complexity of cultural forms and our engagement with them. Spirit communication was once an unorthodox religious practice within the modern spiritualist movement, but it quickly became part of entertainment and communications industries. Today paranormal matters invade primetime, TV psychics are celebrities, historical buildings are famously haunted, and magicians exploit paranormal beliefs. There are recurring themes then and now. These themes include the re-imagining of historical spirit forms or folk legends for contemporary times; the search for evidence through personal experience; mind, body and spirit practices that unite various paranormal beliefs as part of personal empowerment; and sceptics who encourage critical thinking on paranormal claims. What is different today is that paranormal beliefs, ideas and practices are less associated with religious thinking and more about lifestyle trends. There is a cycle of culture where new products, services and events connect with a never-ending search for unique, alternative and extraordinary experiences.

Researching the paranormal

This book offers a popular cultural ethnography of the paranormal. These are novel cultural formations with few existing frames of reference. The paranormal is a neglected area of research in media, communication and cultural studies. An absence of dialogue on this subject makes it a challenge to research. For example, how do we study people's engagement with cultural experiences that they believe go beyond reality? With no main frame established on how you research cultural engagement with the paranormal there is a need to establish a discursive space. Such a space becomes made through trial and error. There are many threads of research on the paranormal in psychology, history, and anthropology, to take a few examples, but what are the relevant threads for a popular cultural ethnography? This problem takes time to solve.

Another problem is why study cultural engagement with the paranormal at all. If it is a neglected area of research perhaps there are good reasons why this is the case. For example, paranormal beliefs may be better left to psychologists because they are so related to how the mind works. If the aim of audience research is to provide rigorous and critical thinking on individuals and publics then the paranormal is perhaps an alien entity in this rational world. But, here is an even bigger problem. Polls data indicate lots of people claim to believe in some form of the paranormal. There are many examples of ghost walks, theatre shows, art exhibitions, films, photography and the web, TV shows, and radio programmes about the paranormal in mainstream and alternative culture. When assertions are made that people who believe in the paranormal are gullible, delusional, suffering from an over active imagination, and sometimes just plain crazy, there is a very real need to ask people what they understand is going on.

The approach used in this research is informed by cultural sociology in that it starts from a position that cultural practices associated with paranormal beliefs and ideas can be studied in a sociologically rigorous way. Cultural practices are perceived as the things people do with products and representations that are richly varied, distinct to social contexts and culturally specific to place, space and time. This book explores 'how culture works in practice and how practice makes and remakes culture' (see Calhoon and Sennett 2007: 10). However, it extends beyond this approach and its emphasis on people as a social group. The aim of this research is to reach out and explore the diversity of contemporary culture around the phenomena of the paranormal. To that end, the work is rooted in audience research in its emphasis on reception. As a popular cultural ethnography, it extends beyond texts or genres to cultural experiences. The research offers original and empirical data regarding audience responses to the representation of spirits and magic in a range of media, and their personal experiences of the paranormal and psychological entertainment in tourism, live events and theatres.

This project used a combination of a deductive and inductive approach to the sociology of the paranormal in popular culture. Theoretical and empirical studies from a range of areas in media audiences, cultural history, media and religion, social psychology, cultural geography, anomalous psychology, and discursive parapsychology, worked alongside the data design, collection and analysis of cultural practices. The fieldwork included individual and group interviews, semi-structured focus groups, household in-depth interviews, and participant observation in Britain. The sample included participants with a range of positions, audiences of magic entertainment, paranormal drama, reality TV, films, photography and the web, from sceptics to believers, to those in between. Over a hundred men and women aged 18–65+ took part in focus group interviews, 15 individual and expert interviews were conducted, 27 households interviews took place with 70 participants, and there was participant observation of ghost hunting events with approximately 70 participants. See Appendix for full details. The data and analysis informed each other and led to a specific approach that combines qualitative media audience research with critical social and cultural theory.

Although this is a study of novel cultural formations, there are existing discourses that can help in analysing how and why people engage with paranormal phenomena. One of the most influential studies in sociology is by Avery Gordon in *Ghostly Matters* (1997). She argues hauntings 'are part of social life.' If we want to study life then 'we must learn how to identify hauntings and reckon with ghosts, must learn how to make contact with what is without doubt often painful, difficult and unsettling' (1997: 23). Ghostly matters refers to what is there and not there: 'the intricate web of connections that characterises any event or problem' (20). For Gordon, ghostly matters are:

> a paradigmatic way in which life is more complicated than those of us who study it have usually granted ... haunting is a constituent element of modern life. It is neither premodern superstition or individual psychosis; it is a generalisable social phenomenon of great import. To study social life one must confront the ghostly aspects of it.
>
> (1997: 7)

Gordon argues the statement 'life is complicated' may seem banal, but nonetheless it is 'a profound theoretical statement – perhaps the most important theoretical statement of our time' (1997: 1). People are beset by contradictions and have complex identities and experiences.

This book is inspired by *Ghostly Matters* in the way Gordon understands hauntings as social experiences: 'haunting is the sociality of living with ghosts, a sociality both tangible and tactile as well as ephemeral and imaginary' (1997: 201). Gordon analysed the subjects of torture and slavery within contexts of history and psychoanalysis, and ideas of power, knowledge and resistance. Hauntings are the unseen forces in modern society. For Gordon, when ghosts speak they tell us of violence and injustice and the possibility of reconciliation. In this research, the focus is on the voices of people rather than ghosts. When people speak they tell us of cultural experiences and explore questions of evidence, interpretation and the possibility of other spirit forms, entities and states of consciousness. Their knowledge is based on physical, emotional, psychological and social understanding. There is an intricate web of connections between audiences and what they do with paranormal matters. There is what Roger Silverstone (1994) called a double articulation of paranormal matters which are material and symbolic. These are matters which are real to the people who experience them and they are symbolic of social relations. These are people who take up Gordon's call to ghostly arms and do so in complicated ways.

Another source of inspiration is the related idea of connected lives in *The Purchase of Intimacy* (2005) by Viviana Zelizer. Her research in family law analyses 'how people and the law manage the mingling of what sometimes seems to be incompatible activities: the maintenance of intimate personal relations and the conduct of economic activity' (2005: 1). Legal case studies reveal how 'people couple, care and participate in household economies' (306). Zelizer rejects 'dichotomous theories of sentiment and rationality' (25), arguing that reason and emotion are not separate spheres but mixed together: 'money cohabits regularly with intimacy, and even sustains it' (28). For Zelizer:

> people create connected lives by differentiating their multiple social ties from each other, marking boundaries between those different ties by means of everyday practices, sustaining those ties through joint activities ... but constantly negotiating the exact content of important social ties ...
>
> (32–33)

It is this sense of the ongoing 'relational work' in 'all social settings, intimate and impersonal alike' that underpins her analysis of human experience (ibid).

The idea of connected lives is useful to an analysis of paranormal matters because, like economics and intimacy, this is 'a profoundly relational world' (Zelizer 2005: 306). This is not a world 'peopled with characters that play out fixed roles based on gender, sexual orientation, religion or ethnicity', nor a world made up of only individuals with self-interests (306). 'There is not one strategic actor moving against another. Instead, we find people locating themselves within webs of social relations' (306). Connected lives signals how:

> people are continually involved in maintaining, reinforcing, testing, and sometimes challenging their relations to each other. In fact, their sense of themselves intertwines closely with the meanings of their relationship to others.
>
> (ibid)

Cultural engagement with paranormal matters is about social relations where a sense of self intertwines closely with that of others.

Some of these ideas of ghostly matters and human relations are explored in literary, philosophical and religious studies of re-enchantment. Such research offers new perspectives on rationality and irrationality in theories of modernity (see Landy and Saler 2009 amongst others). Like Gordon and Zelizer, these researchers perceive the human condition as complex, containing ambiguous thinking on issues of reality and illusion, or reason and emotion. What has commonly been referred to as opposing arguments of enchantment and disenchantment become blurred in research on re-enchantment. In histories of secular magic, for example, Simon During argues that magic shows have always been and continue to be a major influence on 'modern culture's understanding and judgement of itself' (2002: 1). Some researchers consider ideas of re-enchantment and modernity with religious beliefs. For example, audience research on religion, including supernaturalism and alternative spiritual beliefs, has explored uncertainty and metaphysical thinking amongst American teenagers and adults (Hoover 2006, Schofield Clark 2003). Rather than secular enchantments like magic and illusion, this work addresses the return of religious thinking in the world, from orthodox religions to progressive spirituality (Lynch 2007). Work in media and religion has focused on how contemporary religious beliefs are articulated in the market place (Hoover 2006, Schofield Clark 2007). This kind of research is comparable to that of cultural engagement with the paranormal in the ways people's beliefs are a basis from which a market arises in popular culture.

Cultural histories provide a valuable frame of reference for the long held associations with spirits, magic and psychological entertainment in early modern and modern popular culture. There is a tradition of 'ghost making' and media technologies, such as phantasmagoria in the early development of magic lantern slides, photography, cinema and new media. This research has given a historical overview of spirit photography, cinema and theatre, or ghost stories in literature (see Davies 2007, Harvey 2007, Kaplan 2008, Nead 2008). There are histories of magic and stagecraft, and the reception of magicians and mediums during the nineteenth century (see Lamont 2006 and Steinmeyer 2003 amongst others). Histories of mesmerism, the spiritualist movement and mediums explore tensions between religion and science in the Victorian period in Europe and America (Blum 2007, Melechi 2008).

This book extends the studies by Jeffrey Sconce (2000) and Marina Warner (2006) into 'haunted media' by exploring engagement with contemporary representations of spirits and magic. In *Phantasmagoria* Warner argues that the 'language of spirit' remains dynamic in our culture. Spirit forms are a 'work of art continuing over time, similar to a cathedral or another grand and sacred artefact' (2006: 12). The language of spirit has the capacity to 'institute forms, meaning and experience' (376). She writes 'contemporary media of representations … convey a plural and liable theory of consciousness that installs virtual presences, phantoms, hauntings, and doubles in the ordinary way of things' (ibid). For Warner the power of contemporary spirit forms is in the mesmerising spectacle they create: 'they wrap us in an illusion of phantoms and phantasms, turning reality into dream, dream into act, and myths into realities' (ibid). This is an idea of audiences as disembodied spectators. Sconce also notes in the history of spirit forms and electronic presence conceptual models that favour disembodiment, where the audience is often associated with metaphors of simulation and fragmentation (2000: 172). He writes: 'fantasies of electronic disembodiment began as belief in the social deliverance to be achieved through the spiritual telegraph', continuing through the history of radio and television 'with a belief in an autonomous electronic reality', and also appearing in ideas of cyberculture and virtual reality (2000: 200). Sconce challenges these conceptual models as constructions that work within wider social and cultural anxieties about new technologies and narratives of the self. In different ways, both Warner and Sconce suggest that ideas of audiences in spirit forms have been dominated by discourses of disembodiment. As Warner notes, audiences have become associated with zombies and a soulless state. In this book audiences tell us about their participation in 'the language of spirit.' Rather than zombies, audiences are an embodiment of ideas of identity, the self, consciousness and death.

What can be seen from these approaches to paranormal matters is that many of the books and articles have been published recently. This is not to say that there is anything new about relations between the paranormal, magic and illusion, psychology, sociology and popular culture. History tells us otherwise. Rather, current interest in this subject suggests that it is now on the radar of researchers in a range of disciplines as posing a set of intellectual problems that need to be addressed. It is timely that media researchers get in on the act. The paranormal turn in popular culture continues to run its course and the more we can understand how this is happening the closer we come to understanding why this phenomenon is taking place.

Overview of the book

Chapter Two, 'Spirit Histories', examines the story of ghosts as one of change and uncertainty. Spirit beliefs and forms in the nineteenth century provide a rich history of the production and reception of cultural experiences where things are not quite what they seem. Ghost shows, spirit photographs, trick ghost films, and theatrical illusions drew on a state of uncertainty in the nineteenth century and they illuminate the selling of an ambiguous cultural experience to mass audiences. Chapter Three, 'Paranormal in Popular Culture', critically analyses a range of contemporary paranormal forms, experiences and practices, across entertainment. There are recurring themes in popular culture of fascination with the dead, the selling of cultural experiences, and the search for the authentic, across drama, novels, film, art and theatre, non-fiction publishing, reality TV, photography and the web, and tourism and leisure. The common understanding of the paranormal as things you can't explain, or don't understand, makes it a rich area for an eclectic range of representations, products, and services. As paranormal beliefs and ideas move from the margins to the mainstream the meaning of the paranormal changes meaning. It becomes less associated with religion and alternative spiritual thinking and more connected with lifestyle and entertainment.

Chapters Four to Seven offer thematically driven case studies of the cultural and sociological practices associated with paranormal beliefs and ideas. 'Armchair Ghost Hunters' examines responses to reality TV. Ghost hunting shows induce a state of uncertainty where the spaces in between scepticism and belief are explored. Audiences are aware of their role in what one person described as 'waiting for a haunting to happen.' In this way the media is a resource for identity work and a playful experimentation with paranormal beliefs. Chapter Five, 'Psychic Tourists', examines the growth of ghost tourism and ghost hunting events. Here, the way people participate in their own production of beliefs is by going on a sensory journey where strong emotions and physical and cognitive responses contribute to a powerful live collective experience. Raymond Williams' concept of a structure of feeling is used to examine the fixity and flow of sensory journeys within an organised cultural event. Chapter Six, 'Experiences', explores paranormal beliefs and how these are imagined in popular culture as self-empowerment. Such ideas can be seen in the ways people tell their stories of paranormal phenomena and how they interpret self-experience as evidence. Matters of authenticity and authority are explored by participants in their tales of the extraordinary. In this way, narratives of the self and issues of authenticity are part of wider debates about trust in the media and a crisis of evidence in paranormal and truth claims. Following on from this, Chapter Seven, 'Beyond Magic', examines the magician Derren Brown and his style of mentalism which is a form of magic that has the appearance of psychic powers. Brown constructs magic tricks that rely on contemporary cultural practices and as such his live magic events highlight common knowledge of paranormal beliefs and psychology as powerful explanatory frameworks.

Chapter Eight, 'The Audience is the Show', presents the overarching concept of the book in the ways people produce beliefs within an entertainment and communication environment. Through an analysis of histories of audiences, magicians and mediums, the idea of an attentive audience is expanded to one that co-performs and co-produces a cultural experience in live events. The concept of the audience as the show is one where types of live collective experiences rely on a high degree of audience participation, such as magic, or medium demonstrations, and in different contexts political and religious events. In the concluding Chapter Nine, 'Transformative Acts', the concept of the audience is the show is situated within the social and cultural context of contemporary paranormal beliefs in Western societies. Cultural histories of anxiety, changing practices of death and dying, and psychological theories of coping strategies for fear of death, are some of the explanations for why paranormal beliefs are part of mainstream culture today. Within the context of entertainment, people can participate in one of the greatest mysteries of what happens to us when we die.

Notes

1   See 'They See Dead People' *People Magazine*, 7 November 2005, Vol 64, No 19. Accessed online at www.people.com 29 January 2009.
2   See official website www.parapsychologicalassociation.com, accessed 16 January 2010.
3   Gallup News Service, 'Three in Four Americans Believe in Paranormal', David W Moore, accessed online at www.gallupnewsservice.com 29 January 2009.

4 The results showed no statistically significant differences among people by age, gender, education, race, region or religion. A survey by the National Science Foundation of 2001 showed some minor differences across social groups, in particular, gender where they found more women with paranormal beliefs than men, except on the subject of UFOs when the gender difference was reversed.

5 National Science Foundation, Division of Science Resources Statistics Chapter 7, Science and Technology: Public Attitudes and Public Understanding, accessed online at www.nsf.gov/sbe/srs/seind02/c7/c7s5.htm 30 January 2009.

6 See World Values Survey 2008, accessed online at www.worldvaluessurvey.org 29 January 2009.

7 See 'They See Dead People' *People Magazine*, 7 November 2005, Vol 64, No 19. Accessed online at www.people.com 29 January 2009.

8 Bianco, Robert. '2008 in Review: Television' *USA Today*, 22 December 2008, accessed online at www.usatoday.com 16 January 2009.

9 See *Time*, Lev Grossman, 23 November 2009, accessed online at www.time.com/time/magazine/article/0,9171,1938712–1,00.html#ixzz0d8zrS5L3.

10 Jones, Oliver. (2008) 'He Sees Dead People' *People Magazine*, 9 June 2008, accessed online at www.people.com 14 January 2009.

11 See Phil Hogan, 'Who ya gonna call?' *The Observer Review*, 18 March 2007: 13.

12 Xan Brookes, the *Guardian*, Monday, 30 November 2009. Accessed online at www.guardian.co.uk/film/2009/nov/30/paranormal-activity-oren-peli 11 February 2010.

13 Jason Solomons, the *Observer*, 29 November 2009. Accessed online at www.guardian.co.uk/film/2009/nov/29/paranormal-activity-review 11 February 2010.

14 Kharif, Olga. 'Scaring up Paranormal Profits' *Business Week*, 12 May 2005, accessed online at www.businessweek.com 28 January 2009.

15 See Elsa Wenzel (2007) 'Believe it or not' CNET News.com, 20 July 2007, accessed 18 October 2008.

16 See Dixon, Rachel (2009) 'How Britain Became a Nation of Ghost Hunters' the *Guardian*, 30 October 2009, accessed online at www.guardianunlimited 4 November 2009.

17 See BBC news 'Ghost Capital's Tourist Hopes', Friday, 9 August 2002, accessed online at http://news.bbc.co.uk/2/hi/uk_news/england/2183197.stm 20 October 2009.

18 Accessed online at www.londonparanormal.com/lgf.htm 4 June 2009.

19 Londonist, accessed online at http://londonist.com/2009/04/londonist_goes_ghost_hunting.php 4 June 2009.

20 See 'In a credit crunch, there's more to life than x-factor and gossip' *Marketing Week*, 4 September 2008, accessed online at www.marketingweek.co.uk/previous-issues/2008.publication 18 October 2008.

21 Mooney, Bel. (2008) 'Apocalypse Now?' the *Daily Mail*, 8 August 2008, accessed online at www.dailymail.com 16 January 2009.

22 Online at www.oft.gov.uk/news/press/2007/18–07 20 October 2008.

Chapter 2

Spirit histories

Owen Davies (2007) argues that the history of ghosts over the past 500 years is a remarkable story of the survival of spirit belief. It is also a story of change and uncertainty. At times of war, civil unrest, political and economic crisis, people turn to spirit beliefs as one way of coping with change. Prior to the 1800s, supernaturalism, folklore and spirits were common to European culture, in the oral tradition, artefacts and printed matter. These spirit beliefs and representations were produced within the context of religious and pagan practices. With the revolution in commerce and communications during the nineteenth century, spirit forms changed from a religious to secular realm. Ghosts, ghouls and witches were perceived as old-fashioned thinking and superstition. Spirit beliefs continued to exist but were framed in the social context of the industrial revolution and scientific progression. Nineteenth-century spiritualism marked a new and significant chapter in the story of ghosts. Modern spiritualism offered an alternative form of spirit belief outside of dominant scientific and religious thinking. It offered hope in an afterlife during a time of cultural and moral imbalance.

The story of ghosts in the nineteenth century shows how spirit forms and beliefs were produced within a state of uncertainty. These cultural forms invited multiple meanings. On the one hand, the representation of demons, witches, ghosts and magic were a major part of nineteenth-century popular culture, such as stories of haunted houses, public attractions, séances and spirit photographs, stage illusions and ghost shows. These representations were popular in part because they drew on a longstanding cultural fascination with ghosts and provided familiar stories for mass consumption. Phantasmagoria, trick ghost films and theatrical magic used spirit forms as secular attractions. On the other hand, spirit photography, film, and medium demonstrations were examples of how spirit beliefs were maintained through popular cultural forms. The double meaning of a medium signalled the web of connections between technologically based communication and spirit communication during this period. The multiple meaning of spirit forms and new technologies was incorporated into the construction of live performances in public séances, magic acts and variety shows where things were not quite what they appeared to be. In this way, the

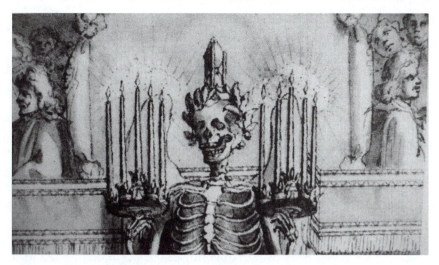

Figure 2.1 Death candelabra at a church funeral

production and reception of ghost shows, spirit photographs, trick ghost films, and theatrical illusions during the nineteenth century illuminates the selling of an ambiguous cultural experience to mass audiences.

Historical spirit forms

In the early modern period spirit belief was closely connected to religious and pagan practices. In a history of night time, A Roger Ekirch cites the proverb 'night belongs to the spirits' to highlight how people believed Satan embraced darkness, rejecting the light of God's word and calling forth his army of demons, hobgoblins and witches to his 'dark world' (2005: 16). Ghosts, boggles, boggarts and wafts were prevalent in nearly every European culture during this period: 'denied entry to the light of God, according to Christian tradition, they almost always appeared at night' (ibid). There were Irish banshees, Hungarian vampires, German werewolves, and ghost dogs roaming the streets of Newcastle. Cautionary tales of spirits, demons and witches were part of rural traditions, connecting with temporal rhythms such as day and night, summer and winter, and also pagan festivals, such as All Hallows' Eve and Midsummer Eve (ibid). A writer in the *Spectator* in the early 1700s commented:

> There was not a village in England that had not a ghost in it, the churchyards were all haunted, every large common had a circle of fairies belonging to it, and there was scarce a shepherd to be met who had not seen a spirit.

(Cited in Ekirch 2005: 16–17)

Ekirch notes 'the late eighteenth century folklorist Francis Grose estimated that the typical churchyard contained nearly as many ghosts at night as the village parishioners' (140).

Historical ghost stories are moral tales. Some ghosts had a reason for returning to haunt the living, whilst others existed as a memorial for the dead. In 1660 the ghost of Robert Parkin appeared in the Westmorland parish church crying 'I am murdered, I am murdered, I am murdered.' An enquiry was undertaken to restore justice to the victim (Davies 2007: 5). 'Chapbooks with titles such as *A Dreadful Warning to all Wicked Persons* reinforced the message: murderers beware; the ghosts are out to get you!' (ibid). Ghosts appeared in bedrooms warning loved ones of their departure from this world. Those who had not received proper burials haunted battle fields, bridges and parish boundaries. Stories of haunted highways were connected to the common practice of burying the bodies of suicides at crossroads in order to prevent the return of the unsettled spirit to the local community. A stake was driven through the heart of the corpse. This tradition from the early modern period was still being recorded in eighteenth-century newspapers and periodicals: 'consider for instance the corpse of the murderer and self-murderer David Stirn, which was dissected in September 1760 and buried with a wooden stake driven through it at a crossroads near Black Mary's Hole, Clerkenwell' (Davies 2007: 51).

Owen Davies in his social history of hauntings writes 'a ghost needs to be located in time to make sense of it' (2007: 40). Ghost sightings and popular accounts of spirits tend to be located in moments of political and social change. War, religious and political unrest, violence and mass trauma, new scientific developments, challenges to orthodoxies, all contribute to the historical contexts for hauntings. For example, during the Reformation Protestant theologians denounced ghosts as a product of superstitions and Catholic ideas. Instead of disappearing, ghosts remained in British culture haunting places of historical importance. The Civil War was 'strong in the collective memory and popular literature, and consequently numerous historic ghosts are dated to this conflict', such as the haunting of Heath House in Shropshire by a Roundhead (Davies 2007: 40). The dissolution of the monasteries also provided ghost stories of nuns and monks haunting former sites around Britain. Later in the eighteenth and early nineteenth centuries the Parliamentary Enclosure Act provided another context to ghost legends. Local communities used parish boundaries of crossroads and rivers to keep ghosts away. When these natural boundaries were removed ghost stories depicted hauntings in these altered spaces.

The historical context to ghosts highlights a transformation of spirits from religious to secular realms (Warner 2006). Such a transformation is crucial to the way spirit beliefs and stories became intricately connected with the development of popular culture. The example of the magic-lantern illuminates how optical technologies were used to affirm religious beliefs and then later to create entertainment experiences. In the seventeenth century, Jesuit priest Athanasius Kircher conducted early experiments with magic-lantern slides in Rome. For Marina

Warner lantern shows 'reveal an intrinsic, unexamined equivalence between the technology of illusion and supernatural phenomena' (2006: 139). Kircher's study of physical laws and optics led him to develop an idea of the 'radiation of imagination.' The experience of being at a magic-lantern show with slides of demons, ghouls and goblins transformed material objects into phantasmagorical experiences (Warner 2006: 140). These experiences should be understood within the context of the time where illusion and imagination were part of the formation and management of religious belief. A century later, after the French Revolution, Etienne-Gaspard Robertson's gothic moving picture show promised to raise the dead. Through experimentation with moving projectors, arrangement of lenses and the use of music, Robertson gave audiences spirit forms that appeared to move in the flickering light and shadow. Some of his shows were staged in an abandoned Gothic convent, creating an eerie atmosphere in which audiences were promised 'the terror which shadows, symbols, spells, the occult works of magic inspire' (cited in Warner 2006: 149). This was a live spectacular that turned the imagery of spirits into secular entertainment.

Magic-lantern shows are one example of how spirit beliefs became caught up in a general development of mass entertainment. Oral stories of ghosts had been written down before but it was during the 1800s that ghost stories began to be mass produced. The tradition of collecting and publishing folklore developed during this period as part of a re-invention of the past for European cultures (Sassoon 2006: 85–87). Regional and national folklore was used as a political and cultural means of nation building during the Empire period. Catherine Crowe's bestseller *The Night Side of Nature* (1848) was a book that drew on ghost stories from friends, books and newspapers, and 'turned its author from a little-known writer of children's stories to a celebrity advocate for the occult' (Blum 2007: 14). In another example, Icelandic sagas containing stories of trolls and ghosts were popular in Victorian Britain. The Brothers Grimm heard fairytales from educated women who in turn heard stories from their nurses and servants. They re-packaged these tales for middle class consumers. By the turn of the nineteenth century Grimm's fairytales were outselling every German book apart from the bible (Sassoon 2006: 99).

Two issues arise from this glimpse into historical spirit forms and beliefs. First, beliefs were located within religious and pagan practices. It was common in the early modern period for the practice of magic and healing, and ghosts and supernaturalism, to be combined within a framework of religious beliefs. Fear of ghosts was also a fear of the occult and the Devil with his army of night workers. The historical context to ghosts indicates beliefs and practices were closely connected with social and political changes, and cultural and moral instability. Ghost stories became narratives of personal, social and religious significance. Second, in the early development of popular culture spirit beliefs began to be relocated from religious to secular contexts. People still believed in ghosts but the way their beliefs became expressed in cultural forms gradually changed. Fear of ghosts was a sign of superstition and old ways of thinking about religion and supernaturalism. To make sense of ghosts in these contexts is also to make sense of cultural engagement at these historical junctures. The next section examines the nineteenth century and the social history of spirit belief during this period of great change. Connected to this development is the nineteenth-century explosion in commerce and technologies which exploited spirit forms and beliefs as mass entertainment.

Victorian spiritualism

Deborah Blum in *Ghost Hunters* (2007: 8) writes about the Victorian period as an era of 'moral imbalance – religion apparently under siege from science, technology seemingly rewriting the laws of reality. Finding some balance, a way to make sense of existence in the changing world' became imperative. There were scientific developments which impacted on ways of seeing the world. The study of clouds helped develop meteorology. Louis Pasteur's germ theory revolutionised medicine. Electricity powered generators and gave light. Electricity also re-animated corpses, as Duchenne de Boulogne discovered in his physiological research on emotions. The work of naturalists Charles Darwin and Alfred Russell Wallace on the theory of natural selection challenged religious orthodoxy. Darwin's *On the Origin of Species* (1859) sold out in its first print run, sparking intense public debate amongst scientists and the clergy. It was in this historical context that the perception of spirits changed: 'until the rise of spiritualism in the nineteenth century, the main reason for wishing to encounter the dead was in order to banish them rather than seek their spiritual guidance' (Davies 2007: 71). Modern spiritualism offered guidance in a changing world.

Spiritualism drew on the writings of the Swedish scientist Emmanuel Swedenborg. In the mid 1700s Swedenborg wrote in a trance-like state on his alternative meaning of the Scriptures. His 'theory of correspondence' outlined a connection between this life and a spirit world, where invisible forces connected these parallel worlds together (Blum 2007: 12). Good spirits could help people to see God's other realms. Evil spirits blocked spiritual correspondence, casting shadow on the spiritual light from the other side. This theory of correspondence was preached in Swedenborgian churches and societies across both sides of the Atlantic. American spiritualism developed Swedenborgian ideas alongside concepts of spirit guides and metaphysical thinking from Eastern and Western religions and philosophies. This unorthodox religious movement travelled to various countries, where it developed within specific cultures and belief systems. In Britain, leading figures already involved in experiments in somnambulism and mesmerism took up spiritualism. The socialist Robert Owen became a convert, promoting the spiritualist movement as democratic, empowering ordinary people to converse with spirits. Other socialists toured secular societies, 'advising working men to interrogate the spirits, to glean as much knowledge as they could of the one place that knew no distinction of rank' (Melechi 2008: 172). The former Chartist David Weatherhead funded the *Yorkshire Spiritual Telegraph* to promote British spiritualism to the working classes. In Brazil, the French educator and medium Allen Kardec developed a form of spiritualism that included:

> communication with the dead via mediums, the existence of a spiritual body that can affect the health of the physical body, and a theist moral system that governs reincarnation across various existences according to a law of karma.
>
> (Hess 1994: 16)

In other countries in Latin America, what became known as spiritism was developed by European or American educated settlers. For example, spiritism in Puerto Rico was established in the 1870s by wealthy intellectuals who studied in France and Spain.

Spiritualism sought guidance from the dead on how to live a better life. Spirit guides communicated through mediums who called themselves spirit talkers or communicators. Reputedly there were 30,000 mediums working in America during the 1850s and 60s (Melechi 2008: 170). Mediums varied in their abilities. Mental mediumship involved trance-like states and visions, with messages from the other side. Physical mediumship involved rappings, table tilting, telekinesis, other forms of spirit writing on slate or paper, spirit photography, levitation, healing, and materialisation of spirit forms or fluids. The first mediums to gain popularity were the Fox sisters, two farm girls in up state New York who invented rapping in 1848. Their spirit guide, Mister Split-foot, spoke to them in the form of raps (once for yes, twice for no). The telegraph had not long been invented and rapping was promoted as a spiritual telegraph. The Fox sisters became famous, appearing in private salons and performing séances at P.T. Barnum's New York City museum of attractions. Blum writes: 'in the same way that the *Night Side of Nature* was considered the most influential publication of its kind, these mediums would be hailed as the most revolutionary ghost talkers of their time' (2007: 16). Other professional mediums also became international celebrities and were the subject of press attention and controversy. The American Davenport brothers toured around the world with their séances. They were bound by rope in a wooden cabinet and communicated with spirits through rapping and the materialisation of musical instruments. The British medium Florence Cook was tied up in a cabinet and materialised the spirit form 'Katie King' who spoke with eloquence on a variety of topics. As a trance medium, Cook's control would bring forth other spirits, offer advice, and interact with the audience. Daniel Dunglas Home performed séances in private salons where he produced messages from the dead, table tilting, and extraordinary feats such as levitation.

Blum writes in the early 1850s America seemed 'possessed' with spirit communication. For example, invitations to tea and table talking were common (2007: 21). The practice of table tilting involved sitters placing their hands lightly on the surface of a table and waiting for vibrations or movement which would indicate spiritual presence. Table talking usually involved a medium who was invited to join the sitters and through a similar process speak with spirits. The planchette was a pencil attached to a piece of wood shaped in a heart. It was on rollers so when people touched the planchette and called on spirits it moved around making barely decipherable letters or drawings. Slate writing involved a medium asking sitters to pose questions and writing would materialise on hand-held slate boards. The talking board was a variation on the planchette and swept across America, 'catching everyone from working men to children in its fascination' (Blum 2007: 21). A simple to use device made of a board with the alphabet and the words yes and no printed on its surface, users would sit with their fingertips on a pointer or glass and watch for it to move across the surface, spelling out messages. Blum cites one man who told the *Tribune* 'I know of whole communities that are wild over the "talking board"' (111). Sears Roebuck mass marketed and re-branded them as Ouija boards, meaning yes in French and German.

John Durham Peters notes how this cross-fertilisation of 'spiritual and technical realms' was influential in establishing 'a vocabulary and vision of communication' (1999: 95). Not only was there the spirit telegraph, but a wide variety of popular devices for communication with spirits and humans. A crucial feature of this cross fertilisation is 'the element of structural doubt built into the communications' (95–96). This structural doubt is articulated in debates at the time regarding the reality and illusion of spirit communication. There was a strong sceptical position put forward by some scientists. The physicist Michael Faraday published a letter in the *Times* of London in 1853 explaining how the talking table moved as a result of people unconsciously pushing it. He wrote 'if spirit communications, not utterly worthless, should happen to start into activity, I will trust the spirits to find out for themselves how they can move my attention' (cited in Blum 2007: 21).

Criticism of fraudulent mediums also cast doubt on the authenticity of spirit communication. The success of spirit shows such as those performed by the Davenport brothers drew attention in the press, leading the editor of the *Boston Courier* to offer a $500 reward to any medium who could demonstrate real spirit communication. Harvard University investigated the Davenports' show, reporting that the performance was an illusion. Magicians sensed an opportunity to promote their own work through the exposure of another profession, offering 'honest deception' rather than dishonest spiritualism. The poem 'Mr Sludge' by Robert Browning satirised fraudulent mediums – 'Now, don't sir! Don't expose me! Just this once!' Blum notes:

> The fact was, too many actual Mr Sludges existed, and too many of them shared their secrets. Professional magicians and actors took to the stage, performing to packed houses, showing that they too could conjure like the Davenports, or, as one theatre poster declared, could reproduce 'All the Tricks of the Spirit Conjurers.'
>
> (2007: 29)

Some mediums came out in public denouncing the profession. Daniel Dunglas Home explained some of the illusions behind the séance in his book *Lights and Shadows of Spiritualism* (1877). One of the Davenport brothers would reveal the rope tricks used in their act to the escapologist Harry Houdini. The mechanisms by which a fraudulent medium could deceive their audience were speculated upon in the press, by journalists, magicians and scientists. The séance phenomena which were allegedly evidence of spirit communication were openly criticised and these debates part of popular discourses on spirit belief.

At the same time, and within the same debates, spirit forms and beliefs remained open to multiple interpretations. For example, when Harvard scientists declared the Davenports a hoax they were unable to prove exactly how the séance was produced. The public did not stop going to see their shows despite the newspaper's attack because they would rather trust the brothers than lofty academics (Blum 2007). The case of Daniel Dunglas Home is a good example of how spirit belief and representations were criticised as illusion and also believed as evidence of an afterlife. Peter Lamont (2006) in *The First Psychic* argues that Home became a symbol for that which could be explained and that which was beyond explanation in late nineteenth-century society. Home amazed his audience with extraordinary feats of spirit messages and levitation. Many witnesses were dumbfounded and unable to attribute rational explanations to what they had seen and felt during his séances. For example, *Experiences in Spiritualism with D.D. Home* (Lord Adare 1869) offered testimonials by eye witnesses who had seen him levitate. Home was tested by scientists who declared him the first psychic, coining a new term for his special powers. He was accused of fraud, and even exposed other mediums, and yet there was never a clear case made against him, nor could other magicians and mediums replicate his extraordinary feats. In this way, Home symbolised how ambiguity was part of popular discourses on spirit belief and modes of communication.

In a chapter titled 'a spirit of unbelief' Blum (2007) writes that Alfred Russell Wallace, who helped develop the theory of natural selection, turned to spiritualism because he felt a moral duty to study more than the physical. He perceived 'dark spots in the polished progress' of evolutionary man, where despite the newfound ability to measure the speed of light, man had also invented the machine gun (Blum 2007: 38). He did not reject the theory of evolution, but argued that there were limits to natural selection. In his search for a higher power Wallace attended mesmerists and mediums to investigate supernatural realms. He thought of this 'as a scientific expedition into the dark jungles of spirit phenomena' (ibid). Wallace was one of several prominent Victorian scientists and philosophers who took part in what Blum describes as the 'greatest ghost hunt of any age' (2007: back cover). As Melechi notes 'religious doubt and scientific fervour were conjoined in the Victorian séance room' (2008: 5). William Crookes, a chemist who discovered the neurotoxin thallium, set out to debunk Wallace's arguments by testing mediums only to discover something inexplicable in their spirit communications. Like Wallace, Crookes was denounced by his fellow scientists for investigating supernaturalism. Darwin wrote 'I cannot disbelieve Mr Crookes' statement, nor can I believe his result' (cited in Blum 2007: 52).

Blum suggests these early psychic experiments showed scientists struggling to research what we know now as the structure of the atom, or 'the energy embedded in subatomic particles like the electron' (2007: 52) 'The sense of natural sources of energy, of physical explanations waiting to be found, simmered in the scientific community' (ibid). The Society for Psychical Research (SPR) was established in 1882. As the first president, Henry Sidgwick was joined by fellow philosophers and classicists Frederick Myers and Edmund Gurney who were responsible for investigating spirit apparitions and thought transference. The Society attracted over 200 members including Wallace and Crookes, the poet Tennyson, art critic John Ruskin, author Mark Twain, amongst others. The SPR collected hundreds of personal accounts, observed private séances, tested and exposed fraudulent mediums. They looked for rational explanations for psychic claims. The element of structural doubt was built into their approach to psychical research. At the same time, within this structure, was a belief in the possibility of a source of psychic energy yet to be discovered within orthodox science.

The philosopher and psychologist William James established the American Society for Psychical Research. In his groundbreaking book *The Principles of Psychology* (1890) he offered an explanation of human behaviour that was not bound to either traditional religion or philosophy. This was 'a world less mechanical, more infused with human possibility – including the possibility of psychic phenomena' (Blum 2007: 169). James discussed telepathy, trance personalities, or spirit possession, as evidence of the importance of understanding the mind and states of consciousness (Blum 2007: 169). In *The Will to Believe* (1896) James argued that those who believed in religion, morality and science, were connected by their faith, the difference being that scientists denied any belief that was not verified by proof. 'The pursuit of truth, even when it might seem illogical by the rules of science, was always worth the risk' and to 'reach the stubborn mysteries of the universe one had to be willing to believe that the most unlikely paths might lead in that direction' (Blum 2007: 214). In 'The Confidences of a Psychical Researcher' (1909) James wrote that after 25 years conducting experiments and reading literature on psychic phenomena he had reached a state of uncertainty:

> I confess that at times I have been tempted to believe that the Creator has eternally intended this department of nature to remain baffling, to prompt our curiosities and hopes and suspicions, all in equal measure, so that, although ghosts and clairvoyances, and raps and messages from spirits, are always seeming to exist and can never be fully explained away, they also can never be susceptible of full corroboration.
>
> (580)

This state of uncertainty provides a context to understanding spirit beliefs and cultural forms in nineteenth-century society. In one way, spirit belief was a means of coping in an uncertain world, as Blum and Davies suggest. Spiritualism provided hope of afterlife through an alternative belief system than that of traditional science or religion. In another way, spirit forms were open to multiple interpretations. As Durham Peters points out a structural doubt was built into communication acts between mediums and their spirit guides and in witnesses' accounts of alleged séance phenomena. People couldn't be sure that what they were seeing and feeling was real or an illusion. In the next section, developments in nineteenth-century popular culture provide other aspects to the story of ghosts and a state of uncertainty in cultural experiences.

Nineteenth-century popular culture

Prior to the 1800s, much cultural consumption took place in aristocratic circles. Opera, theatre, musical recitals, reading novels or poems, were the tastes of the aristocracy. Donald Sassoon points out: 'it is an inescapable fact that wealth provides the leisure time required for cultural pursuits' (2006: 7). The nineteenth century was the start of an 'extraordinary expansion of cultural consumption' (Sassoon 2006: xiii). For industrialised countries like Britain and America 'it was as if history had speeded up; what had previously taken decades or centuries was squeezed into a few years' (2006: 293). The revolution in manufacturing, commerce, communication and transport contributed to an unprecedented growth in cultural markets. From 1800 to 1900 European populations exploded, doubling in size from a total population of around 195 million to 422 million (2006: 3–4). During this same period there was large-scale migration from rural to urban communities. In 1851 Great Britain had more people living in urban than rural areas. London was the largest city in the world. From 1851 to 1915 around 40 million Europeans emigrated to the Americas and Australia. The rise of the working and middle classes in cities created bigger and more diverse cultural markets. Increases in literacy, high speed printing presses, and a removal of stamp duty for newspapers, contributed to the widespread production and distribution of newspapers, novels, poetry and essays. Thirty million copies of newspapers were published annually in Britain (Sassoon 2006: 313). In 1881, around six million penny publications, weeklies and monthlies circulated in London (Briggs and Burke 2006: 159). The developments of faster travel and modes of communication ensured that 'books, newspapers, periodicals, musical scores as well as musicians, actors, storytellers and singers could move around more rapidly' (Sassoon 2006: 7). As a consequence 'local markets turned into national and international ones' (ibid).

The nineteenth century was also 'a revolution in communications' (Sassoon 2006: 596). In a short space of time the invention of the telegraph and telephone fundamentally changed the experience of communication at a distance. Sassoon gives the example of the time it would take to post a letter to India. In the 1830s a letter posted in London travelled by boat and took around five months to reach India. The opening of the Suez canal in 1869 meant that a letter travelled by steam train, boat and camel and reached India in 35 days. Telegraph wires linking Britain with India in 1870 ensured a cable reached India in five days. By the invention of the wireless telegraph in 1889 a person to person telephone call meant someone in London could communicate with someone in India instantaneously. As Tom Standage has shown in *The Victorian Internet* (1998) the telegraph opened up a whole new way of communicating across time and space. No longer did people need to rely on messengers to communicate with absent others, they could do it themselves (Sassoon 2006: 597). Jeffrey Sconce notes 'the electronic circuitry of the telegraph made possible the instantaneous exchange of messages in the complete absence of physical bodies' (2000: 21). As one telegraph enthusiast explained at the time – the world had been made into a 'great whispering gallery' (cited in Sconce 2000: 22).

The photograph was another 'momentous technological revolution' (Sassoon 2006: 339). A camera used light and chemistry to capture a moment in time, making a permanent image of real life. 'Louis Daguerre, one of the reputed inventors of the new technology, found the "democratic" possibility of photography appealing' as he believed ordinary citizens would be able to participate in their own reproduction of images, just like artists and illustrators (Sassoon 2006: ibid). In a short amount of time the bulky equipment, complex chemicals and film development that was part of the early process of photography was transformed into a hand camera. The first Kodak camera was marketed with the slogan 'you press the button, we do the rest' (cited in Nead 2008: 112). According to Linda Nead, the revolution was not so much in the invention of the photograph but in visual representation, where the hand camera 'created a new aesthetic and a new way of looking' (2008: 112). The 'in your face' hand camera was part of changes in social interaction, where ordinary people could transgress assumed codes of behaviour by taking and displaying photographs in public and private places (ibid).

The cinematograph drew on developments in optical technology, such as the photograph, kaleidoscope, or magic-lantern slides. Film was 'part of a world of vibrant, modern mass entertainment, which was driven by the engines of competition and novelty' (Nead 2008: 123). Early cinema was promoted as a novel attraction. The first British screening of the Lumière Cinématographe occurred in February 1896 in the Polytechnic of Regent Street, known for magic-lantern shows and photographic demonstrations. A month later cinema was part of the Empire Music Hall programming in Leicester Square (ibid). What marked cinema from other attractions was it offered 'the collective viewing of recorded images in motion' (Sassoon 2006: 792). In the early days of cinema a typical film lasted one or two minutes, often using sight gags, or optical illusions which were already an established repertoire of live shows. Sassoon comments 'film pioneers, as they experimented with new technologies, sought to imitate live performance.' Significantly what was being sold to audiences 'was not an object (like a book or a record), but the experience of the performance – like a live show' (2006: 796). Until films became longer and more complex in storylines they were rarely the main attraction in a show. Sassoon gives the example of a programme for a theatre in London in 1910, 'a typical music hall mishmash' containing:

> a juggler, a comedienne, an Italian violinist, Miss Margaret Cooper and her piano, the first appearance in England of the great Russian ballerina Anna Pavlova and finally a series of films including 'Paris the Gay City' and 'Arrival of Lord Kitchener at Southampton.'
>
> (2006: 800)

Robert C Allen's historical research in early cinema highlights how 'going to the show' included a variety of entertainment where film was one of many competing attractions. Most people's experience of cinema in rural North Carolina in the early 1900s was part of a line-up of live entertainment (Allen 2008).

Two key issues arise in this environment of attractions and variety shows. The first is that new technologies were sold as cultural experiences. This historical context leads Allen to ask the question 'what was cinema?' The experience of early cinema was connected to live shows, events and festivals. It was not the film itself that was sold, but an experience similar to a live performance. Similarly, Brian Winston in *Technologies of Seeing* (1996) analyses the invention of photography and cinematography within the historical context of a social need for new forms of communication. Cinema appeared in 1895 not simply because that was the year it was invented but also because of the 'arrival of the urban mass theatrical audience' and 'the broader implications of the move from "show" to "show business"' (Winston 1996: 38). What was cinema becomes a question that has to be addressed in the context of a cultural experience that was produced within nineteenth-century show business.

The second issue is what was an audience? Theatrical audiences did not come into being fully formed as what we know today as the experience of going to the movies or seeing a play. Nineteenth-century audiences learned how to watch live performances. They participated in the shaping of a show as a collective cultural experience. And they did so in diverse ways. Late nineteenth-century audiences were made up of elite aristocracy, middle and working classes. Each group developed their own understanding of the experience of being an audience at a show (see Butsch 2008, Sassoon 2006). The upper classes traditionally paid little attention at the opera for example, using the performance as a backdrop to a social gathering. The middle classes were developing a new style of cultural appreciation and attentiveness for performances, looking for value for money. And the working classes traditionally were rowdy and talked back to the performers, but this was changing with new theatrical policies and crowd control. There is a connection between the selling of new technologies as cultural experiences in nineteenth-century popular culture and the shaping of experiences by audiences (see Chapter eight). The final section explores how ghost beliefs, ghost shows and theatrical magic contributed significantly to ways of seeing communication technologies and ways of experiencing these cultural forms.

Multiple meanings

Familiar spirit forms were staples of early European popular culture. 'Indeed, they would not have been convincing if they had departed from the tradition' (Warner 2006: 224). Medieval illuminations of spectres in white returned as phantoms in magic-lantern shows, variety acts, photographs and films of ghosts. At the beginning of the nineteenth century magic-lantern shows offered a combination of ghostly images and stories as live entertainment. Lonsdale advertised his 'Spectographia, or Phantomimic Illusions' at the London Lyceum with the offer of the 'representation of Traditional Ghosts and Supernatural Appearances ... accompanied by such amusing Relations and explanatory Details as naturally attach themselves to the subject' (cited in Davies 2007: 195). As the novelty of magic-lantern shows wore off performances expanded to include complex illusions. For example, Oehler combined 'ghost projection onto smoke with a technique borrowed from the Invisible Girl illusion, which was one of the most celebrated attractions of the early nineteenth century' (Davies 2007: 196). 'Pepper's Ghost' was another example of a ghost illusion using screens, angled mirrors and actors. It was patented, highlighting the business of illusions in theatrical magic (see Steinmeyer 2003). Travelling ghost showmen pitched at fairs and races, and hired venues, to put on productions such as 'Phantaspectra Ghostodrama'.

Ghost showmen became early cinematographers, reprising illusions in short films. Linda Nead in *The Haunted Gallery* (2008: 1) notes:

> the Lumiere Brothers advertised their first public film exhibition with the words 'for only one franc see life size figures ... come to life before your very eyes.' It was an invitation to a séance in which the medium – in all senses of the word – was film.

George Méliès and George Albert Smith were early trick film makers influenced by stage magicians and ghost showmen. Méliès produced films that were markedly different from those of the time. Most films in variety shows depicted a recreation of everyday life, from sitting on a train to watching crowds go by. Méliès made *The Vanishing Lady* (1897), in which a woman transforms into a skeleton. Another of his trick films was titled *The Apparition, or Mr. Jones' Comical Experiences with a Ghost* (1903). Smith ran a pleasure garden in Brighton, and alongside gypsy fortune tellers, photography, magic-lantern slides, and trapeze artists, he also produced one-minute ghost films such as *Photographing a Ghost* (1898) (Davies 2007: 210–11). Spirit forms in early films were often comic in nature, highlighting audience awareness of ghosts in music hall or variety acts, and debates in the press regarding ghost hoaxes. *The Haunted*

Curiosity Shop (Paul and Booth 1901) was a film about a shopkeeper's antics with Egyptian mummies, ghosts and dwarves. Later films addressed the topic of fraudulent mediums, such as *Spiritualism Exposed* (Payne 1913).

According to Davies ghost belief was vibrant during the late Victorian period, even in towns and cities where magic-lantern shows, Pepper's Ghost and trick ghost films toured. He writes:

> If anything, it may have stimulated urbanites to go out into the streets and try to see the real thing for themselves. Ghost projection opened up new realms of possibility. In a sense, by creating realistic ghosts, scientific endeavour reduced the gap between reality and belief ... as well as being an imaginative tool for simulating spirits, it also captured the actual dead for posterity and brought them back to life over and over again. They looked directly at the audience through the camera lens and even talked to them. They may not have been ghosts, but if the dead could break the fourth wall of cinema then, despite the objection of physics, it seemed less implausible to the human imagination that they could also travel through the fourth dimension.
>
> (2007: 215)

Jeffrey Sconce in *Haunted Media* (2000) also points out how the reception of new communication technologies sparked interest in spirits. The telegraph was an invention 'developed in the rationalist realm of science and engineering that revolutionised society and laid the foundations for the modern information age' (2000: 23). The spirit telegraph helped to promote spiritualism and communicating with ghosts.

These multiple meanings were a central feature of the reception of spirit forms during the nineteenth century. The word medium became part of common language during the 1850s. In the context of communication technologies, medium referred to the platform through which messages could be conveyed from one person to another, or to many. In the context of spiritualism the word medium meant 'a person who provided a medium through which spirits could connect to the world of the living' (Blum 2007: 21). Sconce notes 'the historical proximity and intertwined legacies of these two founding "mediums", one material, the other spiritual, is hardly a coincidence' (2000: 24). The very nature of communication technologies was thought to be other worldly. This is an example of what Roger Silverstone (1994) calls a double articulation, where cultural forms are material objects and symbolic of social and psychological matters. Scientific developments and new technologies proved ghosts were an example of old-fashioned superstition and not to be believed in the rationalist age of industrialisation. At the same time, communication technologies sparked a curiosity, or belief, in supernaturalism. Photography and film symbolised invisible forces and supernatural elements in a secular realm. In this context, a double articulation of a medium contributed to a state of uncertainty about communication technologies and spirit belief.

Spirit photography is a good example of the double articulation of meaning associated with this cultural form. Tom Gunning notes: 'while the process of photography could be thoroughly explained by chemical and physical operations, the cultural reception of the process frequently associated it with the occult and supernatural' (1995: 64). The lens technology used in magic-lantern slides was a means of imagining physical and spiritual presence. Whereas magic lanterns projected light, the camera took in light. The reception of early photographs was associated with supernatural powers that captured the source of light inside the body, giving rise to 'the idea that the camera steals the soul' (Warner 2006: 194). Light could be interpreted as the light of God in Christian theology, and the spirit or soul in other religious and pagan beliefs. Accounts of travelling cameramen in North America and China contained examples of the fear and wonder with which the camera was received by indigenous peoples. Spirit photographs 'revealed reality beyond the surface of the physical: things which were previously and normally out of sight could now be perceived' (Harvey 2007: 74). In Western societies a common type of spirit photography captured images of a phantom, usually appearing near the sitter. Warner (2006) argues the dark chamber of the séance was transformed into the apparatus of the photograph. Ghosts were invisible to the naked eye but made visible through the psychic projection of the sitter and photographer.

As early as 1856, Sir David Brewster had published on how to create a ghostly image using long exposure times. The London Stereoscopic Company exploited Brewster's idea, selling a series of staged images of spirits titled 'The Ghost in the Stereoscope'. Not long after, William H Mumler published a photograph of his dead cousin in 1862 and set up shop in Boston and New York as a 'Spirit Photographic Medium.' In Britain, Frederick Hudson established a studio, working closely with the celebrated medium Georgina Haughton. He sold reproductions of spirit photographs at retailers. Public discussions of spirit photography included awareness of this form as an illusion and interest in the possibilities of psychic powers. 'The Society for Psychical Research, stage magicians and photographers regularly debunked photographs and demanded more credible evidence' (Davies 2007: 208). Critics pointed out photographs of mediums emanating ectoplasm looked suspiciously like cotton wool which had just been invented for dressing wounds. A high-profile law case exposed Mumler as a fraud, but at the same time failed to prove how the deception was produced. Mediums and spirit photographers continued to make a living. In this cultural context, spirit photography offered multiple meanings. When crowds came to the Cheapside showroom to see Brewster's stereoscopic ghosts, the reception of these photographs would have included 'expressions of wonder, humour, scepticism mixed with discussion on the reality of ghosts and tales told of recent sightings' (Davies 2007: 204).

There is an ambiguous articulation of spirit forms produced during the nineteenth century. The example of photographers and magicians exposing the spirit photograph as a hoax is not an isolated case. Those people who saw public photographic exhibitions or bought reproductions of spirit photographs were engaged in a wider debate about illusion and evidence. Ghost shows and trick films explained how spirits were optical illusions. Theatrical magic used variations on Pepper's Ghost in stage shows which purposely drew attention to the trick without revealing the method behind it. Audiences at these shows collectively experienced a demonstration of the construction of illusion. At the same time audiences attended medium demonstrations and public séances where they witnessed phenomena that they could not explain in rational terms (Blum 2007). There was debate about fraud and tricks used by mediums and psychics which sparked interest in witnessing such alleged psychic phenomena at first hand. Ghost hunting became a leisure activity. One public lecture titled 'Gossip about Ghosts' by former chemist George Tweedie claimed 'spook hunting has recently become as fashionable as Slumming', another middle-class cultural experience (Davies 2007: 207).

Nineteenth-century spirit forms produced a state of uncertainty. Spirit photography and film were technical apparatus and possessed supernatural forces. Theatrical magic was a stage illusion and symbolic of things which were beyond explanation (Lamont 2006). The multiple meaning of spirit forms and new technologies was incorporated into the construction of live performances in public séances, magic acts and variety shows. Professional mediums and magicians shaped their performances on the centrality of ambiguity. Magical entertainment focused on complex mechanical, optical and physical conjuring which aimed to leave the audience with multiple explanations, masking the method behind the illusion (see Chapters seven and eight). These professionals worked with audiences in their experience of these performances. They drew on audience participation. Attentive and inattentive audiences became incorporated into the development of these professions and style of entertainment. In this way, the production and reception of ghost shows, spirit photographs, trick ghost films, theatrical illusions, illuminated the selling of ambiguous cultural experiences to mass audiences.

Conclusion

Ghost shows have been part of the industrialisation of mass culture, providing a traditional set of stories and images to be used in the move from show to show business. The nineteenth century is rich in histories of spirits and magic, and media and communication. To make sense of ghosts in this historical context is also to make sense of cultural forms and how people engage with them at this juncture in time. The story of spirit belief in nineteenth-century Europe and America is one that connects with other historical accounts of spirits in previous centuries. People turned to spirit beliefs as one means of managing great socio-economic and political changes, alongside moral and cultural imbalance. The rise of modern spiritualism in the nineteenth century is one chapter in a long history of spirit forms and beliefs as sociological and psychological processes. But spirit belief in this period also marked a development in seeking guidance from spirits, in actively searching for proof of an afterlife through spirit communication. Spirit forms during the nineteenth century were associated with communication of every kind, technological, face to face, and at a distance. And spirit communication was tricky. An element of structural doubt was built into modes of communication (Durham Peters 1999). This doubt reflected discourses of spirit belief at the time. Spirit communication was both an alternative belief system to those of dominant scientific and religious thinking and a cause for doubt as proof of an afterlife was elusive. A structure of doubt was emblematic of spirit forms and beliefs and the ways people engaged with them.

The centrality of ambiguity that was established during this historical juncture is one that continues throughout the twentieth century. Technological developments in radio, television and the web continued to be associated with spirit forms, such as radio and trance states, television and altered states, and the internet and virtual reality. The more technological devices that were taken up in society the more complicated communication became. The web of connections across multimedia environments is rich territory for spirit forms. Nineteenth-century production and reception of spirit beliefs and cultural forms tells a story of change and uncertainty which continues to dominate contemporary paranormal beliefs in popular culture. In many ways entertainment and leisure industries and audiences are continuing to develop ambiguous cultural experiences.

Chapter 3

Paranormal in popular culture

'Something is happening ... '

The paranormal is part of mainstream popular culture. The front cover of Take a Break's *Fate and Fortune* uses a pun on 'girl's night out' as a playful reference to Halloween attractions. Readers can hold a dinner for the dead, visit a haunted house, predict the future, cast a spell, meditate and make a jack-o'-lantern. Have a 'ghouls night out' and explore your dark side. According to the *Economist* Halloween could be the new Christmas, with record sales in ghost products and haunted happenings. Halloween is part of paranormal trends. Polls around the world indicate 50 per cent of people in these countries hold at least one paranormal belief. In such an environment it is open season on ghostly matters. Resurgence in paranormal beliefs gives momentum to a range of representations of ghosts, supernaturalism, angels, and fringe science, across multimedia environments. In popular culture, paranormal attitudes and beliefs are being transformed into lifestyle choices. Spirits are becoming a way of life.

As paranormal ideas and beliefs become part of popular culture they change meaning. The extraordinary transforms into something more ordinary. A wide definition of the paranormal includes eclectic beliefs and practices, from spirits and vampires, to angels and aliens. People don't have to be religious to believe in spirits, nor do they need to know about science to explore altered states of consciousness. Cultural practices loosely associated with the paranormal range from media and communication, to tourism, leisure, health and well being, psychology and self-help. Professionals within psychic and paranormal industries are not only mediums or clairvoyants, but people whisperers, angel communicators, reality adjustors. One of the implications from this transformation of meaning is that what people think of as paranormal is changing, and what they understand as a paranormal experience is open to multiple interpretations.

Paranormal beliefs

Social trends suggest widespread belief in the paranormal. In Britain, various polls indicate paranormal beliefs have risen from around 10 per cent in the 1950s to

Figure 3.1 'Ghouls Night Out'

almost half the population of today. A recent British poll showed 64 per cent of people in the survey believed there were powers that could not be explained by science, the same amount of people who believed in God. Forty-nine per cent of people believed in ghosts and 41 per cent believed in communication with the dead (French, cited in Waterhouse 2008: 8). 'A 2005 Gallup survey showed three out of four Americans harbor at least one paranormal belief, and that one in three believe in ghosts—up from one in four in 1990.'[1] Gallup surveys in 2001 and 2005 indicated rising belief in four paranormal phenomena, haunted houses, ghosts, communication with the dead, and witches. A recent American poll signalled nearly half the population believed in extrasensory projection.[2] The National Science Foundation in America claims an increasing belief in pseudoscience – phenomena which have no agreed scientific explanation.

In *The Psychology of Paranormal Beliefs* Irwin outlines various aspects of the paranormal (2009: 4–5). These include superstitions (good and bad luck); psi processes (extrasensory perception); divinatory arts (astrology); esoteric systems of magic (magical spells); new age therapies (crystal powers); spiritism (spirit communication); Eastern mystico-religious beliefs (reincarnation); Judeo-Christian religious beliefs (angel communication); extraterrestrial aliens (alien visitations); and cryptozoological creatures (legendary monsters). The list is not exhaustive and people can have more than one belief in any of the above. There is debate about whether traditional religious beliefs should be included under the umbrella of the paranormal. Irwin cautions against leaving out religious beliefs because of connections between angels, miracles and the paranormal. Another category that could be included in the list is that of traditional folkloric beliefs such as vampires or werewolves.

Irwin defines paranormal beliefs by referring to what they are, who holds these beliefs, and how they believe:

> as the concept is popularly used, a paranormal belief is defined on a working basis as a proposition that has not been empirically attested to the satisfaction of the scientific establishment but is generated within the non scientific community and extensively endorsed by people who might normally be expected by their society to be capable of rational thought and reality testing. For these people the belief is phenomenologically a part of their sense of reality and truth rather than 'a proposition they endorse.' Like other types of belief, a paranormal belief will either be intuitive or reflective; will have cognitive, affective and (sometimes) behaviourable components, will be distinct from a value or simple statement or preference, will be relatively stable and therefore somewhat resistant to the influence of counterargument; and will be dimensional, that is marked by various degrees of endorsement between the poles of extreme scepticism and extreme gullibility.
>
> (2009: 16–17)

The paranormal is a concept loosely based around science, but understood primarily within non-scientific communities. It's a concept endorsed by people capable of rationality, and yet rational thought and reality testing is equally open to interpretation and specific to cultures and contexts. Paranormal beliefs are not only propositions to be endorsed but part of the fabric of people's lives and their understanding of reality and truth. The nature of paranormal beliefs makes them important to people, but at the same time relatively unfixed and unstable within broader concepts of reality and truth. The ways people believe are varied, involving feeling, thinking, evaluating, sensing, and acting, all components that shift in weight and meaning as people put their beliefs into practice. And there are modes of belief and scepticism, with people positioning themselves within a wide spectrum. As Irwin points out, 'the complexities of the development of paranormal beliefs' challenges 'simplistic characterisations of paranormal believers' (2009: 128).

Amongst people in this study, the paranormal includes 'things that cannot be explained.' It's a wide category inhabited by a mix of divergent beliefs. Irwin points out the porous meaning of the paranormal implies 'some beliefs may not be regarded as paranormal forever' (14). Rather than resist the openness of the paranormal, people in this research study tend to embrace it. They adopt a philosophy of possibilities. One of the most common phrases on the topic is 'you have to keep an open mind.' Paranormal beliefs symbolise possible worlds. One person explained:

> I am sceptical, but I wouldn't rule out paranormal things completely because obviously none of us know what it is. I think that certain people who experienced certain things that they can't explain, if they have an open mind to it maybe it could be paranormal … I think it's a lot to do with how an individual views certain events or experiences. You just don't know.
>
> (30-year-old female library assistant)

In terms of cultural practices, the paranormal opens doors into possible worlds.

A shift in meaning from spirit belief to paranormal belief highlights popular construction of the term today. Spirit beliefs were connected to modern spiritualism, a nineteenth-century unorthodox religious movement which included Eastern and Western philosophies and religious practices. The spirit telegraph or spirit photograph were examples of how these religious beliefs were explored within Victorian society and culture. Today, in Western popular culture, there are paranormal beliefs which are related to paranormal photographs, paranormal romance, paranormal activities. There is parascience, parapsychology, parahealth. Hess argues 'paraculture' includes aspects of modern science, spiritualism, new age practices, Eastern and Western philosophies, the psychology of the human potential, indigenous religions, neo paganism, Wicca and goddess religions, alternative therapies and exercise, and environmental and ecological practices (1993). This person commented: 'it's almost a genre really, things with no definite explanation under one heading – aliens, ghosts and sprits' (20-year-old male student). The paranormal is a powerful term because it signifies something beyond definition. One woman explained her understanding as 'something you can't logically explain or something that doesn't fit into what is considered as normal. So I say, something happened to you, or something you experienced that there is just no logical explanation for it at all' (25-year-old female human relations trainer).

Other terms associated with paranormal beliefs include psychic and occult. Irwin's definition does not include either but there are areas of spiritism and communication with the dead which include Ouija and séance practices, and occult folklore related to vampires, werewolves and other legendary monsters. In *Beyond Entertainment*, Sancho (2001) surveyed and interviewed a representative sample of over 3000 British people about their attitudes and beliefs towards psychic matters in the media. 'For most respondents, psychic was familiar, mainstream and relatively comfortable' (2001: 11). Psychic meant 'positive intent with positive consequences', it was thought to be 'enlightening and about information gathering' (ibid). Sancho noted 'there has been a shift in society regarding the way many alternative practices are viewed. Most respondents considered things like acupuncture, Feng Shui, homeopathy and yoga as familiar and mainstream. They were widely regarded as activities which contributed to one's physical and mental well being' (2001: 8). She also noted 'psychic practices, such as horoscopes, astrology, faith healing and clairvoyance were regarded as relatively mainstream and predominantly harmless' (9). However, respondents made a distinction between psychic matters and occultism which 'was associated with Satanism, black magic, Ouija and voodoo' (ibid). Occultism was considered fringe and 'as having negative intent.' The area of spiritism and 'supposed contact with the dead' was somewhere in the middle, depending on the intent of the medium. People differentiated between the calling of loved ones in the spirit world, and calling on negative forces which was thought to cross over into occultism (2001: 10).

In this study people used the word psychic to mean a loose set of beliefs and practices associated with divinatory arts, new age therapies and Eastern-mystico religious beliefs, although there are some connections with psi processes such as telepathy and spiritism practices. The occult was rarely referred to and thought to be outside the parameters of the paranormal. As with the participants in Sancho's study, it was important to people that their paranormal beliefs were understood in relation to positive intent. There were common discursive strategies to differentiate paranormal practices from other areas perceived as taboo. Jokes about black magic, satanic worship, or digging up graves were often used to make a distinction between paranormal beliefs and occultism. References to psychics were made to differentiate professionals from ordinary people. There was a difference between ordinary people with psychic abilities who were perceived to have positive intentions to help people, and professional psychics who charged by the hour and were perceived to have negative intentions to exploit people. Context is crucial and people choose when and how to express their beliefs with care.

The question of whether different kinds of people have a propensity to paranormal beliefs should be treated with caution. Research on this matter is inconclusive. There are debates amongst psychologists as to the wording of questions and scales used in paranormal belief surveys. In terms of age, Irwin reports there are no definitive findings so far on younger and older people and paranormal beliefs. Most survey results found no correlation between socio-economic status, or education, and paranormal beliefs. Irwin comments on gender and the endorsement of most but not all paranormal beliefs as slightly stronger amongst women than men, as reported in polls data worldwide (2009: 55–56). Women reported more beliefs in astrology, extrasensory perception, new age practices, psychic healing, and superstitions. Men reported more beliefs in UFOs, extraterrestrial aliens, and extraordinary life forms (2009: 66). Witchcraft had mixed findings on gender. Using different indices for paranormal beliefs in survey research Irwin found slight differences amongst men and women for paranormal concepts and new age beliefs. These results were confirmed by some studies, for example Sjödin analysed Gallup polls data in Sweden and found 'women generally hold more beliefs than men' (2002: 84). However, other studies showed no differences at all. Irwin notes 'sociocultural structures evidently influence the form or type of the paranormal beliefs embraced by a person' but methodological problems mean it is difficult to say one way or another which sociological variables have a significant impact on paranormal beliefs (2009: 34).

In this research, the context within which people express their beliefs suggests age and gender differences. This is related to life stage and cultural preferences, with younger people framing their scepticisms and beliefs somewhat differently than older people. Issues of age and religion were taken up by Lynn Schofield Clark (2003) in her study of young people, religious faith, and representations of supernaturalism and occultism in the media. As with this study, she used socio-logical approaches in qualitative research, looking at connections in the lives of people. She found young people who were uncertain about religion were inter-ested in exploring various beliefs related to the paranormal and supernaturalism. In terms of gender, there was a general approach by participants that combined both scepticism and belief in the paranormal, but was framed and understood somewhat differently by men and women. Males were more sceptical of the paranormal than females (by their own definition). However, this did not mean to say men did not believe in the paranormal, but that they framed their scepti-cism and belief in relation to scientific and evidentiary matters. Conversely, females were more believing of the paranormal than men (by their own defini-tion), but this did not mean women were uncritical of the paranormal; rather they framed scepticism and belief in relation to personal, emotional and spiritual matters. A point of connection was that men and women prioritised personal experience as proof of their paranormal beliefs, something common to other studies on 'beliefs as part and parcel of a fundamentally subjective perspective on life' (Irwin 2009: 76).

Most research in paranormal beliefs has taken a sceptical perspective. Sceptics view these beliefs as a personal and social threat (Irwin 2009: 20–21). There is a presumption that beliefs are false and therefore promote uncritical thinking, poor-value judgements, gullibility and susceptibility to fraud. *Paranormal Claims* (1999) includes a range of sceptics, often within psychology or science, who express concerns about such beliefs. Irwin surveyed literature from psychology and various studies on people who hold paranormal beliefs. One issue includes whether people are delusional. Irwin argues although paranormal concepts can be part of a delusion this is 'not evidence that paranormal beliefs are themselves delusory' (Irwin 2009: 9). There is a difference between beliefs as phenomen-ological and part of people's sense of reality and truth and beliefs as an indicator of psychopathology. Another issue is irrationality. In Irwin's definition he speci-fically argues that people who hold paranormal beliefs are capable of rational thinking. Studies in creativity and reasoning style indicate complex thought processes underlying paranormal belief (Irwin 2009: 90).

A sociological perspective has an understanding of the paranormal as practised by people in this study and does not presume the truth or falsity of these beliefs. The issue of respect is crucial. As surveys show, many people believe in the paranormal and many claim to have had a paranormal experience. To understand people's experiences includes respect for a diversity of positions, across a spec-trum of scepticism and belief. One participant commented: 'it's respecting each other, accommodating each others existence' (43-year-old female student).

Participants are familiar with discourses associated with a diversity of positions. Criticism of people who hold paranormal beliefs is common knowledge. By the same token, criticism of people who presume there is no such thing as the paranormal is also common knowledge. In this study no one wanted to be perceived as an extreme believer or extreme sceptic because both positions had negative connotations. One identity is perceived as gullible and irrational, the other hyper critical and a killjoy. There are assumptions about people who hold paranormal beliefs which are taken up and debated by participants who define themselves as moderate sceptics or believers, or people who just don't know one way or the other, by the far the most common position in this research. This woman summed it up as 'I don't believe in ghosts and don't disbelieve either' (38-year-old housewife). There are discursive strategies used to deal with assumptions about paranormal beliefs which centre on scepticism and belief, where people construct an identity that contains both positions at the same time. Lamont (2006) calls these discursive strategies an avowal of prior scepticism or belief, where people tell a story about themselves as a former sceptic turned believer, or vice versa. The research here supports a sociological understanding of people as capable of holding both positions at the same time. The sceptic and believer is a dual identity position that draws on assumptions about paranormal beliefs. It connects with broader sociological theories regarding rational and irrational thoughts, feelings and emotions (see Gordon 1998, Landy and Saler 2009 amongst others).

The next section examines cultural trends. These are trends observed and commented on by participants in this study. Paranormal romance, ghost hunting TV, or psychic services highlight how a range of paranormal beliefs are the basis for cultural practices, such as reading psychic magazines, or going on a ghost tour. Cultural and entertainment industries take paranormal beliefs and turn them into revenue streams. Although cultural practices are related to beliefs, they are not the same thing. For example, a belief in psi processes, such as extrasensory perception, may be based on personal experiences, information and knowledge on psi from published sources, press accounts, or popular science books. The television series *Fringe* (ABC, USA) is about psi processes as re-imagined and represented in mainstream drama, where character, narrative, and aesthetics are paramount. Someone who believes in psi may or may not watch *Fringe*, but they will certainly know the difference between the two. This connects with much audience research which has found critical engagement with the media, and complex responses to media messages. Popular culture plays with paranormal concepts. And people learn how to play with these concepts as related to, but also separate from, paranormal beliefs in society.

Paranormal trends

In a history of European culture Donald Sassoon reflects on some key themes recurring from the 1800s to present day. One of these themes is 'the desire to see the unique', whether that is the arias of an opera singer in the 1800s, or the inauguration ceremony of the new President of the United States of America today (2006: 1365). Sassoon argues our intrinsic desire to see the unique in popular culture has increased rather than decreased over time. A related theme is the selling of culture as an experience. Early cinema was sold to mass audiences not as a film they could own, but as the experience of a performance. Theatre, live events, and public shows are based on the selling of an experience, such as being at a music festival, or going to see a play. Another theme is that of fascination with the dead, from the magic-lantern shows of the 1800s, waxwork exhibitions, or the gothic literature of the Victorian period, to the horror films of today. All three themes are apparent in contemporary examples of the paranormal in popular culture. The paranormal offers the promise of something unique, it is by its very definition 'scientifically inexplicable', and associated with unusual and strange people and happenings. It offers the promise of a unique experience. By far the most common way of selling paranormal matters is as a cultural experience, such as visiting a psychic, or going to a haunted castle. Many TV shows such as *Paranormal State* are about the second order experience of being at a haunted place. And the paranormal offers the promise of a unique experience about the living and the dead. Fascination with issues of life after death, and life before death, recur in magazines, books, or live demonstrations, around spiritism and mind, body and spirit practices.

The business of Halloween is one example of how the themes of uniqueness, cultural experiences and fascination with death and afterlife come together. Retail figures for Halloween have increased in America, with around $5 billion for 2009. According to *Business Week* 'Halloween's popularity is part of the post-September 11 nesting craze. Richard Laermer, author of *2011: Trendspotting for the Next Decade*, says fantasy is absolutely crucial for stressed-out adults right now.'[3] The *Economist* reported that Halloween could be the new Christmas. In New York City the haunted house attraction 'Nightmare' has seen its visitors grow from 6000 in 2003 to an estimated 35,000 in 2007. The company uses the internet to survey New Yorker's worst fears and then recreates those in 23 rooms, each with a different spirit.[4] 'Nightmare' makes $1 million in revenue during Halloween. In this example, familiar themes of phantasmagoria, spirit forms, or gothic horror from the past are recreated for contemporary times. The fantasy of 'Nightmare' works within a specific setting of New York City, set against the backdrop of recent history and trauma concerning the terrorist attacks on the World Trade Centre and subsequent wars in the Middle East. It shows how paranormal themes work within social and cultural contexts.

Spirit forms

Historical spirit forms reappear in contemporary examples of paranormal media. As noted by Marina Warner, phantasmagoria explicitly reference earlier spirit forms, making these representations familiar to the public. Much paranormal media today draws on Victorian representations of ghosts, giving a gothic tone to contemporary spirit forms. The retro Victorian take is made obvious in the picture of a transparent female form in Victorian clothing used to illustrate the book *21st Century Ghosts: Encounters with Ghosts in the New Millennium* (Karl 2007). A twenty-first-century ghost can appear as a familiar form, even if it is encountered through new media technologies, such as the 'ghost in the machine' account of a former lady of the house appearing as a shadow on digital copy paper. These ghosts are historical figures. They are striking examples of how popular history re-imagines the past as troubled spirits who appear today in famously haunted locations.

Spirit forms often appear as an unusual light source. The familiarity of this type of spirit is explained by examples of representations of ghosts as light sources in early modern accounts and pictures of ghosts where spheres or patches of light were seen at haunted locations, or along woodland paths (see Davies 2007). Spirit photography was popular during the late nineteenth century and the First World War. The spirit photographer claimed the camera was a conduit to the spirit world, for example capturing the image of a deceased child in the photograph of a grieving mother. Such an image would appear transparent, often as an unusual light source. As Kodak invented an easy to use camera, more spirit photographs emerged by members of the public who were visiting historic places, or attending séances with mediums. These photographs often depicted a ghostly light source. The ectoplasmic spirit photograph referenced the ghost light in the form of a luminous substance emerging from a medium's body.

In digital photography the ghost light is re-imagined as an orb. In an article in the magazine *Paranormal* 'Orbs – just a load of balls?' the UK-based investigatory group Para.Science described the orb as 'the craze that swept through the paranormal world.'[5] Photographs of orbs show small circles of light, or lines of light known as tracer orbs. Videos of orbs show dancing light sources. Para. Science noticed that the appearance of orbs as ghost manifestations in digital photographs and videos happened during the daytime and at night, in haunted and non-haunted locations: 'there was something terribly wrong – they surely couldn't be paranormal, there was just too many orbs!' (ibid). They looked at 10,000 digital pictures from the internet and concluded: 'orbs are not really paranormal manifestations: the combination of camera design, software and lighting, together with the dust and water vapour suspended in the air all play a part in the creation of these interesting but ultimately explainable phenomena' (ibid). Despite such claims, many paranormal websites show images of orbs photographed by members of the public debating whether these forms are evidence of spirit presence. Orbs are common knowledge amongst people who attend ghost hunting events, or watch reality TV. For example, this male participant at a ghost hunting event came from an investigation in the cellars of an old building saying 'I think I got an orb. I don't know if it was an orb, but it was a ray of light that went downstream. Not dust, possibly, it might be, an orb.' Whether orbs are real or not, they represent a re-imagining of ghost lights for contemporary digital culture. Orbs also are spirit forms for mobile phones.

For example, one woman commented on watching mobile phone footage of an orb in her daughter's bedroom: 'In the pitch black and then the light came from nowhere. It was a thrill to watch it. When I saw it I went cold' (41-year-old female dance/choreographer).

The lifestyle magazine *Country Living* offered DIY tips to its readers on how to display 'paranormal portraits' for a Halloween theme (see Figure 3.2). This is a good example of how the spirit photograph of the Victorian period is now called a paranormal portrait. The associations of the spirit photograph with the unorthodox religious movement of modern spiritualism are lightly mocked. Here the paranormal is a lifestyle matter, not a religious belief. It connects with the revival of the Victorian gothic as a lifestyle trend. In Spooner's cultural analysis of contemporary gothic she argues this revival is self-referential (2006). Making mock paranormal portraits is one way of restaging the spirit photograph in a modern domestic setting – 'you'll never look at loved ones the same way after transforming their images into a ghostly display.'

A series of exhibitions on spirit photography at the American Museum of Photography ('Do you Believe?', 2000), and the Metropolitan Museum of Art ('The Perfect Medium', 2005), reframed the history of photography in light of contemporary ideas on fantasy, surrealism, fakery, and the unconscious. These exhibitions illustrate how historical spirit forms can be critically re-examined in contemporary culture. In the exhibition 'The Disembodied Spirit' (Bowdoin College Museum of Art, 2003) various film-based works by artists such as Bruce Nauman, Bill Viola, or Tracey Moffatt explored the history of spirit photography in contemporary representations of ghosts. According to the curator Alison Ferris 'the representation of ghosts can be understood as more and other than novelties and can, in fact, open the way for new understandings of vision and reality in our contemporary, digitized, hypermediated world' (2003: 1). She explained:

> artist's recourse to the ghostly often functions as a by product of technological advances ... it is no coincidence that ideals of a disembodied self ... evolved directly from radical technological innovations, in as much as these utopian visions offered new possibilities for life and experience within a drastically changing world.
>
> (2003: 2)

These artists used the spirit photograph of the past to explore their anxieties regarding alienation of the self within a digital environment. For example, British artists Jon Thomson and Alison Craighead used search engines as inspiration for *e-poltergeist* (2001), where the chaos of search and retrieval was experienced as disembodied and unnerving in their digital installation.

Many historical spirit forms in paranormal media can be understood in relation to Marina Warner's argument of the metaphor of spirit in *Phantasmagoria* (2006). Spirit forms in sculpture, fine art, film, photography and digital arts are part of 'the logic of the imaginary.' Examples include the Greek gods 'who

Figure 3.2 Paranormal Portraits

summoned mists and clouds in which to wrap themselves and their protégés from harm', or renaissance 'theories of the inner eye and fantasy' (2006: 13). Warner outlines how metaphors of spirit have changed and what this suggests about the contemporary self and modern ideas of individuality and consciousness. 'The faculties of what used to be called the soul – fantasy, memory, sensations, emotions – now exist in symbiosis with televisual communications', with an image-world that is denatured, unsettling, hallucinatory, and chaotic (19). Metaphors of spirit can appear as historical figures connected to social injustices or personal trauma, exploring issues of memory and emotions in popular history. The image of the ghost light of the past can exist in symbiosis with digital technologies, producing unstable discourses of authenticity regarding spirit communication. The metaphor of spirit can become a sign of disembodiment in the form of paranormal portraits as lifestyle trends. And it can be part of concerns about changing ideas of the self and identity in chaotic times, as *e-poltergeist* suggests.

Beyond death

USA Today claimed the oddest trend of 2008 was dating the dead: 'Death isn't just proud these days, it's practically exultant.'[6] *True Blood* (HBO 2007–) takes vampires to the modern-day American South, where vampires have rights, drink synthetic blood, and try to live as humans rather than the undead. The central character Sookie falls in love with Vampire Bill. Their relationship explores the ups and downs of dating the dead. The world of Sookie is one inhabited by several paranormal entities – she is telepathic, her boss at the local bar is a shape shifter, and other legendary monsters populate the local area. *True Blood* is based on the bestselling books in the *Southern Vampire Mysteries* by Charlaine Harris, with nine novels released in eight countries so far. Stephanie Meyers' series of vampire romance novels *Twilight* are also popular; the fourth in the series *Breaking Dawn* sold 1.4 million copies in a day, with an initial print run of over three million. Her books have been made into Hollywood films – the soundtrack of the first film was the biggest selling album of 2008 in America. According to the *Financial Times* 'escapism from dark economic times is contributing to a boom in vampire-themed entertainment.' 'Paranormal romance accounted for 11.8 per cent of all romance fiction – the largest category in the book trade – in 2007. This was up from 9 per cent in 2006 and 4 per cent in 2002, according to the Romance Writers of America, and was expected to grow further in 2008.'[7]

A related trend is television drama about altered states, or fringe science, such as extrasensory perception, or time travel. Many top ten TV shows on American networks include characters with paranormal powers. *Heroes* (NBC, USA) is a drama series about ordinary people who discover they possess a special power to heal the sick, or fly. *Fringe* (Fox, USA) follows a special FBI team and their investigations into phenomena outside of mainstream science, like telepathy where one person can read the mind of another. *Flash Forward* (ABC, USA) explores the possibility of time travel and the existence of different realities. Similar to *The X Files* (Fox, USA) of the previous decade, this type of television drama takes niche scientific research and popularises it for mass audiences. Channel controller of Five (UK), Richard Woolfe commented: 'those sorts of

Figure 3.3 Paranormal romance

shows that would have lived in the peripheries of the TV universe on niche channels now live in the mainstream. It encourages debate and that is exciting.'[8] When Five screened *Flash Forward* in Britain they followed the show with a documentary about the possibility of time travel and a related online forum for fans.

A significant element of the paranormal in popular culture is its symbolic power to bring the dead back to life. Within spiritism practices the word death is rarely used. When people go to see a medium, or watch a demonstration on television they will see someone who speaks of spirit. There may be messages from dead relatives or loved ones but this does not mean to say their life is over, they continue in spirit. Whilst different beliefs and practices exist in spiritism, with some following modern spiritualism, and others a mix of Eastern and Western philosophies, esoteric writings, fringe scientific theories, and pagan practices, what unites these approaches is a positive perspective on death. The titles of non-fiction books reflect this perspective, such as the bestselling book series *From the Other Side* by psychic author Sylvia Browne. People who professionally work within spiritism call themselves mediums and psychics, and also spirit whisperers, or spirit communicators.

The *Ghost Whisperer* (CBS, USA 2005–) is a good example of the way television drama can represent spirit communication. Jennifer Love Hewitt plays a newly wed medium helping troubled spirits come to terms with unfinished business and pass on to the afterlife. The series attracts eight to ten million viewers and has won its Friday evening time slot across all demographic groups. According to CBS' Scott Koondel, 'the show is about a strong woman who owns her own business and is married to a firefighter, so women relate to that. It's family-oriented ... And it offers scary stories and high-end special effects.'[9] The series contains life-affirming stories of how family and loved ones communicate with each other in this life and the spirit world. CBS advertises the show as 'Home but Not Alone.' James Van Praagh is the creator, co-executive producer, and also a spirit communicator. He modelled the character Melissa on the medium Mary Ann Winkowski. The star is a believer in spirits, explaining: 'I'm sort of a control freak and for me death is a concept that's always been very difficult ... If there really is a different adventure afterwards, then that is a lovely thought. That makes you feel not necessarily good about dying, but better about it.'[10]

Televised recordings of medium demonstrations highlight the way an audience engages with the concept of death as afterlife. In shows such as *Crossing Over with John Edwards* (Sci Fi, USA), or *6th Sense with Colin Fry* (Living TV, UK) the medium conducts a platform reading of a studio audience. Their performance involves communicating with their audience, passing on messages which are acknowledged by participants as spirit relatives or loved ones. Speaking with spirits is represented in these demonstrations as authentic communication with the dead. Rarely are the dead referred to, but rather these are messages from spirits, and family members appear to audiences as if they are with them in the present moment. It is a collective communication where the close relationship between a medium and their audience is reflected in the sharing of highly emotional and personal stories. One woman who had been to a televised medium demonstration told her story of bereavement:

> When I lost my mum I lost all faith. My mum promised me she would find a way to get back to me and when a year passed and nothing happened I disbelieved. ... I believe if you are in a strong grieving process they are not going to come through, you have to let go so they can come through. They wait until we are ready.
>
> (37-year-old female housewife)

The close relationship with her mother continued, and continues, after death, with messages appearing at moments of positive transformation within her grieving process. After meeting Fry on TV she said, 'seeing is believing.' In her view, Fry provided details that proved the existence of afterlife: 'my mum's last words were "I haven't had a fag today" ... to me I have had proof that my mum is around.'

In the novel *Beyond Black*, Hilary Mantel reflects on the concept of death as a negative to positive transformation within paranormal practices. She portrays a medium working in broken Britain, a land of ring roads and forgotten communities, where people have become disenchanted with the world. Mantel's character of Alison is aware of her role in providing positive messages from spirits for people who are grieving, or troubled with their own journey through life:

> People are right to be afraid of ghosts. If you get people who are bad in life – I mean, cruel people, dangerous people – why do you think they're going to be any better after they're dead? But she would never speak it. Never. Never utter the word 'death', if she could help it. And even though they needed frightening, even though they deserved frightening, she would never, when she was with her clients, slip a hint or tip a wink about the true nature of the place beyond black.
>
> (2005: 193–94)

In this context, deception is not about fraud but rather the reconstruction of death. Mantel's medium perpetuates a positive image because people expect it of her, wanting to transform fear of death into reassurance of an afterlife.

Paranormal activities

In the past, ghost hunters would probably have been priests, or local people of importance, who would drive out an evil spirit from the churchyard, or parish boundaries. There were haunted places, and people visited them, but this wasn't part of large-scale tourism (Davies 2007). During the height of the spiritualist movement in the nineteenth century, people used Ouija boards, or contacted mediums, in order to seek out spirits of the departed. These approaches to spirit communication were part of a general fascination with the dead in nineteenth-century popular culture, for example ghost shows, theatrical plays, and gothic novels. It was during this period that a common representation of the ghost hunter emerged, that of a psychic investigator using scientific techniques to uncover evidence of spirits (Blum 2007). Such an image of a ghost hunter worked alongside that of a ghost showman in the entertainment business. Today, ghost hunting is part of entertainment and leisure industries. The film *Paranormal Activity* (2009) is a good example of how representations of scientific investigation into psi phenomena are popularised within entertainment. The film is a dramatised account of the director's personal experience of a haunting, shot with hand held digital cameras to enhance the aesthetics of reality. The advertisement for the film explicitly references one of the main attractions of ghost hunting by focusing on the reactions of the cinema audience who are visibly moved by something invisible. The relationship between cultural forms and how we engage with them are part of the way paranormal activities are shaped within popular culture.

One of the biggest growth genres over the past few years is ghost hunting TV. This is reality entertainment television where paranormal investigations take place in 'most haunted' locations. Although these television programmes are labelled as

Figure 3.4 'Paranormal Activity'

entertainment for legal purposes, they use real mediums, parapsychologists, and famously haunted houses. Ghost hunting TV exemplifies the way popular culture reinvents itself. Changes to the regulation of psychic television paved the way for new content that went beyond the niche marketing of psychic services on satellite and cable channels. An increase in multichannel audiences, and better market shares for digital and satellite channels, ensured a commercially viable platform for new paranormal TV. This hybrid genre of reality TV and history draws on the social and cultural trends of paranormal beliefs and visiting historic places (the second most popular pastime in Britain after gardening). Richard Woolfe, former controller of Living, described how he commissioned *Most Haunted*:

> I bought every single monthly magazine aimed at women, pulled out the content, laid them across my living room floor, in every single magazine there was some form of paranormal article. This was appearing in written form, maybe TV should be doing something about it. My first day at Living, on my desk in the in tray, on the very top of this pile of post was a proposal for a show called *Haunting Truths*. This was in fact the proposal for what was has become known as *Most Haunted*.[11]

Most Haunted has crossed over to mainstream television with celebrity ghost hunts on the commercial channel ITV. The series screens in other countries, including the Travel Channel in the USA. *Most Haunted* has been so successful for its production company Antix that they launched the Paranormal Channel (2008), with the advert 'tune into the paranormal wavelength.'

Most Haunted offers multiple cultures of viewing. For some viewers in this study the show is entertainment:

> I like the ones with famous people. The one with Robby Williams was the best one ever. You've got to watch that one, that is hilarious, that just made me laugh. He screamed like a girl. I enjoyed it, but still, we don't actually see anything, you can hear little things, but that's just us believing that. I believe in ghosts but I don't believe in that.
>
> (33-year-old female youth worker)

For others the show is an ambiguous representation of fact and fiction:

> I don't know, I want to say I'm mad, but I have felt something when I was watching it … I just get a feeling … I think there is an aspect in the programme that sort of draws me as well. In particular some of the history, these buildings the public don't have access to. I'd like to explore there and they are doing it for you.
>
> (28-year-old male civil servant)

This is an example of what Richard Woolfe describes as armchair detection where the viewer decides for themselves the level of reality within an entertainment show (ibid). It is also an example of the disquieting experience of watching ghost hunting TV. As this woman explained: 'sometimes, I can't watch because I cannot be scared. I still do believe it, but I don't. I don't believe it because it makes me feel better, does that make sense?' (45-year-old female carer)

Most Haunted has spawned many ghost hunting shows. The *Observer* newspaper commented:

> The digital and cable channels are so full of bumps in the night and psychics putting the willies up each other that they barely have room for bid-up shopping and unwinnable premium-line quizzes. Take *Ghost Towns*, in which 'acclaimed spirit medium' Derek Acorah (a man possessed if ever you saw one) explores Britain's most 'paranormally active' hot spots, or *Ghost Homes* (people jumping out of their skins in the comfort of their own living rooms) … Paranormal TV is coming out of the walls.[12]

Hollywood Reporter also noted 'the ghost-hunting genre shows no signs of slacking on cable TV, with ratings continuing to grow for several shows' in America.[13] *Ghost Hunters* on the Sci Fi Channel is based on the Atlantic Paranormal Society (TAPS) where two plumbers by day turn into ghost hunters by night. The show has been syndicated to NBC and Oxygen, with a spin-off show *Ghost Hunters International*, radio programme and magazine, as well as several books on paranormal investigations across America. A & E show *Paranormal State*, about a group of college students from Penn State University, and also commissioned *Paranormal Cops* for 2009, based on police officers in Chicago who moonlight as ghost hunters. Alongside other ghost hunting reality TV is that of scientific investigations of paranormal claims, such *X-Testers* on Discovery.

The search for an authentic experience drives much online paranormal activities. As this man said: 'unless you are there, or experience it first hand, it's just entertainment' (31-year-old male retail worker). 'Onestopparanormalshop' sells starter ghost hunting kits (electro-magnetic field readers, motion sensors, night vision cameras, electronic voice listening devices). *Business Week* reported:

> Scores of small businesses, selling ghost-hunting equipment, ghost investi-gation services, and even ghost counseling, are booming outside of their prime season, Halloween … How big is the paranormal market getting? It's hard to tell, as most businesses in the field are small, privately owned, and don't report revenues. But owners say they're getting a boost from the reality show *Ghost Hunters* … Alamo City Paranormal in San Antonio, Texas – said to be one of the most haunted regions of the country – claims to own $80,000 worth of special ghost-detecting gear and charges $50 and up for its investigations.[14]

Websites contain films, photographs and reports of paranormal investigations. Included in the 'top paranormal sites' website is the online ghost hunting community 'ghostsamongus' which hosts live ghostcams. Other sites include a package of amateur footage, reports, blogs, and live chatting, such as 'I am Haunted'.[15] These online paranormal activities illustrate the significance of evidence within paranormal cultural practices, described by one participant in this study as 'I want to believe, but I just need proof' (22-year-old male student).

Alongside the growth in reality TV and web investigations is the popularity of ghost tourism. Ghost hunting events offer customers a unique cultural experi-ence. These organisations make a distinction between the real experience of a ghost hunt and those represented in the media. The distinction is based on an understanding of what is normal within paranormal investigations. A newspaper report used the juxtaposition of fake TV and real ghost hunting to comment on the differences:

> Don't believe what you see on TV. Ghost hunting is boring. There is no traipsing loudly through cemeteries. No spooky séances. No startling at every sound. Real ghost hunting requires hours of sitting in silence and a sceptical mind, explains Jan Gregory, founder of Vancouver Paranormal … But the

popularity of shows such as *Most Haunted*, *Paranormal State*, *Ghost Hunters* and *Ghost Trackers* has proven to be a double-edged sword for real-life ghost hunters. It has brought a legion of new people to the pastime, but most of them are going about it all wrong. 'I'm tired of people doing it the way they do it on TV,' Ms. Gregory says. 'All they do is give ghost hunting a bad name.'[16]

The recruitment organiser for a local paranormal investigatory group in England mirrored the distinction between the mundane reality of ghost hunting and its representation on TV: 'scientific investigating in the real world is nothing like what you see on TV. Some people think that the ghost-chasing antics of entertainment programmes like *Most Haunted* are the reality of research, but that could hardly be further from the truth.'[17] In a satire of sensational ghost hunting TV, comic effect is used to critique the success of drama series such as *Medium* (NBC) with Hollywood actress Patricia Arquette, and psychic detectives such as Allison du Bois, author of *New York Times* bestseller *Don't Kiss Them Goodbye*. *The Onion* is a satirical news network – 'making you seem better informed.' In a spoof news item on 'Today Now!' paranormal detective Leonard Higgs explained how 'using ghosts to solve crimes actually involved a lot of paperwork' (see You Tube, 4 September 2008). As the news anchors try to spice up the interview by showing clips from *Medium* and asking about sensational cases, the paranormal detective only becomes more morose, complaining about the mundanity of his job. The banner running across the screen reads: 'being a detective who talks to ghosts not as exciting as TV.'

Paranormal activities in popular culture raise more questions than answers. The issue of evidence is ambiguous and makes the paranormal open to a number of interpretations. When nothing happens on a ghost hunt this can be proof of the paranormal. For example this man said: 'I would quite happily sit here for nine hours and not hear or see anything. You know you have given it a go' (32-year-old male train driver). One participant explained her experience of watching *Most Haunted*, a show that in ten years has never caught ghosts on camera: 'sometimes they would show absolutely nothing happened because that made it much more believable' (24-year-old female online marketing worker). In this ambiguous environment the issue of personal experience is important. Television shows or websites may encourage debate but for many people in this study they need to see it to believe it. As one woman said 'anything I see on telly I'm naturally sceptical about everything. I think it has to be personal experience' (25-year-old female sales executive). In the next section, there are a range of cultural experiences that extend beyond entertainment or tourism into lifestyle where people can explore paranormal matters for themselves.

Mind, body and spirit

Paranormal cultural practices include the area of mind, body and spirit. The category has transformed from its early association with the new age movement to mainstream areas of lifestyle, health and well being. Mind, body and spirit publications and practices are broadly associated with personal empowerment, including spiritual intelligence, metaphysical thinking, Eastern and Western religious practices, and the psychology of the human potential. Publications target consumers looking for help in relationships, physical health, spiritual well being, or business acumen. An eclectic range of paranormal beliefs and practices can be found in magazines, books, audio and visual step by step guides, and personalised gifts, such as angel cards, or tarot charts.

Hay House is the most well known of the publishing companies in the mind, body, spirit category. It was founded by self-help guru Louise Hay, author of *You Can Heal Yourself*. Hay became known in the 1970s and 80s within the gay community for her work with AIDS patients where her approach to the treatment of illness was through the power of the mind. Today Hay House books and related merchandise are international hits. Authors include motivational speakers, positive thinkers, psychics, angel therapists, water therapists, amongst others. A quick look at Hay's bestselling titles highlights a metaphysical and spiritual approach to life. There are nine books by spiritualist author Marianne Williamson, including four *New York Times* bestsellers, the work of motivational author Wayne Dyer, who has written 30 books, four in the *New York Times* bestseller lists, and psychic author Sylvia Browne whose many books include *New York Times* bestsellers *From the Other Side* series. The newest growth area is self-help for young people, including children's picture books and teenage guides to success. As the *New York Times* points out:

> Though you may not know it, you live in Louise Hay's world. Are you a black man who thinks psychics are nonsense but reads the affirmations of Tavis Smiley? Hay House has a special imprint just for Smiley. Are you a TV-loathing snob who occasionally condescends to watch PBS? The pledge-drive specials that Hay House has produced for Wayne ('Inspiration: Your Ultimate Calling') Dyer have helped raise more than $100 million for public television – they are one of PBS's most-successful fund-raising tools.[18]

In 2007 Hay House 'sold 6.3 million products, taking in $100 million, 8 per cent of which was profit.'[19] Hay Publishing has sold over 40 million books in America alone. They claim 'we think a lot of those people have been helped. You hear people coming up to our authors, and the way they thank them, you know they've been helped.'[20]

Hay specialises in reaching people across a range of platforms. Marianne Williamson's 2008 book *The Age of Miracles* was number two on the *New York Times* bestseller list. She hosts a daily 'Course in Miracles' radio programme on the 'Oprah and Friends' network, referring to the daytime chat show with Oprah Winfrey. She co-founded The Peace Alliance, a grass roots campaign supporting legislation to establish a US Department of Peace. Her official website includes meditation tapes, e-newsletters, and live events, including regular lectures, seminars and study cruises. Motivational author Wayne Dyer regularly appears on television and radio; his official website has the banner 'welcome *Ellen* fans', referring to an American daytime chat show with Ellen Degeneres. Dyer's self-help guide *Change Your Thoughts – Change Your Life: Living the Wisdom of the Tao* is available in book form, audio CDs, advice cards, and on demand streaming. The *New York Times* notes:

> The Hay House audience is different. They don't just want to read Sylvia Browne's books, or see her do psychic readings on a talk show. They want to see her live. Hay House authors do those seminars time and again, with punishing travel schedules. Nancy Levin, the event director, was on the road with one author or another 200 days last year. John Holland toured 23 weeks last year, Sonia Choquette 19 weeks. Esther and Jerry Hicks are on the road all the time: they live in their touring bus. At the events, the speakers' paraphernalia are sold. Doreen Virtue, for example, is known less for her books than for her decks of angel 'oracle cards' that can be used as a divination tool. (Hay House has sold eight million Doreen Virtue card decks, in 12 languages).[21]

One of the successful touring events that Hay House organises is I Can Do It!, where for the price of around $450 people can see and meet the authors for themselves. In the I Can Do It! event in Las Vegas (2008) there were 7200 attendees. I Can Do It! events take place around the world, for example in London, or as an I Can Do It! cruise.

Paranormal beliefs such as divinatory arts, psi processes, esoteric systems of magic, new age therapies, Eastern mystico-religious beliefs and Judeo-Christian religious beliefs are represented in many print forms as personal empowerment. For example, the women's magazine *Soul and Spirit* included the following free products related to a range of beliefs: a crystal bracelet, a meditation DVD, a sun catcher necklace, a wall calendar and angel advice cards – 'find out which arch-angel can change your life!' Beliefs are framed as resources for self-improvement. Heidi Sawyer is one of the magazine's experts in psychic development. A Hay House author (*Why My Mother Didn't Want Me to be a Psychic* 2009), Sawyer explained 'we may envy the psychics and mediums who seem to just "know" the answers, but in fact, we all have a sixth sense that can be easier than you think to tap into.'[22] From simple meditation techniques, to free online psychic tests, the beginner can 'unlock' the extras senses. A participant in this study commented: 'everyone has the ability to do it … it is just training and practicing. It is almost like having a radio station and trying to tune into the right frequency. I think there is a strong connection between mind, body and spirit' (28-year-old female administrator). In this way, a belief in extrasensory perception is framed as a resource to be tapped into for personal empowerment.

Women's magazines illuminate the transformation of meaning from para-normal beliefs to lifestyle practices. For quick comparison, men's magazines are

Figure 3.5 Angel advice cards

aimed at readers interested in hauntings, aliens and legendary creatures. For example, *Paranormal* features news and in-depth articles on parapsychology, UFOs, history and folklore. The front cover of a 2008 edition of *Paranormal* included the title 'Paranormal Apes', the front cover of a 2009 edition included 'Aliens Among Us?'. Women's magazines restyle paranormal beliefs as personal transformation. Something about sorcery in a men's magazine is an article about the history of protective charms, whereas women's magazines have spells for new beginnings, and how to increase fertility, in regular columns where readers are encouraged to write in and join the coven. These magazines can be found in nationwide bookstores and supermarkets in Britain. Readers can also find similar mind, body, and spirit articles and columns in other mainstream publications, where psychic love advice, or angel guidance, are on offer alongside fashion and celebrity gossip.

Take a Break's *Fate and Fortune* claims to be 'Britain's best loved mystic magazine.' It was launched in 2001 by H Bauer publishing, a unit of the privately owned European publishing house Bauer Verkgsruppe, which has 240 magazines in 15 countries. Bauer UK owns 80 titles, read by 26 million adults. Some of their titles include *TV Quick* and *Bella*. Bauer also owns Emap radio and consumer magazines, including titles like *FHM* and *Heat*. *Fate and Fortune* is aimed at women, aged 25–54, working and lower middle class. It invites readers into mystic and paranormal realms – 'welcome to our world.' The magazine

features 'psychic and spooky' reader stories, regular columns by celebrity mediums, astrology charts and psychic readings, in particular responding to readers'
letters – 'send psychic stars your questions.' The front cover of *Fate and Fortune*
January 2009 included headlines of psychic lifestyle transformations such as
'2009 Love Forecast', or the new psychic house doctor – 'she can heal your
home.' *Spirit and Destiny* claims to be the UK's No 1 spiritual lifestyle magazine.
It is owned by Bauer, targeting middle-class women aged 25–44 (with a readership of around 66,000 in the second half of 2008). The magazine is 'for women
who want the best possible future.' The front cover of the January 2009 edition
included the headlines 'get a new life: can a mystic make the most of your future?',
and 'get in touch with your guardian angels.' *Soul and Spirit* is 'your spiritual life
coach.' It's owned by Aceville Publications, who also have titles like *Grow Your
Own* and *Slim at Home*. It has a list of authors from Hay House, like Louise Hay
and Doreen Virtue. The front cover of the January 2009 edition included the
headlines 'new year, new you' and 'find out how to boost your sixth sense.'

In the novel *Beyond Black*, Hilary Mantel describes a psychic hen party, where
the organisers offer party packs–'mini-sizes of aromatic oils, three-pack of incense
sticks, candle in tin, you know the sort of thing … an evening of pampering,
relaxation and prediction' (2005: 325). The medium has to sneak off and deal
with unwanted spirits:

> It's a presence in there … blowing out candles. Cara tried to get it in a
> corner, but we don't want to be frightening the punters. I'm just popping
> over the road because there's a bunch of grannies standing by the hedge …
> Spirit grannies. Great-grannies. Great-greats … I have to explain to them …
> that they're not wanted. I have to put it so as not to cause pain.
>
> (327)

The crossover from paranormal to lifestyle practices creates contradictions in the
meaning of these experiences. These parties are more about the living than the
dead. Another psychic changes profession to become a life coach: 'I'm writing a
book. A new one. *Self-Heal through Success*. It's using the ancient wisdom traditions for health, wealth and happiness. Believe the world owes you: that's what
I say' (255). The paranormal as personal empowerment highlights how alternative beliefs become part of mainstream culture and change the meaning of the
paranormal in the process.

Sceptics

Scepticism is a significant aspect of representations of the paranormal in popular
culture. The term sceptic is commonly understood as 'rational thinker.' It is a
feature of a rise in paranormal beliefs that scientists, psychologists, journalists,
writers, magicians, and other interested groups provide alternative explanations for alleged paranormal phenomena. One participant in this study described

a 'resurgence of rationality' in the media. High-profile sceptics include the American magician James Randi who runs a foundation that challenges pseudo scientific claims. The Amazing Meeting (TAM) is a conference for sceptics sponsored by the Randi Foundation. The BBC news reported on a TAM meeting in London in 2009 with the headline 'When sceptics fight back.'[23] Psychologist and magician Professor Richard Wiseman, author of *The Luck Factor* (2008), explained: 'a lot of sceptics feel very isolated … It's not a popular position to be saying "Father Christmas does not exist" so it motivates people and acts as a springboard for people to see what we're up to.'

Ben Goldacre's *Bad Science* (2008), and related newspaper column and website, critiques the reporting of science in the media. He offers tools for rational thinking and assessments of scientific claims in health and alternative medicine. He writes:

> Without anyone noticing bullshit has become an extremely important public health issue … working in the NHS you meet patients from every conceivable walk of life, in huge numbers, discussing some of the most important issues in their lives. This has consistently taught me one thing: people aren't stupid. Anybody can understand anything as long as it is clearly explained – but more than that, if they are sufficiently interested … but journalists and miracle-cure merchants sabotage this process of shared decision-making, diligently, brick by brick.
>
> (317)

He highlights systematic misrepresentation of science in the media. For example, the assertions of individual entrepreneurs are reported as facts in the press, or authority figures in alternative health are presented as mainstream experts. He argues the kinds of advice given in women's magazines for healing through the power of the mind acts as a barrier to important lifestyle advice such as healthy eating and regular exercise.

Jon Ronson's *The Men Who Stare at Goats* (2004, also made into a Hollywood film in 2009) is an investigation into the American military and extraordinary beliefs in paranormal matters. He traced the journey of a 'madcap vision' of a First Earth Battalion by a US soldier dealing with post-combat depression in the 1970s through the intelligence and psychological operations divisions of the United States military. Ronson interviewed General Stubblebine, the US army's chief of intelligence in the 1980s, who believed in psychic powers and wanted to establish 'an army of soldiers who could bend metal with their minds and pass through objects' (2004: 77). He found connections between the new age thinking of Jedi soldiers, or psychic spies, and the torture of prisoners of war in Iraq:

> The First Earth Battalion Operations Manual had encouraged the development of devices that could 'direct energy into crowds.' History seems to

show that whenever there is a great American crisis – the War on Terror, the trauma of Vietnam and its aftermath, the Cold War – its military intelligence is drawn to the idea of thought control. They come up with all manner of hair-brained schemes to try out, and they all sound funny until the schemes are actually implemented.

(214–15)

Ronson's investigation into the irrationality of the 'war on terror' during the Bush administration showed chilling consequences of psychological operations. An estimated $20 million was spent by the CIA and Department of Defense on psychic warfare.

Chris French runs an academic research unit that investigates alleged paranormal phenomena. He argues the media routinely misrepresent reality, often ignoring sceptical explanations for paranormal matters. In one example of the filming of an allegedly haunted house a team investigated strange sounds coming from the wall:

> people had often reported hearing this sneezing sound ... the first night of the filming there was actually sneezing sounds recorded and played back next day, and it was definitely there ... The following night, we go back again and the sneeze sound was heard again and identified ... and what might have looked like a real haunting was in fact an automatic air freshener ... there was no question at all, that was what we recorded. Once the programme was broadcast, they made a big deal of this sound recording, but no explanation was offered whatsoever ... that's not good TV.[24]

Similar to Goldacre, Professor French believes the sceptical explanation is often missing or misrepresented in the media and this prevents the public from assessing all the evidence for and against paranormal claims.

The magician Derren Brown specialises in mentalism, a form of magic that appears as psychic powers. In his show 'Messiah' (2008, Channel Four), Brown exposed pseudo psychics and preachers by becoming accepted and endorsed by members in America. He explained:

> I've found the idea of raising questions much more interesting and powerful than trying to force my opinions on anyone – so with that as a background I feel very strongly that belief-systems that limit us in any way should be questioned. Belief-systems can be very beneficial of course. But when we're being asked to make life-decisions based on the information coming from a psychic, or a preacher, or an author or teacher, then that strikes me as something that is worth checking and really worth looking at. Is that information credible? Where is that information coming from? I think that's something really worth questioning especially when there is a huge potential for fraud and charlatanism.[25]

His type of magic asks questions about beliefs and relates these to illusion and psychology. A former Christian, Brown became disillusioned with his faith:

> Around the same time of me coming out of Christianity I had already started performing. I slowly realized that true belief of any kind – Christians, new-agers, committed cynics – all fall prey to a similar circular, self-fulfilling logic. I saw that although my faith was culturally endorsed, it didn't stand up to any more scrutiny than the wackiest new-age belief. In the end what it boils down to is if things make us feel good then we believe in them; we take them on board. There's nothing wrong with that. That's kind of what we do as human beings. We're very suggestible around authority figures and if an authority figure tells us things then we tend to believe them and a month later we're coming out with those same opinions as if they were our own. It's absolutely part of what makes us human but equally part of what makes us human is the ability to recognize that as a pattern and question it.
>
> (ibid)

In one televised conjuring trick Brown appeared to touch a young woman without laying a hand on her. The explanation was one based on the psychology of fear. One viewer noted: 'she said she was scared of the dark, and I kind of wonder how much of her imagination was just going into overdrive, because she was in a situation she wasn't comfortable with' (33-year-old female analyst). Such a conjuring trick draws on the common idea of the power of suggestion. One participant commented:

> I like the fact that I still can kick my fears away. I don't quite believe in anything but suggestion ... so, yeah I like the fact that I can keep my fears away, because I know it's suggestion, it is a medical thing, you can really induce people to do something ... my feet are on the ground.
>
> (37-year-old female conference producer)

Grounded in rationalism, there is a pleasure in using critical skills in reconstructing the apparent methods behind these conjuring tricks.

Although Brown focuses on psychic matters, he also references new age beliefs or alternative medical practices. As such, he draws on anti-science, or bad science (Goldacre 2008). A participant in this study noted:

> He's done a show with Richard Dawkins so I have seen him very much as part of, kind of, a resurgence of rationality. I just feel his techniques are more popular. I have to say, I am a really, really big fan. I love his shows, really clever and charismatic. I tend to be sceptical myself, so I completely like the way he is expanding that at the same time.
>
> (25-year-old female teacher)

While Goldacre writes about the claims of homeopathy, Brown performs an elaborate conjuring trick 'The System'. Here, horse racing is the subject of the trick – the myth of the perfect system for winning racing bets – but the explanation for the method behind the trick is one based on science – the placebo effect. A woman believes in the efficacy of a system for horse racing because it appears to work for her. However, there is no system and her chances of winning are based on a law of average that of the many people who place bets a few will win. Whatever complex methods Brown uses in the creation and performance of this conjuring trick, the explanation he offers is one based on science and the placebo effect.

In a review of Brown's book *Tricks of the Mind* (2006) Hilary Mantel commented on a sceptical position to the paranormal. She argued there is a 'difference between explaining and explaining away' (2006: 3) where one approach dispels a myth and another explains the social context to the myth:

> The more the debunkers stamp and shout 'These are the laws of nature', the more some of us hope they will be broken. The psychic trade (a stench in the nose of rationalist piety) is full of frauds, for sure, and lottery tickets are a government-sponsored racket. But the sentiment that 'It Could Be You' is incontrovertible, and hope keeps people going. Psychics are soft targets and there seems no point in attacking them and their audiences, or any other group of believers, without noting the social context in which belief flourishes.'
>
> (2006: 1)

For people in this study, there is a sense of the necessity of a collective voice for rationalism and sceptical thinking. Many viewers are attracted to Derren Brown because he provides an entertaining way of encouraging people to question and debate beliefs. At the same time, there is also a sense of the possibility of paranormal phenomena. Most participants who believed in some form of the paranormal were aware of the discourses of rationality used in the media. People have information and misinformation about the paranormal and rational explanations working together. As Mantel notes, many people know the national lottery is a government-sponsored racket but that doesn't stop them buying a ticket. The social context to belief and scepticism highlights the complex and contradictory nature of people and their experiences.

Conclusion

Polls on paranormal beliefs suggest over 50 per cent of people in countries around the word believe in extrasensory perception, unexplained phenomena, hauntings, or witchcraft. The entertainment industry has transformed paranormal beliefs into revenue streams. What was once considered niche is now mainstream. Psychic cable channels sit alongside network successes such as the *Ghost Whisperer*.

The clinical practice of hypnotism is popularised by self-empowerment. The academic specialism of parapsychology modifies into ghost-hunting reality TV. The scientific study of psi phenomena, like precognition or psychokinesis, becomes a subject of popular television drama *Fringe*. Spiritual and folklore practices turn into publishing phenomena. Angel authors top bestseller lists with celestial advice and help. A new trend in dating the dead sees paranormal romance a worldwide success with the vampire books and TV drama series *True Blood*, or the novels and films in the *Twilight* series.

Recurring themes include the re-imagining of historical spirit forms or folk legends for contemporary times; relationships with loved ones or relatives who have passed to the other side; the search for evidence through personal experience; mind, body and spirit practices that unite various paranormal beliefs as part of personal empowerment; and a resurgence of rationalism that encourages critical thinking on paranormal claims. The process of going mainstream creates a paradox. As paranormal beliefs become part of popular culture, the meaning of the paranormal changes from something extraordinary to something more ordinary. Beliefs become lifestyle practices. But, as people become familiar with representations of the paranormal they also continue to search for unique experiences. As one person explained 'I have to see it to believe it.' Thus, new forms of cultural practices emerge which emphasise personal experience as proof of the paranormal. And in the cycle of culture, new products, services and events connect with a never-ending search for unique experiences.

Notes

1 See 'They See Dead People' in *People Magazine*, 7 November 2005, Vol 64, No 19. Accessed online at www.people.com 29 January 2009.
2 Associated Press and Ipos (2007) American poll conducted 18 October 2007.
3 Young, L. and Siddiqui, S. 'Grown-Ups: Embrace Your Inner Goblin' *Business Week*, 31 October 2008, accessed online at www.businessweek.com 28 January 2009.
4 See 'The business of horror', 25 October 2007, *The Economist*, accessed online at www.theeconomist.com 29 January 2009.
5 See Paranormal, 'Orbs – just a load of balls?' October 2008, Issue 28: 62–63.
6 Bianco, Robert. '2008 in Review: Television' *USA Today*, 22 December 2008, accessed online at www.usatoday.com 16 January 2009.
7 Edgecliffe-Johnson, Andrew. 'Vampires set to provide ray of hope amid gloom' *The Financial Times*, 21 November 2008, accessed online at 18 January 2009.
8 Interview with author 1 December 2009.
9 Albiniak, Paige. '"Ghost" with the Most; CBS hit "Whisperer" to haunt Sci Fi, We and Ion', *Broadcasting & Cable*, 5 May 2008, accessed online at www.broadcasting&cable.com 16 January 2009.
10 Develyn, Darren. 'Whisperer lays body fears to rest' *Daily Telegraph*, 17 December 2008, accessed online at www.dailytelegraph 16 January 2009.
11 Richard Woolfe, Channel controller Five, former controller of Living TV and Sky channels. Interview with author 1 December 2009.
12 See Phil Hogan 'Who ya gonna call?' *The Observer Review*, 18 March 2007: 13.

13 Hibberd, James. 'A& E puts a collar on 'Paranormal Cops' series' *Hollywood Reporter*, 7 January 2009, accessed online at www.reutersnews.com 16 January 2009.
14 Kharif, Olga. 'Scaring up Paranormal Profits' *Business Week* 12 May 2005, accessed online at www.businessweek.com 28 January 2009.
15 See Elsa Wenzel (2007) 'Believe it or not' CNET News.com, 20 July 2007, accessed online at news.cnet.com/2100-1008_3-6197680.html 18 October 2008.
16 Leung, Wency 'Real ghost hunting – not that fake stuff on TV' *Globe Life*, 25 July 2008.
17 See 'Want to become a Ghost Investigator?' *Swindon Advertiser*, 6 August 2008, no author listed.
18 Oppenheimer, Mark. 'The Queen of the New Age' *New York Times* Magazine, 4 May 2008, accessed online at www.nytimes.com/2008/05/04/magazine/04Hay-t.html 30 January 2009.
19 Oppenheimer, Mark. 'The Queen of the New Age' *New York Times* Magazine, 4 May 2008, accessed online at www.nytimes.com/2008/05/04/magazine/04Hay-t.html 30 January 2009.
20 Oppenheimer, Mark. 'The Queen of the New Age' *New York Times* Magazine, 4 May 2008, accessed online at www.nytimes.com/2008/05/04/magazine/04Hay-t.html 30 January 2009.
21 Oppenheimer, Mark. 'The Queen of the New Age' *New York Times* Magazine, 4 May 2008, accessed online at www.nytimes.com/2008/05/04/magazine/04Hay-t.html 30 January 2009.
22 January 2009 issue 12 of *Soul and Spirit*, page 36.
23 Arran Frood, 'When sceptics fight back' *BBC News*, 7 October 2009, accessed online at http://news.bbc.co.uk/2/hi/uk_news/magazine/8291688.stm 7 October 2009.
24 Interview with author 11 June 2008.
25 Derren Brown official website, in response to his television show Messiah (7 January 2008, Channel Four).

Chapter 4

Armchair ghost hunters

'You do kind of believe it a little bit.'

Reality paranormal TV is an example of armchair ghost hunting. As a sub genre of reality TV, these kinds of shows depict ghost hunting as it happens, following paranormal teams on night time investigations in allegedly haunted locations. For legal purposes, these programmes are labelled as entertainment alongside other psychic services. Shows such as *Most Haunted* specifically leave issues of evidence and authenticity open to multiple meanings, allowing audiences to decide for themselves what may be happening. The tension between the entertainment frame and the reality claims in ghost hunting TV is the basis from which these shows are produced and engaged with by audiences. Audiences are invited to join investigations by watching and listening, using webcams, texting comments, and sharing their thoughts and feelings. Audience awareness that paranormal phenomena are extremely rare and difficult to document makes the chances of a haunting being captured on camera highly unlikely. As one viewer said of ghosts 'you can't make them jump through hoops.' At the same time hope is built into the production of the show and audience engagement with it in the possibility that something paranormal might happen on TV.

As armchair ghost hunters audiences have ambiguous responses. In 'The Shawl' by David Mamet the play follows encounters between a medium and their client. A woman wants to make contact with spirits to help her deal with bereavement and a medium exploits the situation, using fraudulent means to make money. However, the story is not what it seems as the woman becomes sceptical of psychic claims and the medium hides the true extent of his gift. In watching the play, the audience is put in an uncertain position. In a similar way, reality paranormal TV is based on the centrality of ambiguity. There are audiences who find the shows entertaining, there are others critical of the way the media construct ghost shows. And there are audiences who also want to believe in spiritism and hauntings. In this sense, audiences have a common understanding of William James' concept of 'the will to believe' (1898). As one viewer put it, people are 'waiting for a haunting to happen.' Ghost hunting TV is an

Figure 4.1 Ghost hunting TV

example of how this distinctive type of popular culture creates ambiguous cultural experiences. As such, the media are a resource for identity work and a playful experimentation with paranormal beliefs.

Ghost hunting TV

The mockumentary *Ghostwatch* by the BBC (1992) is an infamous example of a hoax that was believed to be real and caused widespread panic amongst viewers. *Ghostwatch* was a 'live' television special, with children's television presenter Sarah

Greene and chat show host Michael Parkinson. A team of investigators went to a haunted house, reporting on location to Parkinson in the studio. The alleged paranormal activities in the house included strange sounds, unusual light sources, and blurred images. These indistinct forms helped draw attention to the reactions of the investigators who became increasingly more frightened as the night wore on. The abrupt ending to the live transmission left the investigatory team in danger and viewers very much in the dark. After its transmission, the BBC received thousands of complaints, causing a public reaction similar to Orson Welles' famous radio broadcast of *The War of the Worlds* in the 1930s. Just as the radio listeners of Welles' broadcast were taken in by the verisimilitude of the 'live' radio news broadcast of an alien invasion, so too were television viewers taken in by the 'live' ghost hunt. The *War of the Worlds* appeared so real partly because it tapped into debates about aliens at a time of economic crisis where people were fearful and uncertain of their future in the interwar years (Sconce 2000). *Ghostwatch* appeared so real partly because it connected with debates about the paranormal at a time of anxiety during the end of the millennium. The power of 'live' television can be seen in the public reactions to *Ghostwatch*, where the drama was enhanced by the appearance of being part of something unexpected happening there and then. A viewer recalled their experience as a child: 'I saw *Ghostwatch*. I was very young, I completely believed it and it terrified me. I was at my friends at that time, and I had to phone my parents. I didn't want to go home. I was terrified' (27-year-old male security worker).

A decade later, after the terrorist attacks of 9/11, *Most Haunted* appeared on British television. Richard Woolfe, Channel Controller of Five, and former controller of Living and Sky channels, explained how the show was commissioned when he first arrived at Living:

> I was a complete and total sceptic and I thought this would be bonkers, but I absolutely loved it. It was a great way to bring the paranormal to a wider audience. It brought history to people. There was fantastic showmanship and entertainment, the 'do we believe?' element that psychics supplied. There was the fantastic storytelling ability of Yvette Fielding. It is ten years since *Most Haunted* started and we haven't captured any ghosts on camera and there is still the fantastic ability for the show to attract audiences ... *Most Haunted* remains the brand leader in this type of genre.[1]

As Woolfe notes, the show combined a history of ghosts, with the showmanship of a medium and their ability to connect with audiences, and the emotional reactions of a former children's television presenter. *Most Haunted* managed to capture an elusive search for ghosts and turn it into a long-running reality entertainment series. It did so at a time when anxiety about 9/11 and the subsequent 'war on terror' led many people to look for alternative explanations and ways of perceiving the world. A social trend in paranormal beliefs and practices helped to create a cultural trend in ghost hunting TV.

Living's brand became connected to paranormal entertainment. Richard Woolfe noted 'we found out that although Living was a female skewed channel, this was a way for partners, husbands, boyfriends to watch the channel, a shared viewing experience' (ibid). A small digital channel was attracting two per cent of the adult audience share and up to two million viewers for its live shows, such as the three-day event *Most Haunted Live from Romania* (2005). With more than 12 series, *Most Haunted* is a firm favourite of Living. The acquisition of the CBS drama *Ghost Whisperer* adds to the channel's paranormal theme. Other shows include *Crossing Over* with the American medium John Edwards, *6th Sense* with the British medium Colin Fry, *Psychic Detectives* where three psychic mediums investigate past crimes, *Street Psychic* with British medium Tony Stockwell, and *Psychic Sally* with celebrity medium Sally Morgan. As paranormal matters take to mainstream channels in the form of drama such as *Being Human* on BBC, or celebrity ghost hunting on ITV, Living shows itself as at the forefront of a phenomenon.

In this study, audiences described *Most Haunted* as 'ghost hunting kind of reality', 'kind of non fiction reality', or 'paranormal documentary.' The combination of reality and documentary genres, and paranormal activities, signals a hybrid genre. This 21-year-old male student summed it up: 'that's hard to put into a genre. It's not exactly reality TV, or documentary, I think documentary probably would be closest but documentary really doesn't entertain us, *Most Haunted* does really.' The look of the show is instantly recognisable. One viewer said 'the way they made their own film, green and jerky and sort of down hill, seemed to make the atmosphere' (25-year-old male marketing assistant). Sound is also a key part of the show. One viewer described *Most Haunted* as 'lots of screaming.' A distinctive combination of sound and vision creates a viewing experience that is 'almost like sensory overload' (22-year-old male student). As the show is shot as if live, and actually live for special events, it uses hand held cameras and on-scene night time footage to create a distinctive viewing experience of reality entertainment.

There are also references to gothic horror in this hybrid genre. One TV critic described the show as 'demented gothic titles and rattling dungeons and *Blair Witch*-style images of people recoiling from sudden instances of jiggery-pokery.'[2] TV critic Charlie Brooker said *Most Haunted* was 'an allegedly "factual" cross between *Scooby Do* and the *Blair Witch Project*.'[3] These two viewers explained:

It's exactly when you are watching horror movies, home by yourself.

(20-year-old male student)

The first time I watched it in the dark and I was like, you know, pretty scared, and then I turned the lights on, and it wasn't that scary any more [laughs].

(24-year-old male computer programmer)

There are mock gothic title sequences and a mock documentary style. When the *Most Haunted* team visited Madame Tussauds in London the description of the location playfully referred to the pleasures of horror (Hills 2005) 'where fear, dread and eerie dopple-gangers await in the most famous tourist attraction in the world.'[4] Yet another genre in the mix is that of soap opera with its cast of characters and serial drama. Woolfe commented: 'it's a zoo format with lots of people on the screen. A variety of historians, mediums, cameraman, sound-men, it is a fantastic way of bringing the show to life. Television is littered with examples of this.'

One of the significant aspects of the series is the development of the live event which made *Most Haunted* more of a participatory show. An audience reacts in real time to the investigations on location, and audiences at home can interact with the event via texts, emails and webcams. Woolfe (2009) explained:

> After *Most Haunted* took off I came to my team and said 'right this is a real phenomenon, why don't we do *Most Haunted Live* at Halloween.' The most exciting thing about that was saying come along to Dudley castle on Halloween night, and I remember putting out five hundred chairs and I said to my team do 'you think anyone is going to show up for this?' By about six o'clock one of my team said 'quick, quick come here,' and there were about four hundred people queuing up, and I suddenly realised we had an extraordinary phenomena on our hands. What I learned about *Most Haunted Live* is I have never, ever known a show where if you give someone a ticket they will come. They are amazingly loyal fans.

More than loyal, fans understand that paranormal matters are best experienced live. This is one of the ways *Most Haunted Live* connects with other spirit forms as cultural experiences. In this way the producers offer fans a televised investigation which is like a live performance.

At the same time, something similar was going on with reality TV which was also experimenting with live events. After changes to the regulation on psychic and occult matters in 2001 (by the former Independent Television Commission), a more relaxed framework allowed for the paranormal to be shown on television as long as it was either presented as entertainment, or part of a serious factual investigation. The timing was crucial as this was also the period when reality TV, in particular formatted reality gameshows such as *Big Brother*, had taken over British schedules. Audience research indicates people watch reality TV formats like *Big Brother* looking for a glimpse of reality within factual entertainment (Hill 2005). The makers of *Most Haunted* have to label the show as entertainment, but they also want audiences to look for the reality within this entertainment frame. Going live makes audiences participate even more in a reality game. According to Woolfe:

> It is the ability to be an armchair detective. You can be really spooked by it, and it is great to enjoy that experience from the comfort and safety of

the armchair. What I love about the show and the stance of the channel is that it is not for me to say whether this is true or not. All I wanted to do was present the evidence. I believe our audiences are grown up enough to work it out. Is that rubbish, interesting, paranormally significant? There is the evidence. You take out what you want from it. I know there were audiences who were fascinated by it and examined every frame, and others enjoyed the show as entertainment.

In its early development *Most Haunted* invited viewers to make up their own minds. It positioned audiences within a state of uncertainty. This position is one that is common to spirit forms in popular culture and allows for multiple responses. It is also a position which works best in a live performance where uncertainty links with tension, heightened senses and emotional drama. It invites debate, criticism and reflection. It gets people emotionally and psychologically involved. These ingredients would also become hallmarks for successful reality event shows.

The cast of characters reflects the way the show invites multiple responses, from sceptic to believer. Dr Ciarán O'Keefe is a trained parapsychologist who is profiled on the official website as 'the soft-spoken voice of reason.' He offers a psychological explanation:

> I don't think there's anything paranormal going on at a séance, I think that when something physical happens like the table moves, it's merely down to trickery or unconscious movement. When information comes up or people report subjective experiences like temperature drops or feel dizzy, or tired this comes down to psychology. People are sitting around the table and they have the desire to communicate with the spirits. It's a huge psychological phenomena.[5]

His position is one also adopted by viewers. For example 'when they are actually doing whatever they are doing, getting scared in the room together, I am not really sure what I am supposed to be watching. It's just people getting scared in the room together' (25-year-old male marketing assistant). To watch the show from a sceptical position is to see it as entertainment: 'it's quite a set up where you have a small number of people in quite a small area and they kind of, I don't know, as soon as one of them gets a feel of something, then they start feeling panic or horror. I love it because I find it is really entertaining' (26-year-old female office worker).

The presenter Yvette Fielding is described on the official website as 'the face, heart, soul and scream of the world's leading television ghost hunt.' She defines herself as an open-minded sceptic. In an interview Fielding explained 'you can't make up people being physically sick, hit by stones and chairs and doors being slammed in their faces. My hair has been pulled, I've had slaps across the face and I've even had my bottom pinched!'[6] Viewers can adopt several positions towards the presenter. One man commented on the reactions of the presenter

and team: 'I don't disbelieve. They were genuinely convinced there were something happening there' (28-year-old male sales worker). Another person said:
'I don't believe that for second. And it's really weird because I remember her
from my childhood from *Blue Peter*, so I really want to believe her. I really want
to believe that that's real, but I just don't think it is' (25-year-old female human
resources trainer). Such opinions have been incorporated into the production of
the show: 'I think they have learned by experience because even she says no.
Everybody is saying "can you hear that?" And she comes and says no, no,
no' (36-year-old female care worker). The presenter tells an emotional story that
can be interpreted in different ways as authentic reactions to a spooky place and a
performance for a televised ghost hunt.

The medium in *Most Haunted* occupies a position of believer. As Woolfe
pointed out this is not a simple position but one that asks the viewer 'do you
believe?' Different mediums work on the show, often one medium working full
time for a series with another assisting. On the official website the resident
medium defines themselves as an open-minded believer. Outside of the series,
these mediums are celebrity figures who have a reputation built on public
demonstrations, one-to-one sittings, magazine and newspaper articles, and other
television appearances. As celebrity mediums their reputation is both enhanced by
being on the show and at the same time put at risk because of their involvement
in a reality TV series. For audiences, the medium in *Most Haunted* is the most
appealing and challenging character for them to engage with as they directly
address an audience about the question of belief. This form of communication
between a medium and their audience is one common to psychic-sitter interactions where the question of scepticism and belief is negotiated through matters
of authenticity and expertise (Wooffitt 2006). A medium's reputation precedes
them. It is common knowledge that 'there are good ones and fake ones'
(39-year-old housewife). Even when a medium has a positive reputation, their
appearance on the show can be problematic. As this woman explained of one
medium she had been to see live on stage and thought very good: 'when he did
Most Haunted, he stepped back and just agreed with everybody else. He didn't
do it for very long either. So I think he just thought "well, this is fake and I've
got a name"' (34-year-old woman). Viewers internalise the question 'do you
believe it?' One person reflected: 'I don't know if I believe. I want to believe
them. Maybe, when the medium says their feeling and then they put the facts
on the screen, and they get it right, that's got to be true, surely. I want to believe
in them' (29-year-old female retail manager). A straightforward rejection re-
positions a medium as an entertaining character: 'I always think mediums are
least believable of the whole stuff. Very funny. I completely don't believe that
they are actually contacting ghosts. They believe it themselves, don't they? But
I don't think so. It's very entertaining' (35-year-old female sales worker).

When viewers are asked to decide for themselves if they believe it
or not they make up their minds within a context of debate about the
reputation of professional mediums. *Most Haunted* attracted controversy when a

parapsychologist accused a medium of faking it. O'Keefe explained to the tabloid newspaper, the *Mirror*, that he made up the name of a dead jailer called Kreed Kafer (an anagram of Derek Faker) and gave it to a crew member on a shoot at Bodmin goal: 'I honestly didn't think Derek would take the bait. But during filming he actually got possessed by my fictional character!'[7] These viewers discussed the scandal:

> It was really damaging, and a piece came out, I think it was in the *Daily Mirror*, where they exposed him as being a fake.
>
> (29-year-old female)

> He was set up by one of the crew. He was possessed, when he was saying the name of the person it was actually an anagram of Derek fake, or something.
>
> (27-year-old male)

> And it was quite big scandal about it everywhere. And then, it kind of ruined the spell of it really.
>
> (29-year-old female)

The medium denied the charges and went on to establish another show. A fakery scandal like this highlights audience engagement and disengagement with the show. One person explained: 'I always believe the least about the mediums. The guy that used to be on, he was possessed all the time. Just ridiculous!' (32-year-old male designer). Another woman commented:

> I kind of fell out of love with *Most Haunted*. I thought it was quite realistic, and I became more and more sceptical as time went on after the scandal. It seemed to be so real. I'd be freaked out by it really. But then after I became sceptical of that particular show.
>
> (28-year-old female public relations worker)

Such comments signal how recurring debates about reality and illusion, and authenticity and deception dominate modes of engagement with reality TV and with interactions between a medium and their audience.

Another debate which impacts on ways of engaging with the series is reality TV as a hybrid genre. The show mixes drama, horror, history and documentary in a highly stylised way. In discussions of reality TV audiences acknowledge that if reality TV was real they would be 'watching someone sitting down watching telly all day' (Hill 2005). The drama necessary to reality TV makes it both entertaining and a source of contention as what is real becomes caught up in a staging of reality (see Kilborn 2003). This person commented on the problem of a hybrid genre for *Most Haunted*:

> It's overdramatised, all this stuff. But I think it gets viewers to feel like you are involved in it. I think they have to because if they didn't that would be

very boring, basically, just like a history programme with a ghost at the end. People would switch it off. It would be really dull.

(35-year-old female administrator)

There are several ways of interpreting this show as both real and stylised at the same time. As this specific example is also about 'do you believe in ghosts or not?' genre hybridisation connects with the complex matter of paranormal beliefs. The same viewer who said the show was overdramatised reflected on whether that meant everything about it was unreal:

I don't know, I still kind of do believe this stuff happened. I know everyone else thinks it's fake, but I don't know. I think stuff probably happens and maybe in various episodes they might create some stuff to keep audiences viewing. If nothing happened everyone would think 'oh this is rubbish' so maybe, but I don't know.

(35-year-old female administrator)

But in the beginning, sometimes they would show absolutely nothing happened. And it's a shame because that made it much more believable because of the unpredictability of whether something would happen or not.

(24-year-old female online marketing worker)

In a reality TV show about ghosts an absence of drama can signify a haunting presence. It is the common notion of less is more. For *Most Haunted* there is a balancing act between keeping viewers interested through heightened drama and emotional reactions of the team and keeping viewers believing in the reality claims within the show.

From this brief discussion of the production of *Most Haunted* and the multiple positions of the show as reality TV and ghost hunting TV the key issues of scepticism and belief come to the forefront. These issues are articulated in the context of reality TV and the question of authenticity in an entertainment pro-gramme. Audiences can adopt a critical position with regard to reality TV which is a common way of managing the border crossings of fact and fiction in this hybrid genre. They begin from a position of distrust, approaching reality TV as entertainment with moments of authenticity in a performative environment (Hill 2005). These issues are also articulated within the context of paranormal beliefs and the question of authenticity in alleged séance phenomena, or a medium and spirit communication. A sceptical position is a strategy for belief management. People start out as a sceptic, approaching paranormal claims as a critical thinker, weighing up other explanations alongside paranormal ones. In one way these identity positions are similar. People who watch reality TV are fully aware of cri-ticism of the genre as trash TV, unreal and staged. They have taken on board comments made by reality refusniks and incorporated them into their own iden-tity positions as viewers of reality TV. No one wants to be perceived as unaware of critical debates about this genre. Thus, these debates are part of the way audiences engage with it. People who believe in some form of the paranormal are also aware of criticism of mediums and the difficulty of proving paranormal claims. Comments by sceptics have become incorporated into their identity work as they articulate their beliefs to others. No one wants to be seen as uncritical, gullible and naïve when it comes to paranormal matters. Scepticism has become part of the way people manage their paranormal beliefs.

One viewer noted: 'it makes it a lot more believable saying someone doesn't believe it' (23-year-old female). Such a comment signals the complexity of both the production and reception of ghost hunting TV. To engage with *Most Haunted* from a generic perspective highlights border crossings of fact and fiction, which are connected to issues of authenticity, performance and entertainment. To engage with it from a paranormal perspective highlights all of these issues and connects with matters of evidence and belief. This is why in the following analysis there is an emphasis on the ways audiences engage with ghost hunting TV as an ambiguous cultural experience. People can laugh, and shout and scream at ghost hunting TV as entertainment and they can also use it as a resource to explore what they believe or disbelieve about paranormal claims.

Audience as disbeliever

Audiences in this study have multimodal responses to ghost hunting reality TV. These are people exploring paranormal ideas and practices within an entertainment context. Their state of uncertainty, to refer to William James (1909), is influenced by genre knowledge and critical engagement with media representations. And awareness of critical thinking and psychological explanations for alleged paranormal phenomena. The best way of describing the multimodal responses of audiences to ghost hunting TV is to picture them going through a revolving door of scepticism and belief. It is a revolving door marked with genre signs, fiction and fact, understanding of mediated representations, and the construction of reality for entertainment purposes. This revolving door is also marked with psychological signs, disbelief and belief, understanding of deception and self-deception, and misunderstanding of paranormal ideas. And it is also a revolving door that makes people feel there are things which are beyond explanation. To describe audiences as going through a revolving door of scepticism and belief may imply they are caught up in circumstances beyond their control. But this is not the case. People know which way round they are going through the revolving door.[8] Audiences provide the momentum themselves. In this way, they help to produce beliefs and disbeliefs in paranormal matters.

Peter Lamont has identified a discursive position of an 'avowal of prior scepticism' (2007). This position as a former sceptic was used by mediums in the late nineteenth century to situate their belief within the context of criticism of psychic fraud. By acknowledging criticism and confronting fraudulent claims, a medium could reinforce their own apparently authentic psychic powers in opposition to others. An avowal of prior scepticism operates as 'a social and discursive form of "belief maintenance"' (Lamont 2007: 693). The function of an avowal of prior scepticism is to 'demonstrate social competence to a potentially sceptical hearer', emphasising an event as factual, 'allowing speakers to present themselves as reacting normally to an extraordinary event' (2007: 683). Such discursive tactics are not restricted to paranormal beliefs but are also common in accounts of extraordinary events (see Lamont 2007: 683–84; Wooffitt 1992). In relation to the existence of paranormal phenomena, Lamont points out that an avowal of prior scepticism functions both as a demonstration of social competence and as an establishment of social identity. Belief in the paranormal is often associated with 'gullibility and wishful thinking', whereas sceptics are associated with critical thinking (ibid). Sceptical discourses signal skills that are part of Western secular identity formation in late modern society. An avowal of prior scepticism is a strategy for paranormal beliefs to be maintained within a context of critical reflection. In Anthony Giddens' terms, this is part of the reflexive project of the self where sceptical discourses are a resource for the identity work of a person with paranormal beliefs (1991).

Media representations are ripe for critical reflection and act as resources for identity work. In this study, viewers were sceptical of the way the media constructed the paranormal as sensational, dramatic and often comical. Media criticism can therefore be a discursive strategy for a position of scepticism regarding paranormal beliefs. Audiences of *Most Haunted* are media critics and share a general cynicism of the commercial imperatives of the media. One woman summed it up as: 'it's just entertainment. I would see it as entertainment, rather than any kind of reality.' She went on to explain:

> I like that Yvette is just screaming [laughs], and I love when they are trying to convince us that there is something going on the screen, when there isn't actually something going on. 'Did you hear that? Oh my god, did you hear that?' And it's like, no, we didn't. 'Did you see that move?' No, we didn't see it. But everybody was meant to go, 'oh my god, did you see that the glass actually moved.' I think she believes. I think she is just a believer. … Oh my god, oh my god. I have to meet her in person. What kind of person is she if she believes in this kind of stuff?
>
> (32-year-old female interpreter)

The mix of drama and psychological suggestion helps to establish a critical position towards the show and scepticism of paranormal matters in this media context.

Three female viewers reflected on the generic mix of horror and reality entertainment as making them feel scared and silly at the same time:

> It didn't scare me at all. I was kind of trying to get scared, but I couldn't. I was quite entertained by it.
>
> (34-year-old female interior designer)

I thought it's very funny. I love it, I love watching it, very silly. I agree it's very creepy to watch it, so I like it.

(33-year-old female bookseller)

I found it very scary. And then, it's a bit silly. You think 'are you putting it on or not?' And I was sort of laughing and shocked at the same time.

(26-year-old female advertising regulation worker)

Genre knowledge is a resource for maintaining a knowing position on ghost hunting TV. These responses invite physical and emotional reactions akin to watching a comic horror movie. Or, in the following:

I found it comical, not comical, but kind of like, you know, it made me laugh. It seems so forced to me. In that place, you are looking for something and anything could make you creepy, you know. The camera effects and lighting create the atmosphere, and nothing convinced me as far as I'm concerned. Not at all, not convincing at all.

(39-year-old female research consultant)

The mock gothic atmosphere of *Most Haunted* is a resource for a media literate, sceptical identity position. The effective use of drama to enhance a haunted experience for audiences works against an idea of an authentic live ghost hunt where a haunting atmosphere would seem more convincing. This is an example of the way genre knowledge acts as a filter for sceptical responses.

Another filter is psychological knowledge. Audiences have common knowledge of the power of suggestion. This idea is so dominant in popular discourses of paranormal beliefs that it is repeatedly used in discussions as an explanation for alleged hauntings. One woman reflected on the atmosphere created by an old building and the power of suggestion in haunting atmospheres:

It's obviously quite a scary place they are in, and the scary place is having an effect on them, rather than actually anything happening. Even in my house, you can hear noises at night sometimes, and any odd noise when you are in a scary place makes you nervous … I didn't entirely believe in it, you know … I think when you are there for a haunting, you are wanting to be haunted anyway, you know, you are in a small claustrophobic place … they were waiting for something nasty, it's like Madame Tussaud's you know. I believe they were waiting for a haunting to happen.

(retired female)

The explicit reference to spirit forms as a public attraction indicates how ghosts are understood as a dramatic construction in popular culture. The phrase 'waiting for a haunting to happen' is rich in meaning. It suggests a common under-standing of psychological suggestion as an explanation for hauntings. It shows an

awareness of the staging of hauntings. And it highlights how audiences participate in the staging of hauntings. As armchair ghosthunters audiences are not
passively sitting at home waiting for the producers to put on a show; they are
actively engaged in emotional, physical and psychological participation in a
haunting atmosphere.

Psychological analysis of allegedly haunted places indicates that the atmosphere, temperature and visual features of a historic location all contribute to the
suggestion of a haunting. Research on people's experiences of haunted places has
focused on multivariate surveys testing beliefs in the paranormal. Wiseman et al
(2002: 209) call for better understanding of 'the relative importance for haunt
experiences of the variety of environmental and psychological factors.' The role
of the audience in 'waiting for a haunting to happen' in ghost hunting TV suggests
that qualitative research can offer a cultural perspective. These shows exaggerate
the staging of hauntings, adding a created-for-TV environment to the already
existing creepiness of an allegedly haunted house. The psychological factors are
apparent within the media production, where the reactions of the paranormal
investigators are evaluated by audiences. These factors are also apparent in the
way audiences knowingly respond to their own psychological and emotional
engagement with the show as 'waiting for a haunting to happen.'

Audiences can draw on genre knowledge and psychological knowledge to
construct a dual identity position as media critic and sceptic. The following
account of the similarities of real-time and televised ghost hunting link critical
awareness of psychological manipulation and commercialism together:

> I recall visiting a haunted house. It was really a tourist attraction for us, a
> thrill to go. I'll have a look, you never know what's there. So we gave it a
> chance, we went there for a night tour. Nothing, of course, happened.
> Although the suggestion was there to prepare everybody … At the same
> time, they were saying about this programme, these people went there and
> recorded, and apparently everything happened. So I am wondering if these
> ghosts are really keen on appearing on TV.
>
> (37-year-old female conference organiser)

In this example, common knowledge of the power of suggestion combines with
cynicism of the commercial imperatives of entertainment industries.

The reality genre produces a performative reality where the setting is staged
but people's reactions can be perceived as real. These moments of authenticity
within the staging of reality have been noted by researchers as part of the attraction of the genre itself – reality TV isn't real, but reality TV performers can have
real emotions (Hill 2007). This mix of aesthetics and emotions is why commen-
tators have highlighted the similarity of reality TV to soap opera and its melodramatic storylines (Kilborn 2003). Previous studies of soap opera fans showed
that people found an emotional reality to melodramatic soap operas such as
Dallas (Ang 1985). Within the drama of *Most Haunted*, there are flickers of real

emotions within the team, where 'sometimes they are genuinely scared' (47-year-old male day centre worker). The appearance of the investigators is crucial – 'she looked absolutely terrified' (41-year-old female dancer). Viewers reflect on how they might react in allegedly haunted places: 'he looked legitimately really, really scared … if that was me in a real dark castle like that, somebody was knocking on the wall, I would be really scared as well' (19-year-old female student).

The emotional realism of *Most Haunted* begins to signal the way audiences can shift positions from paranormal sceptic and media critic to an ambiguous stance. The woman who reflected how she would feel scared in a dark castle also claimed to be open to psychic forces. She explained:

> I am very sceptical about it … 'wow, it's all true, wow, yeah it's happening', oh dear! … Sometimes, it's like, I am not convinced, but I believe in certain aspects of the psychic itself, but I don't know, it kind of loses the credibility when it goes on TV. I think it becomes a show.
>
> (19-year-old female student)

For another woman the emotional realism of the show opened up the possibility of paranormal phenomena:

> It's frustrating. Did you hear that, and nothing [laughs]. I was quite open minded when I watched it, if you look at their faces and they were genuinely really ill, they were really pale, and absolutely sick. Must be something in it. But I am not quite sure so I tend to be a bit sceptical but also at the same time, looking at, you are looking for reason to believe it because it's been done so realistically.
>
> (49-year-old female teacher)

In this example knowledge of genre and psychology only serves to complicate things and engender mixed responses.

In the following extended discussion of *Most Haunted*, these viewers debated the truth claims made within ghost hunting TV. Their comments highlight the way audiences go through a revolving door of scepticism and belief.

INTERVIEWER: what would you call *Most Haunted*?
EMILY: reality show. (26 year old female receptionist)
KATH: I would call it reality constructed. (24 year old female teacher)
EMILY: but all reality TV shows are constructed.
KATH: oh yeah.
RACHEL: I think it's genuinely some paranormal things happening, but the way they show it is exaggerated. (24 year old female textile designer)
EMILY: I just think it's not real at all. Flick the lights, you can push the door, anyone gets scared if you are in the room with the lights off. Personally I don't believe either.

SHAUN: there was an episode where all the lights were off, 'is there anyone here?', and a rock flies. 'Can you hear that? [knocking the table] … It's just fake. (21 year old male student)

ELEANOR: the time I watched it people were screaming. I don't watch it regularly. I am not sure, I can't tell. (20 year old female construction worker)

MARK: when you watch you want to believe it is true, even though you know that some of the parts may not be true. (20 year old unemployed male)

As these viewers go around the issues of media criticism and paranormal claims they do so within a framework of critical reflection. Genre knowledge enables these viewers to reflect on the staging of hauntings. Emotional knowledge enables them to assess the impact of a haunting atmosphere on people's reactions to scary places. The comment 'you want to believe it is true' touches on the role of the audience as participants in 'waiting for a haunting to happen.' Within the group, there is a collective avowal of scepticism. And at the same time there is a strategic use of media criticism as a stepping stone to the possibility of paranormal phenomena.

Audience engagement with *Most Haunted* offers many opportunities for people to explain why they think the show is unbelievable and to showcase their critical reflection on staged hauntings and psychological suggestion. It also offers people a means to make paranormal claims open to interpretation. For example:

AMY: I am quite sceptical about the programme, and not particularly a sceptical person but I am sceptical about *Most Haunted* … (30-year-old female)

AUDREY: well, I don't believe that for second … I think you know they made a lot of money of out of it and obviously there is a market for it. So, as much as I really want to trust them and believe that I just don't. (25-year-old female human resources trainer)

EMMA: I mean it's good entertainment. If that's all you're looking for, that's what you get. But if you are really too much into it then you are just disappointed, unless you believe it. (25-year-old female teacher and student)

VICKY: …we don't really see much apart from people pushing a glass around. Even when she said 'oh my god, it's moving on its own' but the camera didn't even catch that. It's all about her reaction making us believe that. It's supposed to be our reaction. It's all about entertainment. (30-year-old female library assistant) …

EMMA: when she said, 'ah it's sad.' You know the ghost apparently said help, and I thought, you don't sound very sad if the person is begging for help from other side. You don't sound very sad, or even very surprised. I don't like it really.

AMY: I don't think that you just go into dark buildings and somebody can contact ghosts. That's not really believable. It's not.

LINDA: But they throw in an occasional episode where there are a few knocks and bangs, 'ok we didn't contact anyone in this week', but it's still exciting. (27-year-old female carer)

AMY: but that's really rare.

LINDA: … It's down to everyone's opinions at the end of the day, it's not just what I am saying, the different opinions I have, and if they are true or not. It depends on what you believe or not. You've got to keep an open mind.

These multiple interpretations of the show signal a generally critical position, drawing on genre awareness, emotional realism, and psychological suggestion. Within this framework people are more than TV critics. They react critically to the show because they care about the issue of authenticity within paranormal matters. They want to believe.

What begins to emerge is the use of media criticism as a discursive practice in an avowal of prior scepticism. It is a form of belief maintenance in a mediated environment:

> It's just entertainment more than education. I haven't ever been convinced by anything on television. I read lots of books about experiences. I find that it's more believable than anything else on television. I just feel a bit cynical about television.
>
> (46 year old female personal assistant)

As a media critic viewers can categorise ghost hunting TV as entertainment and not to be taken seriously. This strategy helps in establishing critical thinking within the framework of paranormal beliefs; viewers can be critics and believers at the same time:

> My grandmother is a medium, supposedly, I don't know. She came to stay and my mother was watching *Most Haunted*, and she sat down and watched with her. Coming from somebody who is living as a medium and somebody who believes she has a gift passed down through the family … half way through, she said 'it's a bunch of crap'.
>
> (26-year-old male student)

This is a good example of how the media are a resource for multiple interpretations of paranormal claims.

Audience as believer

Ghost hunting TV highlights the centrality of ambiguity in cultural practices associated with paranormal beliefs and ideas. In this study most people who believed in some form of the paranormal, such as spiritism and communication with the dead, defined themselves as uncertain believers. These people were not sure about their beliefs but expressed hope in the possibility of paranormal phenomena. Their construction of identity and belief was contradictory, mixing metaphysical approaches of openness and positive thinking, with more rational approaches to documentary evidence. These kinds of uncertain believers talked around paranormal claims, reaching no clear conclusions. In research on media and religion, Lynn Schofield Clark indicated uncertainty is not only part of paranormal beliefs but is connected to spiritual beliefs in Western societies (2003). A rejection of organised religion can lead to openness towards spiritual matters. This uncertain position is best summed up by the phrase 'you've got to keep an open mind' (27-year-old female carer). Uncertainty about paranormal beliefs can be understood within late modern society where people reflect on what is going to happen to themselves and their loved ones when they die. It is part of the way people consider alternative explanations to dominant thinking in religion and science on their own mortality.

The idea of 'the will to believe' (1896) by William James is relevant to understanding ambiguous cultural experiences. James' address to the Philosophical Clubs of Yale and Brown Universities (published in the *New World*, June 1896) was a response to the 'snarling logicality' of his fellow scientists who criticised his philosophical writings on the existence of an afterlife (cited in Blum 2007: 213). James established the American Society for Psychical Research (SPR) and was president of the British SPR during the mid 1890s. From a young age he had been fascinated by metaphysical and psychic matters, practising Swedenborgianism and exploring evidence for and against psychic phenomenon. Blum (2007: 8) writes that James' work in psychology, philosophy and psychics 'confirmed his own inclination that the most important lessons might be learned in the most unexpected places.' James' approach to philosophy challenged elitist traditions, 'linking everyday real life experiences to intellectual exploration' (Blum 2007: 5). Blum contextualises 'the will to believe' address within the context of criticism of psychical researchers as gullible and encouraging the public in mystical and superstitious thinking. James argued the world should not only be understood through scientific rationality. Traditional logic dictates that we must disbelieve what cannot be proven scientifically to be true. But James argued that by remaining open to belief people can explore the various ways we understand the world. By choosing to remain open to the possibility of God, a higher power, or other deities, people choose to live as if they believe. James defended 'our right to adopt a believing attitude' in spite of a lack of logic to support such an attitude (1896: 1). A believing attitude is about how our passionate, non-rational nature determines what we believe. It shows how belief is alive to the problems and complexities of real life. As James pointed out: 'the state of things is evidently far from simple' (1896: 6).

A popular form of this idea exists in ways of thinking about a believing attitude: 'I really want to believe there is something, but you just became sceptical of it all on TV. I do believe there is something' (25-year-old male auto electrician). It is articulated in a halfway attitude of belief and disbelief: 'I don't disbelieve they are happening' (49-year-old retired male). There is a sense of a willing nature: 'I don't really know. If it's fake, it's disappointing, you know what I mean? I'd like to believe' (47-year-old male day centre worker). The will to believe becomes expressed as 'we believe what we hope to be true.' The question of paranormal beliefs becomes a living question which is part of the complexities of the real world. Welchman (2006) suggests that rather than perceive James' concept as an ethics of belief, it can be understood as an ethics of self-experimentation. Such an approach takes on board some of the criticisms of James' idea of the will to believe as based on an untenable belief position. Self-experimentation with ethical and moral issues relocates the idea of a will to believe in late modern Western societies. It connects the idea within the notion of the reflexive project of the self where people can draw on everyday social and cultural practices as a resource for identity work.

It is this approach to the audience as believer that highlights the self-reflection and identity experimentation that is part of the cultural practices associated with ghost hunting TV. People play with their own common understanding of a will to believe. In Erving Goffman's terms they perform paranormal beliefs in everyday life (1959). They perform several parts at the same time – media critic, soft sceptic, open-minded believer. It is an ethics of self-experimentation where alternative spiritual thinking is played within an entertainment environment. Such a means of perceiving self-experimentation with moral and ethical issues is also apparent in previous research on reality TV (Hill 2005, 2007). Audiences adopted a shallow ethical position with regard to the fair treatment of non-professionals in reality entertainment programmes. In other examples of health and emergency services reality TV programming audiences experimented with an ethics of care regarding families and human animal relations. In a similar way ghost hunting TV gives audiences opportunities to experiment with paranormal beliefs. It opens up a performative space where people can reflect on alternative identities.

The metaphor of a revolving door captures a sense of the ways viewers go around and around issues of scepticism and belief. In the following discussion two viewers go around these issues:

PAULA: to be quite honest, if you think about it, the show is on for an hour and in that space this ghost has got to appear in that hour [laughs]. Do you know what I am saying? ... all I can say about this programme, every single time they say 'did you hear that?' we can't hear anything. 'Did you see that?' 'Did you see the rock?' How many cameras are in there? We should have been able to see it. This is what they do every single time. It's very irritating to me. There is another thing. If everybody believes something is going to happen, it's going to happen ... It's a phenomenon we don't understand. Unless you are there, or experience at first hand, it's just entertainment, poor entertainment as well. Sometimes I want to believe but, like I said, you don't actually see it or hear anything. Sometimes, I just want to see one thing. The rock going past her head – 'oh my god, I saw that!' But never in their programme have I seen anything. I am such a believer of ghosts and things like that, I swear to God, but in this programme, there's too much talk, there is no action, I want to see action, I want to see – (33-year-old female youth worker)

PETE: But if there is too much action, people don't believe anyway. I am saying that you can't force things. (47-year-old male day centre worker)

PAULA: they are telling us what's happening, you see.

PETE: When they go out and nothing happens, it's very disappointing.

PAULA: but I prefer that because that's more truthful. You can actually think, all right, fair enough, they've been waiting, nothing happened. You actually believe more. You are sitting there and watching that, waiting and anticipating, and nothing. Nothing, every time I watch it, nothing.

PETE: If it's too exciting people don't believe. So it's quite difficult. They can't get a balance.

These viewers know which way round they are going through a revolving door. Their frustrations with the show *Most Haunted* are to do with a perpetual state of uncertainty produced by the programme makers. The suggestion of ghosts – 'did you see that' – only serves to make viewers cry out 'no, I didn't see anything.' The lament 'sometimes I just want to see one thing' is symptomatic of a will to believe. At the same time, and in the same discussion, is an awareness of the messiness of paranormal belief. People play a part in the production of beliefs: 'if everybody believes something is going to happen, it's going to happen.' This raises the complex issue of belief maintenance in a cultural context. As the other participant points out, if nothing happens in a reality ghost hunt does this make it more or less believable? Rationally, viewers know if nothing happens then this is closer to their own understanding of paranormal phenomena as extremely rare and therefore unlikely to occur for television. The absence of evidence makes it somehow more truthful so 'you actually believe more.' Yet, emotionally viewers hope for something to happen. This places their own psychological and emotional investment in 'waiting for a haunting to happen' centre stage. And these viewers continue round notions of truth, trust, evidence and belief in this performative television environment.

Another way around scepticism and belief is to perceive televised ghost hunts as symbolically opening other doors to paranormal matters. Williams (1996) suggests metaphor is important to imagination and embodiment in social interactions. He identifies metaphors of intrusion, transmission and connection in discursive accounts of the paranormal. The metaphor of an open door gives audiences another means of interpreting ghost hunting TV. *Most Haunted* may be made up but 'it has opened a lot of doors' (49-year-old female teacher). The open door metaphor means the show's presence on TV creates a symbolic space within which audiences can explore paranormal beliefs and ideas. This person explained:

Whatever you think of *Most Haunted*, if you have experiences, you felt stupid having them. Now it's actually on television and it's easier to talk about. Did you watch *Most Haunted*?' 'Did you see it?' Did you believe or were they acting up?' It makes it easier to talk about it, you feel comfortable talking about it.

(43-year-old female teaching assistant)

The sociability of reality TV creates a more relaxed atmosphere where people can feel their way through gossip and light conversation to more personal reflections. People can play with the idea of the paranormal beliefs by asking 'did you believe?' and leaving the door open for multiple interpretations.

Once the door is opened, audiences can move from talk about TV to real life. In Wooffitt's (1992) research on tales of the unexpected, the ways people construct narratives of extraordinary events underscores the importance of the mundane in conversational strategies. His discursive analysis highlights how people stress the differences between the normal and paranormal in their accounts of personal experiences. In this study some people use TV as a conversational strategy to stress the difference between fiction and reality. This division ensures that their personal experiences are given greater weight in the discussions. One woman explained:

I am really sceptical about this programme. Personally I do believe in the paranormal because I have experienced things years ago. But I wonder how they are set up, not cynically set up, but set up so you can get a feeling of coldness when you are expecting something. You can get the shivers when you are expecting you might see something. All sorts of physical manifestations happen to you. You can see things because you are hoping to. The atmosphere is created. I feel that, although I have seen things on television, I don't know if it is paranormal or not because I am not there. I have to be there to know whether everything is real or whether it might be my body chemistry and my feeling, the way I feel about the environment ... I'd like to believe it because it gives me comfort for people who have gone. I really would ... When my brother died every light bulb in the house went. There was nothing wrong with the electricity supply. Every single light. There are spirits, they gather around.

(51-year-old female secretary)

In this reflection on mediated realities and personal realities the issue of paranormal belief is experimented with in a number of ways. The discussion begins with a critical statement about reality ghost hunting TV which is a strategy to assert her belief. She is sceptical of the media, critically aware of the importance of suggestion in creating a haunting atmosphere, and reflexive about her own role in this process. This is a good example of an ethics of self-experimentation. She understands that people are willing to believe in paranormal matters. Working alongside these reflections are her personal hopes of an afterlife. The ghost story stands in contrast to the blurred boundaries of mediated realities. It is an experience which involves a mundane reality which is clearly interpreted as evidence of spirits. Different strategies are used to establish paranormal beliefs which in a media context are ambiguous and in a personal context unambiguous.

The distinctions between staged hauntings and paranormal phenomena become important to people exploring their personal beliefs. Within the playful environment of reality ghost hunting TV audiences can experiment with the question of belief. But in real life, this question has greater meaning and more emotional purchase. As one person said: 'if it does happen to you personally you can say for a fact, yes, absolutely with me, it happened to me' (26-year-old male vision mixer). A group of women reflected on living in a haunted house:

SALLY: I don't know if you remember it, when we lived in that place that was haunted? (33-year-old female housewife)

CLARE: do you remember the marching? Sometimes you could hear the crunch when the solders marched. I remember being scared, hearing that in that room. It was horrible. (34-year-old female)

RACHEL: that was spooky. And the taps, the bathroom taps would turn on their own. I think that was spooky. That to me is a haunting. You can see it happen in the room, you know what I mean? You feel someone is touching your hair. (39-year-old housewife)

CLARE: this is what I mean. When you see things you actually experience, and then you've got a programme like that …

CHLOE: when they make it on telly it's like woooo! (56-year-old female homemaker)

The comparison between their haunting experience and the staging of a haunting on TV is clear to see. The key phrase is 'see it happen.' What Avery Gordon (1997) describes as sensory knowledge of hauntings is articulated through the distinction between their personal experience and media experience. One is real, the other fiction. This strategy of differentiating between the media and reality moves some people out of the state of uncertainty and into an avowal of belief. Being a witness to a staged haunting makes audiences sceptical and critical of the media, and playful in their own multiple responses to the question of belief. However, being a witness to a haunting helps to produce a feeling of certainty – 'that to me is a haunting.'

In the above example experience is understood as evidence, promoting a form of solipsism where personal belief is based on experience. In one way reality ghost hunting TV prompts people to get out of their armchair and experience ghost hunting for themselves. As Richard Woolfe said 'It is ten years since *Most Haunted* started and we haven't captured any ghosts on camera.' In the context of reality entertainment this can create an atmosphere of a never-ending search where audiences play a game of ghosts. Audience discussions of *Most Haunted* highlight how distrustful they are of mediated reality and how cynical they are of commercial imperatives. This doesn't stop people looking for glimpses of authenticity in an entertainment frame, but it positions audiences as similar to reality TV audiences in general. But what makes these audiences different from those for other reality shows is their search for evidence of paranormal phenomena. It indicates how being a witness is so important to paranormal matters. These are audiences with great personal investment in finding answers to the question of belief. This is why they are drawn to make comparisons between staged hauntings and their personal experiences. And it is why other cultural practices focus on personal experience. Just as ghost hunting TV took off in the past decade so too did ghost hunting events and ghost tourism which are other cultural experiences on offer to members of the public. In this context the stakes are raised as people want to experience for themselves a haunting atmosphere.

As for an ethics of self-experimentation such identity work around ghost hunting TV is taken into a performative space. It is more of a performance of the self and paranormal beliefs than an exercise in moral and religious thinking. Perhaps ghost hunting TV is a rehearsal space. It creates a playful atmosphere where people can laugh and shout and scream about a televised ghost hunt. They can experiment with different identity positions, and styles of performing the self with other viewers and audiences. A disbelieving attitude is tried out and tested in this rehearsal space. A willing attitude is explored and its impact observed. People begin to try out their own role in the production of beliefs. For some audiences this is enough. But for those who want to find evidence of paranormal phenomena, who want answers to the question of their own mortality, then they look for other ways of exploring the paranormal. Ghost hunting TV can never offer answers; it continually asks 'do you believe?' and leaves audiences to work it out for themselves.

Conclusion

Ghost hunting TV taps into broader trends in hybrid genres and cultural fascination with ghosts. These trends also connect with social trends in paranormal beliefs. Ghost hunting TV is for entertainment purposes only, as it says in the legal statement at the end of each show. But, audiences do not engage with the show as just entertainment. People adopt multiple identity positions as TV viewers enjoying the staging of reality, and as media critics in their engagement with the truth claims made within a hybrid genre of fact and fiction. They adopt positions of sceptics and believers, and explore mixed positions of open-minded sceptics and uncertain believers in paranormal phenomena. These shows provide a rehearsal space for audiences to play with issues of identity and paranormal claims.

As audiences engage with these shows, they go through a revolving door of scepticism and belief. Audiences can never be sure what is going on. It is the suggestion of a haunting that occurs rather than visible or aural evidence caught on camera. There are discursive strategies used by audiences to explore the reality and paranormal claims in ghost hunting TV. There is a common understanding of the concept of the will to believe in the way audiences are aware that there are emotional and psychological factors in paranormal beliefs. As one person commented: 'If you want to believe something, you will try to believe every evidence to believe it' (24-year-old female sales executive). This willing attitude means that paranormal belief is explored as a process of self-experimentation. People work through facts and fiction, mediated realities and personal realities to find out for themselves what they believe or not. This is an example of the media as a resource for identity work in the formation and maintenance of paranormal beliefs and disbeliefs.

Notes

1 Interview with author 1 December 2009. All quotes in this section from this interview.
2 Ibid.
3 Charlie Brooker 'What's on the other side' TV review in the *Guardian*, Saturday, 19 March 2005, accessed online at www.guardianunlimited.com 12 October 2008.
4 See *Most Haunted* website at www.livingtv.co.uk.
5 Accessed online at www.livingtv.co.uk/shows/mosthaunted11/interviews/ciaran-okeeffe.php 18 March 2009.
6 See *OK Magazine*, 29 July 2008 'Yvette Fielding and Karl Beattie' no author listed, accessed online at www.ok.co.uk 18 March 2009.
7 Matt Roper 'Spooky Truth: TV's *Most Haunted* Con' the *Mirror*, 28 October 2005.
8 My thanks to Christine Geraghty for her insightful comments at a seminar in Glasgow University May 2009.

Chapter 5

Psychic tourists

'An eye opening experience'

Ghost walks, all-night ghost hunting, weekend breaks in haunted places, these are just some of the experiences on offer to the psychic tourist. Top ten lists regularly appear for Britain's most haunted village, or America's most haunted hotel. Castles are on the tourism trail as haunted places to visit. Events companies offer nights to remember with celebrity mediums and locations 'as seen on TV.' Such tours or events take traditional ghost stories, history and folklore, and re-package these for the contemporary tourist. The type of ghost walks where actors dress up and spook people are one example of entertainment and spectacle. There are also events where members of the public can be a ghost hunter for the night. Such event organisers take elements from paranormal investigations and parapsychology, mixing this with other alternative practices, deliberately opening up the scientific study of the paranormal to a wide audience.

Similar to other developments such as dark tourism in nuclear hot spots, or extreme sports in wild locations, ghost hunting events offer an unusual, exhilarating experience. This is the commercialisation of ghost hunting as the selling of a unique experience. Events organisers inform their clients that only a small percentage will encounter paranormal phenomena. People understand they are paying for an experience that is by its nature anomalous and therefore highly unlikely to occur. The promise of a unique experience is therefore a strategy that shifts the emphasis of a ghost hunting event away from the elusiveness of scientific proof and towards feelings, emotions, and instincts. There is an emotional geography to an allegedly haunted location which makes ghost hunting events disquieting experiences. Another related strategy is that of sensory engagement. People experience sensory deprivation, listening in the dark, looking at shadows, and in these spaces their senses are heightened. Psychic tourists go on a sensory journey. People use their five senses to experience a place and also draw on their common understanding of a sixth sense. Extrasensory experiences are extremely rare, and yet people on a ghost hunting event invest a lot of emotional and psychological energy in looking for such an experience. Indeed, what many claim

Figure 5.1 London Paranormal, courtesy of Ian Shillito

as extrasensory is created by them – they produce and perform the experience they hope to have.

Ghost tourism

There is a historical tradition to visiting famously haunted places. Owen Davies notes 'ghost hunting as a recreational activity is nothing new. Haunted houses and churchyards attracted large crowds in the past.' However, 'what the tourist industry has done is reformulate and package the experience by creating a synergy between visitor, place and ghost' (2007: 64). The synergy works by drawing on connecting trends in paranormal beliefs, unusual holiday destinations or leisure experiences, and visiting historic locations. These trends work together in attracting people with varied interests in the paranormal, and historical buildings, who want to do something different on a weekend break, or a Saturday night out. Figure 5.2 illustrates an example of a ghost walk at the historic site of Pevensey Castle, where a tour by lantern light on ghosts, poltergeists and 'things lurking in the shadows of the castle' is 'suitable for all ages.' The National Trust explicitly creates a synergy between visitor, place and ghost to attract tourists to their historic and haunted places. The website suggests an itinerary for ghostly encounters where visitors might 'get to see a little bit more than they bargained for.' The book *Ghosts* includes interviews with employees which testify 'Trust houses are bursting with ghosts.' The author Sian Evans writes 'for many staff, volunteers and tenants of the National Trust, the job is sometimes a matter of balancing the normal with the paranormal.'[1]

Local tourism can be promoted by a ghostly theme. The website Paranormal Database lists 65 hot spots across the UK, with over 9000 entries for specific stories and activity reports. There is a wealth of ghost tourism books. The Paranormal Database lists nearly 400, including the international author Peter Underwood, who has written dozens of general and regional guides across Britain. Ghost tourism is part of the branding of an area. For example, a tourist information centre in a small Shropshire town includes books on ghosts, legends and folklore, including the publication *Wales of the Unexpected*. Castles, museums, or pubs can offer ghost tourism as public events. For example, on Halloween 2009 the local pub The Bull in the Thorn, in Derbyshire, offered a three course dinner, psychic demonstrations and a ghost hunt, including vigils,

Figure 5.2 Ghost walks

séances and equipment, all for £79 per person. Or, the Black Country Living Museum offered a Halloween themed evening at £12.95 with psychic readings by gas lamp (at extra charge). The home of the late Queen Mother, Glamis Castle, ran a Halloween night of fancy dress, tours, and tales at one of the reputedly most haunted castles in Britain. These events are advertised in local newspapers, radio shows, and on dedicated websites.

Some of the most popular tourist destinations in Britain are famously haunted. Indeed the book *Ghoul Britannia* (2009) signals the association of ghosts with the entire island. Businesses and places compete for the title of 'most haunted', with lists for the most haunted pub, hotel, castle, village, and city. Europe's Most Haunted city of York attracts four million annual visitors, offers haunted historical buildings such as Theatre Royal, or Holy Trinity church, and runs regular ghost walks with up to 150 tourists at a time.[2] Hampton Court Palace is one of the most visited historic places in Britain. It has three ghost stories associated with the site, including the screaming lady in The Haunted Gallery, the grey lady, and Skeletor, which refers to a ghostly image captured on CCTV. On the official website, one warden explained 'I often walk down the Haunted Gallery and for some inexplicable reason feel as if something is not quite as it should be. Things do happen.'[3]

There are specialist companies for ghostly events. For example, Dead Haunted Nights offers 'a truly spooky night to remember' where a team of mediums, psychics and investigators will take the tourist on a ghost hunt. The company Haunted Happenings claims to have the largest range and number of haunted locations in Britain. On Halloween 2009 they offered nine all-night events, all sold out, with tickets at around £50 per person. For 2010 the event calendar included 40 ghost hunting evenings or weekends from January to March, including 'Dudley Castle Ultimate Experience', 'The Hauntings of Boiling Hall', and 'London Tombs Ghost Hunt' (sold out).[4] Regulars of Haunted Happenings can buy a 'Paranormal Passport' for £190 which entitles them to four events, with one ghost supper and complimentary glass of wine or soft drink. There are corporate events specially designed to demonstrate uniqueness, such as a 'ghost fest' where clients dine and watch paranormal demonstrations. Charities can use a ghost events company to raise money with a difference. For example, the leukaemia charity the Anthony Nolan Trust raises money for bone marrow transplants. It works with Fright Nights. To go on a ghost hunt at the 'famously haunted' Bisham Abbey in Berkshire costs £115 including sponsorship, and in return 'as well as helping a worthy cause' 'participants will be provided with an intimate medium-led all-night experience, with TV clairvoyants as special guests.'[5]

An article in the *Guardian* newspaper on 'How Britain became a nation of ghost hunters' looked at 'a growing number of paranormal-themed experiences springing up around the country.'[6] There are around 2500 ghost hunting groups in Britain, compared with 150 a decade ago. Fright Nights was established 10 years ago and now employs 40 full and part-time staff, with ghost hunts at

Figure 5.3 Ghost tourism

170 locations, with a turnover of £500,000 (ibid). The company attracts 1000 customers a month, each paying up to £75 per event. Fright Nights' customers are 'a complete cross-section of society', varying from 18 to 85, with different religious beliefs, but there is a gender difference 'seventy per cent of ghost hunters are women' (ibid). The owner of the company described ghost hunting

as 'the new extreme sport.' Business is booming in the recession (a 20 per cent increase in customers in 2008–9). The owner was critical of some of the other companies which he claimed were run by amateurs. Sceptics such as Chris French also commented 'some ghost-hunting groups – not all – are deliberate con artists who are just ripping people off for their own benefit ... A lot of people are being ripped off' (ibid). French added reputable companies can offer people the chance to participate in ghost hunts with an experience similar to telling ghost stories around the campfire.

Ghost tourism is a mainstream phenomenon that has little to do with paranormal investigations. Although events companies offer the opportunity to learn about investigatory techniques, and use of equipment such as electromagnetic frequency readers, this is far removed from the scientific study of the paranormal. One parapsychologist claims there are so many ghost hunting events that they get in the way of actual investigations: 'we can't do any real scientific investigation because we can't get to the venues. So I'd like them to bugger off, and go back and calm it down and we could get back in.' The popularity of ghost hunting events means historic venues charge high fees for access, prohibiting real investigatory groups: 'the venues are charging huge amounts of money. From my point of view it has to stop for a while ... I am a ghost hunter. I want them all to stop chasing monsters and leave me alone.'[7] He adds 'people don't want to hear the truth any more.'

Disquieting experiences

According to de Groot (2009) Britain is a society fascinated by the past. History has become a commodity, in television programmes, radio series, websites, through games, re-enactments, museum installations, genealogies, and biographies. The public are keen to engage with the past, watching reality history shows where people live as Victorians, reading books that chart the social history of cod as a cautionary tale of globalisation and mass fishing, investigating the family tree in order to learn who we really are. These are just a few of the ways the public develop their 'sense of the past' (2009: 2), constructing an 'historical imaginary' (3). 'The historical in popular culture and contemporary society is multiple, multiplying and unstable' (4). It is the multiplicity of meaning associated with popular history today that is of importance to the growth of ghost tourism. In a commentary on television history John Corner talks about the way viewers get a 'sense' of the past, playing on the meaning of 'a sensing and then a making sense' (2007: 135). Ghosts bring history to life in the personal, emotional and psychological meanings of spirits. A haunted house, street or village is psychically charged with the past and the present, 'suggesting emotional registers' where 'the dead remain present in life, even when they are apparently absent' (Pile 2005: 171).

In *History and Memory* Geoffrey Cubitt (2008) argues memory is specific to time and place. The past is embodied in the present moment in complex ways (2008: 9). The construction of collective memories of specific events, people, or places, runs alongside, and sometimes counters personal accounts. Ghost tourism manages to blend the social and the individual into a memorable experience for a participant. A ghost story is embedded in its historical context, arising from a specific set of factors that are personal, such as a violent death, and social, such as war. For example the stories of hauntings in the Blair Street Vaults, Edinburgh, are associated with the people who lived on the street, and the disease and mass death that led to the street being built over. A ghost hunt at the Blair Street Vaults connects the past with the present in such a way that spirits embody the memory of this traumatic event, bringing the emotional and personal impact of disease and death into the present day. The ghost stories of the Blair Street Vaults add another layer of meaning to the history and memory of this place and the people who visit it.

Ghost stories reveal the emotional life of the city, what Steve Pile calls the 'double duty' of ghosts to be simultaneously personal and social dramas (2005: 163). Similar to Avery Gordon, Pile examines the 'haunted and haunting emotional life of cities', using London's violent and traumatic past and present to speak of injustice, to highlight the anxieties beneath the surface of cityscapes. As a cultural geographer, Pile is interested in the 'spectral disruptions' of time and space in cities, the way landmark buildings commemorate victims of war, or roadside flowers mark the death of a stranger. He writes:

> Cities haunt us in the sense that they force us – perhaps against our will, perhaps occasionally – to recognise the lives of those who have gone (before). In this sense, the physicality of the city itself shimmers with ghostliness as it becomes a mutable and durable place of memory.
>
> (162)

Pile describes the ghostliness of cityscapes as an 'emotional geography' (163). Ghosts manifest two types of emotional states, evoking the psychologically uncanny effects of city life in a Freudian sense, and also making visible the grief work of the city and its melancholia (163). Whilst for Gordon, ghostly matters can be transformative, allowing us to see social histories behind the multilayered meanings of hauntings, Pile is less convinced, finding the emotional geography of hauntings often incoherent and directionless (164).

New York's ghostly places take on another meaning after the trauma of the terrorist attacks of 9/11. Fictionalized in Patrick McGrath's *Ghost Town* (2005), New York's history of violence is traced through the hauntings of the American War of Independence, the influx of immigrants, and the attacks on the twin towers of the World Trade Centre. In McGrath's stories visiting the city becomes a 'disquieting experience' because it is a place of death and 'the terror of death'. These ghost stories 'expose the traumas and tragedies of the past in a place', they are threshold spaces where feelings and meanings cross over from the past to the present (Pile 2005: 174). Visits to New York and the space where the twin towers once stood are disquieting experiences. The memorial on the site of the twin towers is imbued with ghostly matters, what de Certeau et al (1998: 133) call the 'ghost that ... haunts urban planning.' These hauntings show the 'uncanniness' that lurks in the everyday life of a city, where a population of ghosts teem within urban geography, symbols of the 'strange and immense silent vitality' of a city (1998: 137). The sites of hauntings come to represent the terror of death, and at the same time the emotional life given to these places through the trauma of the past.

People seek out disquieting places. Dark tourism, or emotional tourism, involves visiting sites of the holocaust, nuclear disasters, or war zones. Lennon and Foley explain: 'cultural tourism experiences include several concentration camps ... many of the battle sites of the First World War, Hiroshima, Pearl Harbour ... individual deaths of political figures ... figures from popular culture ... the victims of serial killers' (2000: 10). Ghost tourism can be understood as connected to the development of dark tourism; indeed it may be the precursor to it. In a history of night time, Ekirch (2005) argues that in early modern times the phrase 'night season' referred to the distinctiveness of nocturnal activities. Although artificial illumination means we have lost the use of such a phrase in everyday language, the idea of a night season is still relevant, where the strange, uncanny elements of darkness and all the meanings associated with it are a part of dark tourism.

Pile argues that such tourism practices underscore the emotional qualities of cultural industries (Pile 2005: 171). The focus on emotional tourism helps to explain some qualities of a ghost hunting event, but it doesn't quite capture the force of these experiences. Ghost hunting involves intense sensory experiences. In this way, events can be like extreme sports. They are a safe activity, but nevertheless share some of the physiological responses of extreme sports. Atherton (2007: 43) says extreme sporting activities such as diving in underwater caves, or climbing mountains, are about outdoor kinetic experiences. When people describe extreme sports experiences they often struggle to explain it, saying 'you just had to be there.' Atherton argues that what is meaningful about extreme sports is the energy and enthusiasm for 'being there.' There is a similar energy and enthusiasm for being there on a ghost hunt where the disquieting experiences can make people feel very much alive. As this woman explained 'I was just buzzing the whole blooming night.' The next section explores the emotional and sensory forces of ghost hunting events.

Ghost hunting with London Paranormal

Phantasmagoria offers people 'a fresh, entertaining and alternative night out, at some of the country's hidden spine tingling gems.'[8] According to its official website the company 'produces a variety of themed events under four guises: Ghost hunting with London Paranormal, Haunted History Walks, The Original London Ghost Festival, and Horrorwood Scare Attractions.' The owner Ian

Shillito is a former West End theatre manager and also a sensitive who appeared on the television series *Most Haunted*. He set up his own business with friends and colleagues working to create a different experience for people who believe in the existence of spirits. He explained:

> Hopefully I want people to learn something about themselves, basically, without sounding like a bloody guru. As I say to people all the time in investigations, to be honest with you, you have got make your own mind up. And that's what I offer people. ... I want people to experience history. I want people to experience getting spooked ... They get to really, really experience stuff when on their own, those people have the best time. It is what you're here to do. You are going out into that dark corridor. You are looking in all the corners of the room.[9]

Looking in all the corners of the room describes the literal activity of investigating historic places, and the symbolic activity of looking into all the corners of the mind, body and spirit. People on ghost hunts can learn about themselves through experience.

Ghost hunting with London Paranormal is structured events which build on a set of connecting issues: the hook of history and ghosts, the emotional geography of the site, and the selling of a unique experience. For example an event at Headstone Manor in Harrow offers an unusual 'historic and haunted location.' This provides 'the hook', described by Shillito as 'history, ghosts, an essence of a ghost story.'[10] Headstone Manor is 'currently being restored to its former grandeur, our home for the night suffers from multiple sightings of full bodied apparitions, sounds of babies crying and mischievous poltergeist activity.'[11] London Paranormal ask: 'has the restoration uncovered more than just old timbers? Who or what is responsible for the recent supernatural wave?' The emotional geography of the site is linked to the hook of history and ghosts. Another event includes being locked in for the night at Landguard Fort. The hook is in the opening question: 'ever wanted to sleep in a haunted location?' The mixture of history and ghost story is explicit in the description of the event: 'taking the ghost hunt to the extreme, our spectral hunters will investigate and then sleep at this ghost-ridden and expansive stronghold.' The Fort is 'large, menacing and built to intimidate.' One ghost legend associated with the fort since 1770 includes 'the unfortunate victim of an infectious Plague who was locked in the bastion and left to die a slow, horrible death.' The emotional geography is mapped out in the structuring of the event. London Paranormal explicitly sells an unusual experience: 'this unique find will not disappoint.'

The locations take on a ghostly air. Rather than perceive Headstone Manor as a building site, it becomes a place where walls are knocked down in order to reveal the ghosts within. Once the dust settles an emotional geography emerges, where time and space become disjointed and the ghost legends appear to come alive. The way the places are chosen is to do with the haunted and haunting emotional life of the city. The Old Sessions House at Clerkenwell is a place with a history of injustices, a former law court, on a site close to public hangings, where there are rumoured to be tunnels leading to the Clerkenwell House of Detention. Clerkenwell has many ghost stories associated with its crossroads and underground rivers, said to be conduits for spirits. Davies writes about the case of David Stim in 1760, a murderer who committed suicide, whose corpse was dissected and buried with a wooden stake at the crossroads near Black Mary's Hole in Clerkenwell (2007: 51).

There is a delicate balance between what the team members offer in terms of their skills, personalities, enthusiasm for the paranormal and what participants expect from them as experts. Zelizer (2005: 15) comments that intimate social relations rely on degrees of trust. Such trust can be positive and negative, it can be equal or asymmetrical. In the case of ghost hunting, people are paying for an experience and in this regard they are consumers. Phantasmagoria call them clients, signalling the business arrangement within a ghost hunting event: 'clients range from fans of paranormal TV, open-minded sceptics, blind believers, budding psychics, mums, dads, groups, amateur ghost-busters, and people celebrating birthdays or on work outings.' There can be a range of expectations from such a diverse group – wanting to experience *Most Haunted* for real, searching for evidence, having fun, getting scared out of your wits. Whilst a few will come as a customer – a good night out with friends – many come looking for a paranormal experience. The economics of ghost hunting as a business are secondary to the primary personal, emotional and psychological aspects of these cultural practices.

This mix of economics and intimacy is reflected in the way the team work at a London Paranormal event. Up to 40 people can be split into smaller groups, working with regular team members. Each group will adopt different techniques and practices, using séances, Ouija boards, table tipping, rapping, crystals, dousing, and auras. There is an open and warm atmosphere, light and fun on the surface but with a serious undertone. As Shillito says, the team works well together so when 'something special happens, it's great fun. Feedback is good. People feel involved, part of the team, made to feel welcome. That is really important, one of our unique selling points.'[12] There is an intimacy to the team because they are good friends, and this extends to the participants who are intimately involved in the investigations. Crucially, participants feel they can trust the team. One man commented: 'I prefer London Paranormal, you get more involved. With other groups you are left to your own devices, it's less structured. If anything did happen you would be frightened for your life … Here you are given a sensitive each. You feel more involved, feel safe.'[13]

Shillito ran regular psychic circles with friends and team members, some of whom met at training courses in psychic studies, or through Gay Psychics. He explained at the time:

> In the development circle, we spend time laughing and taking the mickey about each other. Eventually, we meditate together and then anyone who's

got some imagery that comes out on a psychic level, ghosty stuff, we tend to see what happens ... It's an extension of Gay Psychics ... you know, five or six gay guys is actually amusing. It's not like queer eye for the straight guy, that is irritating. It's kind of – I don't know what it is.[14]

Links with the gay community through endorsements by *The Pink Paper*, or charity work with The Terence Higgins Trust ensure a strong gay identity to the group. Shillito has an awareness that as a gay man the paranormal is a means of expressing his identity, his sensitivity to psychic energy. Knowing the history of mediumship, he feels that just as being a medium was an alternative route for women in the Victorian and Edwardian periods to express themselves and their sexual and gender identities in a repressive society, so too today gay men are drawn to the paranormal as a resource for identity work. London Paranormal has a strong gay identity, enhanced by team members and re-enforced by participants who come with an expectation that gay men make good mediums. It is common knowledge amongst people in this study that gay men can be naturally sensitive, both emotionally and also psychically. Such expectations mean that people come to an event expecting a heightened degree of sensitivity from the core team members. This is an explicit reference to the emotional qualities of a ghost hunting event which are used to strengthen the experience on offer.

The experience of being part of the team is not too dissimilar to participants' experience. Indeed, former participants have become team members. For example one woman went on her first location as a punter, and a year later became part of the crew. She explained:

> I am fascinated by the paranormal but scared of people. My fear goes in a different direction. I am starting to develop myself spiritually ... It is like a muscle, if you develop it, it gets stronger. I still am not sure what I believe. ... I like to keep myself open, makes life a bit more interesting ... At first my friends laughed, they thought I was mad. I explained to my mum, it is a passion of mine that is at last being fulfilled ... My dad said 'as long as it makes you happy, as long as you're not digging up graves.'[15]

Many participants can identify with her story, finding a group which she trusts, exploring her psychic potential, opening herself up to the possibilities of the paranormal. The reactions of her parents indicate that her passion comes across to non-believers and makes it more acceptable in her everyday life. The fascination, adrenalin buzz, the personal development in mind, body and spirit: all are elements that participants are looking for in a ghost hunting experience.

A good ghost hunting events organiser has to learn how cultural practices draw on information, emotion, and psychology. Shillito comments that 99 per cent of what goes on in a ghost hunt is not paranormal. Nevertheless he knows 'people want things to happen, they want to get scared. They are not interested in how it happens. Their imagination starts working over and over.'[16]

He gives people information which fuels their imagination, but he also emphasises that an investigation has to rule out what is not paranormal. There is a personal tension for him between knowing what people want to experience as an events organiser and his own experiences as a sensitive: 'you cannot deny they have witnessed something, but I know that it isn't real. But you can't piss on that' (ibid). He deliberately sets up psychological experiments so that people can reflect on the emotion of fear, the psychology of looking in all the corners of the room. In one experiment he called a paranormal *Big Brother* participants were isolated and filmed alone in a dark room. Shillito creates ghost hunts where participants are asked to reflect on what is real or not in haunted places. One participant described his lone investigation in a cellar: it 'gets your exploratory juices going, go and look, much more inquisitive, gets you working in a different way.'[17] Shillito explained a personal test in a disused nuclear bunker:

> I want to go down to the tunnel, a 150 feet below, three floors underground, on my own. I am completely shitting myself at the thought of it but I know that is what I want to do. I don't know why, what happens to us when we get scared? What happens in our bodies that is addictive, like heroin in our bodies, what is it that we love about being scared? I'd love to find out.[18]

The pleasures of fear get the exploratory juices going. Thus the psychology of fear and the emotional adrenalin rush of being in an allegedly haunted space becomes one of the main focuses of the event. This approach foregrounds people rather than ghosts. It emphasises the emotional, sensual and psychological forces at work in cultural experiences.

Sensory journeys

Ghost hunting events take place at night time in the dark. During the course of an evening, there are several investigations where people sit or stand in the dark for up to an hour, quietly listening to each other and the sounds around them, often holding hands. An absence of light or sound induces intense feelings and thoughts. Classen claims we take 'sensory journeys' (1993: 7) where 'we not only think about our senses, we think through them' (9). There is a double meaning to sensory engagement where physical and cognitive processes work together to create an experience. The idea of a sensory journey helps to explain the way ghost hunting events make people feel alive. People become attuned to their senses and think through their disquieting experiences.

Research in parapsychology suggests that psi phenomena are not necessarily connected to the senses (see Irwin and Watt 2007). Psi includes extrasensory experiences like telepathy, clairvoyance, or psychokinesis. There is debate about the mechanisms that cause psi, suggesting a complex and as yet unexplainable combination of cognitive and physiological processes. In terms of experiences in allegedly haunted spaces, studies indicate there may be both a physical and psychological interpretation. Wiseman et al (2002) experimented with visitors to Hampton Court Palace, reputed to be one of the most haunted locations in England. They found electromagnetic fields contributed to the visitor experience, with shifts in strength and variance positively influencing unusual experiences in specific places, such as The Haunted Gallery. They also found other signals could influence ghostly phenomena, such as draughts, odours and light levels. The reputation of such a haunted location was another factor. Wiseman et al concluded there may be physical explanations for why a specific space becomes associated with a haunting which becomes mingled within the social and cultural context of the place. Once this has happened in the case of Hampton Court Palace it is difficult to separate the influence of electromagnetic fields from the psychology of fear and expectations of a haunting.

It is one of the strategies of ghost hunting event organisers to transform the science of investigations into a more sociable and inclusive experience. The structuring of a ghost hunt as a sensory journey is significant because it places emphasis on people and their unique experiences rather than science and the burden of proof. If most of what people experience on a ghost hunt is not paranormal then there is something else they are experiencing which feels strange. Some of this is maybe to do with electromagnetic fields and low-frequency sounds which may make people feel spooked. But some of this is also to do with sensing and making sense of strange feelings in a haunted space. In classical literature the senses were perceived as a media of communication, rather than as passive recipients of data: 'the eyes for example, were believed to perceive by issuing rays which touched and mingled with the objects of which they were directed' (Classen 1993: 2). On a ghost hunt people are more than passive recipients of their physical surroundings, using their senses to touch and mingle with emotional and psychological matters.

Ghost hunting with London Paranormal involves specific activities to help people explore their sensory journeys. For example, at Clerkenwell there was a psychological and sensory experiment where participants sat alone in a dark room with a blindfold on. The room was reputed to be haunted. One woman explained:

> I thought 'oh my god what am I doing?' I am going to be on my own, and I've never really done that. I did feel really scared. It was scarier for the other woman, it was scarier for her. Especially when she was told you're alone in the room, you can take your blindfold off, and she went fuck off! The fear of actually seeing something is greater than the blindfold. I couldn't see anything. It is so easy to imagine you see things, you are looking and the possibility is there ... My heart started beating more ... and you think well I saw it, so it has got to be there.

In the moment, her heart beat faster and she sensed and made sense of her cognitive and physiological responses. The experiment also involved a member of the team secretly remaining present in the room. She did not sense the team member was there until they made their presence known. The idea behind the experiment was to allow participants to reflect on their expectations of a haunting which can overlay physical factors. Another idea was that of visual perception, where the eyes can play tricks on the mind. The visual cortex is the largest of the sensory centres of the brain (Classen 1993: 9). The blindfold experiment played with how people can use other senses than sight to explore presence.

In *Touch*, Laura Marks (2002: xiii) uses an 'understanding of vision as embodied and material' to argue for a 'sensuous closeness' to material objects, such as artefacts or the moving image. She combines vision with touch to explain a mixed mode of engagement. Lawrence Marks claims 'most perception in daily life is multimodal' (2000: 143). In relation to ghost hunts sensory journeys are likely to involve the perception and distinction of one sense modality in relation to another. Synesthesia (Marks 2000) is an anomalous identity experience where 'sensory images or qualities of one modality, for instance vision, find themselves transferred to another modality, such as taste or hearing' (121). In clinical terms most of us experience 'weak synesthesia', often called poetic synesthesia, which involves a metaphor of the senses (123). Strong synesthesia is rare and has been documented with some writers or composers who unconsciously hear words as sounds, or see musical notes as colours. Although there are neural mechanisms underlying synesthesia, Marks acknowledges the importance of social learning and cultural contexts. Most people experience weak synesthesia and draw on systematic intermodal relations, such as the synesthetic connections between temperature and colours, where there is an almost universal agreement that there are warm and cold colours and feelings. There are also connections with low-frequency sounds and darkness, and high-frequency sounds and lightness (128). Many participants on a ghost hunt experience weak synesthesia, metaphorically drawing on multimodal senses, in particular hot and cold colours or light. For example, participants use equipment which measures temperature changes thought to be related to spirit activity. People consciously draw on feelings of temperature change to describe their experience, such as cold, dark shapes. Or participants describe the dark in relation to touch; some rooms feel heavy with darkness, or the dark is crackling with vibrations.

Sensory journeys lie on a continuum of experience. At one end of the continuum are extrasensory experiences. These include intuitive impressions where someone just knows something is going on, hallucinations, such as seeing something that is not visible to others, realistic visual images, like flashes of clothing, and unrealistic images, such as dreams or symbolism (Targ et al 2000: 223). 'The content of extrasensory experiences tends to be personally significant to the experient ... often depicted by experients as very compelling and meaningful' (2000: 224). These experiences contribute to people's sense of self-identity and their journey in life (226). Interpretations of extrasensory experiences are culturally specific; in Western societies they are connected to feelings of confusion, fear and spiritual quests. Significantly, 'personal experience is cited by experients as their principal reason for their belief in the paranormal' (227). Many people on a ghost hunting event are looking for an extrasensory experience. This is extremely rare. Nevertheless people hope to have it. As this woman explained 'I come to these things because I want proof … I believe there are spirits but I have to see it with my own eyes. I have to see it to believe it.'[19] Or, as another participant said: 'it is like your senses, we have some people here who see better, taste better, and smell better, so why can't some people have a different sense?'[20] On a continuum of experience, people are hoping for an intense sensory engagement that is compelling and meaningful to them as evidence of paranormal phenomena.

One ghost hunting event took place at London Dungeon on a Friday 13th. In a maze of corridors a particular exhibit included historical figurines above head height. One of the figures was activated by a sensor and started screaming. No matter how many times participants walked down there, getting lost in the Dungeon, the exhibit managed to scare everyone, as the first person to activate the sensor would jump and bump into the people behind them. The team called this 'the scary way.' It was scary and funny at the same time. Screams of laughter could be heard throughout the ghost hunt as various groups encountered this exhibit. When all of the groups met for a tea break the exhibit still went off. The same thing happened to other exhibits, where sensors were activated seemingly without human help. A few people began to intuitively sense something strange. Another man in a mirror maze felt a tickling sensation on the back of his neck. A woman described 'a feeling of coldness. I get it on one side, you know when someone is in your own personal space. Someone is close to me. I did feel a presence or energy around me.' In these examples people's senses were activated by the space and physical stimuli, by their imagination and fear, and by their expectations of extrasensory experiences.

There is a sociability to sensory engagement. A group bonds quickly and the practices of conducting a séance become a social experience. A good example of this is table tipping and rapping. At the Old Sessions House in Clerkenwell one group was in the cellars, once a holding space for people taken from Clerkenwell House of Detention.[21] The team leader directed the table tipping activity. They informed the group 'what you see is not what it is', and talked of investigating inside the historical layers of the space, looking at 'residual hauntings.' Another team member explained:

> I find it very much works as kinetic energy, which is what we as humans give off, and in order to experience something we need to give this energy. You will always get someone saying it is pushed, it is fake. From my personal point of view there are things I can't explain, from a human point of view I can't explain … Expect everything and nothing to happen … Don't try to push the table because that spoils it for everyone.

The participants held hands and tried not to make any extra movement. Some sounds began, a creaking, clicking noise, then silence. After some time, one of the participants called out, and playfully sang a fragment from the song 'Hey Big Spender'. The tension of straining to hear something disappeared as a few participants and team members sang the opening notes of the song 'the minute you walked in the joint ... '. The team leader called out 'is this what you want spirit, to play?' And there were some rapping sounds that echoed the music and travelled around the table.

Within the group, one team member said it was the anniversary of her father's death 12 years to the day. She heard other sounds moving around the table, the window closest to her rattled: 'I don't know. It is spooky that they called me over today.' Other participants struggled to explain what they thought happened: 'strange how the knocking was in time, it played the tune.' One man said 'it seemed like it was going to kick off but it held back. Normally we can find the energy easily and to me there is a lot of energy here.' His friend asserted 'you do trust the people you are with', implying that the bond within the group would have created a community of like-minded people – 'you want your own evidence.' Such comments signal the sociability of the experience, where the sensations of table tipping or talking are created by the group energy. No one wants the phenomena to be faked, but at the same time they are disappointed when nothing happens. The feeling things didn't 'kick off' was reinforced by a previous example of table tipping:

> Last year the table was moving, it was incredible, it was going crazy. I actually got on the table and I was hanging on for dear life. The table was bucking, I was literally clinging onto the edge of it. It is incredible. When it happens it is really good.

Another man added 'we have been to other locations when the spirit has moved the table, really violent, and the tappings run around the table. That was incredible.' The table tipping in Clerkenwell produced ambiguous associations, but this example shows what people hope will happen to them on a ghost hunt.

Psychologists argue that people make a table tip or talk, consciously or unconsciously. Table tipping can be explained by ideomotor movement, where people unconsciously do something they are trying not to do. Another explanation for what happens on a ghost hunting event involves emotional contagion. Cardeña et al (2009: 33) describe this as 'the propensity to automatically imitate the emotional expressions of others and experience corresponding emotions.' There is a synchrony in the way people emotionally react to each other. Cardeña et al studied the relations between emotional contagion and hypnotism, arguing that it is one explanation for the importance of affectivity in hypnotic responsiveness. People with high levels of emotional empathy had a greater responsiveness to a hypnotic situation where there was a 'proposed enhancement of rapport and purposeful shaping of experience' (35). Similarities to the situation of a ghost hunting event can be found in the way team leaders enhance rapport, and encourage reactivity, emotionality, empathy, sensitivity, and sociability amongst the group. In turn the group responds and encourages such reactions amongst themselves, purposefully shaping their experience. The researchers point out: 'the ability to feel or appear to feel strong emotions, to be able to express them, and to be sensitive to incompatible emotions [are] features that also characterize acting' (35). The performance of emotions within a group situation can help to create and shape an experience.

Sensory journeys are examples of what Raymond Williams (1977) called a structure of feeling. This concept brings two opposites together. It combines the individual and creative elements of personal feelings with the collective and shared elements of social structures. A structure of feeling suggests the fixity and flow of cultural practices on a ghost hunting event. There is a structure to the event which purposefully shapes a disquieting experience. This structure is made up of the event itself, with its group investigations, and references to séance phenomena, and the careful attention of the team to create a safe environment within which to explore paranormal ideas and beliefs. The structure of a ghost hunting event also draws on social issues and values relating to paranormal beliefs, historical events, and a collective searching for evidence of an afterlife. There is a sense that participants at a ghost hunting event know they are part of a collective response to fears of mortality and searching for answers at a time of social and economic crisis in Western society. Other structuring elements include the commercial development of ghost tourism and the positioning of ghost hunting events within tourism and psychic industries. At the same time there is a way cultural practices in turn purposively shape the experience of a ghost hunting event. People react in the moment. Their hearts beat faster, they sense disquieting elements in this live event. There is a performance of emotions, reactions, empathy and sensitivity. These performers are showing how they can feel and sense and respond to each other in the moment.

A structure of feeling connects with Avery Gordon's (1997) point that hauntings are social experiences. For Gordon, ghosts highlight a sensuous knowledge, the knowledge of what we cannot see but feel is present in society. There is a transformative power to this sensuous knowledge because through listening to ghosts people can better understand social injustice and do something about it. What Gordon calls a sensuous knowledge is an awareness of the invisible, of the hidden aspects of history and social issues. In Pile's analysis of the invisible aspects of cityscapes he calls this way of seeing urban spaces the emotional forces of life and death that become visible through hauntings. There is a sensuous knowledge to the cultural practices of ghost hunting events. This is linked to knowledge of hauntings and paranormal beliefs, and to psychological knowledge of haunting atmospheres. There is also an emotional geography to ghost hunting events. There are stories of hauntings and urban planning on locations and an investigation into the forces of life and death in haunted spaces and places.

Whereas Gordon and Pile are both researching the symbolism of hauntings, when people go on a ghost hunting event they are engaging with both real and symbolic matters. They not only have a sensuous knowledge of history and society, or awareness of the symbolism of a haunting in a cityscape. The cultural practices of people at a ghost hunting event show some of the ways people produce beliefs in something that exists beyond our immediate reality. As Shillito commented: 'look beyond what you see there, beyond the surface, we have got to look beyond.' To remain at the symbolic level misses the power of these performative acts to bring into perspective alternative realities. People's sensuous engagement with a ghost hunting event takes them 'beyond what you see there.' Perhaps such intense identity experiences fill the gap in media experiences that remain at the symbolic level. TV series, films or websites can symbolically open doors to the paranormal world, but there is nothing like opening those doors yourself in a haunted house. These identity experiences also work better with others. The sociality of cultural practices is crucial. People perform their identity work together. To say that people go on a ghost hunting event to 'look beyond' is only half the story. They also engage with each other through feeling these shared experiences. Shillito explained:

> We have forgotten how to communicate with each other. Where do you know where people stand around and hold hands in the dark? Mates hold hands with mates, and where on earth does that happen in England? You are blending into one.[22]

Conclusion

Ghost tourism is a growth area. Quite why it has developed so rapidly and with such vigour is partly explained by an increase in paranormal beliefs, diversity in tourism practices, and the popularity of history in contemporary culture. Ghost tourism combines all three in its mix of ghost stories, folklore and memorable historical events, encounters with ghostly phenomena in haunted locations, and ghost walks, talks and hunts in tourist destinations. The development of dark tourism connects with the desire to experience the extraordinary, to be a part of the emotional geography of a building, city, or site of violence. Similar to extreme sports, ghost tourism offers an intense experience that draws on the emotional forces of life and death. It's that adrenalin rush, where the heart beats faster and people are in the moment. Even though ghost tourism draws on history and memory in haunted locations, it does it in such a way that the present seems even more real. It makes you jump.

Event companies want to make you jump. The structure of a ghost hunt takes into account people's desire to have some fun and also explore potentially paranormal encounters. There is a fine line between the pleasures of fear and hope in the existence of spirits. Regular participants learn not to jump at every little thing, wanting to get beyond the fun to the intensity of the experience, where in that rare moment in a darkened room they can say they have seen a ghost. Whilst most people won't have an extrasensory experience, many hope to. It is this hope that makes ghost hunting much more than tourism. There is a charged atmosphere to a ghost hunt precisely because of the emotional and psychological expectations of participants. Research suggests that not only are participants reacting to their feelings and frame of mind, but also variations in electro-magnetic fields, low-frequency sounds, which can influence experiences in alleg-edly haunted spaces. This mix of the physical, psychological and emotional makes for a powerful sensory experience. It creates a structure of feeling, where the structuring principles of the ghost hunt as an event connect to history and ghost stories, paranormal beliefs, and mix with the creativity of people's cultural prac-tices. The event organisers and the participants work together in a purposeful shaping of a unique cultural experience.

Notes

1 See official website for The National Trust, accessed online at www.nationaltrust. org 20 October 2009.
2 See BBC news 'Ghost Capital's Tourist Hopes' Friday, 9 August 2002, accessed online at http://news.bbc.co.uk/2/hi/uk_news/england/2183197.stm 20 October 2009.
3 See official website Hampton Court Palace, accessed online at www.hrp.org.uk/ learninganddiscovery/Discoverthehistoricroyalpalaces/ghoststorieshomepage/ Catherinehowardscreaminglady.aspx 20 October 2009.
4 See official website accessed online at www.hauntedhappenings.co.uk 20 October 2009.
5 See event details in the magazine *Paranormal*, October 2008, Issue 28: 76.
6 See Dixon, Rachel (2009) 'How Britain Became a Nation of Ghost Hunters' the *Guardian*, 30 October 2009, accessed online at www.guardianunlimited 4 November 2009.
7 Interview with author 17 June 2008.
8 Official website, accessed online at www.londonparanormal.com/events.htm 6 June 2009.
9 Interview with author 17 June 2008.
10 Interview with author 23 April 2008.
11 All quotations for this paragraph from the official website, accessed online at www.londonparanormal.com/events.htm 6 June 2009.
12 Interview with author 17 June 2008.
13 Interview with author on ghost hunt at Old Sessions House 31 May 2008.
14 Interview with author 23 April 2008.
15 Interview with author on ghost hunt at London Dungeon Friday, 13 June 2008.
16 Interview with author 17 June 2008.
17 Interview with author on ghost hunt at Old Sessions House 31 May 2008.
18 Interview with author 17 June 2008.
19 Interview with author on ghost hunt at London Dungeon Friday, 13 June 2008.
20 All quotations in this section are taken from interviews with the author on a ghost hunt at London Dungeon Friday, 13 June 2008.
21 All quotations in this section are taken from interviews with the author on a ghost hunt at Old Sessions House 31 May 2008.
22 Interview with author 17 June 2008.

Chapter 6

Experiences

'We feel these things, hear these things, see these things.'

Matters of authenticity and experience are dominant themes in paranormal cultural practices. These themes are framed in different ways. Within the media, there is a crisis of evidence and the paranormal is caught up in a general narrative of distrust in the representation of reality in news, or eye witness accounts. Within personal stories of hauntings, or extrasensory perception, there is a focus on the individual who provides a compelling narrative of experience as evidence. In this context, the paranormal becomes a symbol for popular solipsism, a form of knowledge that prioritises personal existence. These two dominant narratives highlight how matters of authenticity are dealt with in one way that foregrounds rationality and reason, and in another way that foregrounds instinct and identity experiences.

A market has arisen which addresses experiences that go against the grain and prioritise personal existence. Mind, body and spirit is a growth area in the cultural, health and well being industries. It mixes paranormal ideas with popular psychology and personal empowerment. In this way, mind, body and spirit practices, products and services validate identity experiences that run counter to mainstream culture. This is an example of how secular spiritual and magical beliefs are the basis from which an industry can grow and connect with wider trends in alternative medicine, progressive religions and politics, or the ecology and environment. A generation of people characterised as metaphysical and spiritual seekers are participating in what has been called a culture of re-enchantment. A founder of a mind, body and spirit magazine summed up the approach as 'we are all fabulously unique.' This is a culture where alternative identity experiences are a foundation for paranormal beliefs in modern Western societies.

Crisis of evidence

Peter Lamont has argued that nineteenth-century accounts of psychics and debates about spiritualism and fraud can be understood within the context of a

Figure 6.1 Mind, body and spirit magazines

crisis of evidence. The first psychic Daniel Dunglas Home performed a 'bewildering range of inexplicable feats' such as clairvoyance and levitation (Lamont 2005: 3). Home was tested by scientists and the very term 'psychic' was invented to describe the extraordinary feats he performed. 'Many witnesses were hostile to spiritualism, and many remained unconvinced by what they had seen, yet time and again they admitted that they were unable to explain what had happened' (260). Within a crisis of faith in religion and a wealth of scientific discoveries, Home's feats were hotly debated as evidence of miracles and examples of charlatanism. Controversies in the press focused on conjuring tricks and unreliable testimony, but no evidence was found to convict Home of fraud. Matters of authenticity became part of debates about the first psychic. Lamont argues that such a crisis of evidence signals a fundamental problem with trusting evidence from any source:

> If witnesses can report such seemingly inexplicable events, and be so certain that they were not deceived in any way, then we might become more sceptical about testimony in general. And that might change how we read the news or listen to others. Then we might be even more sceptical, and wonder just how plausible deception and unreliable testimony are as explanations. Are we really prepared to accept that so many people could be deceived so often, and that what people say can be so utterly unreliable?
>
> (273)

Scepticism about objective observers and scientific knowledge is just as important as scepticism of psychic or supernatural phenomena. For Lamont, Home reminds us how 'uncertainty is real and certainty an illusion' (269).

Stuart Hoover (2007: 308) notes a recurring theme of authenticity in research on contemporary religion and the media which attempts to explore 'the nature of religion as it adapts and is adapted to new forms and contexts of articulation.' When Schofield Clark (2007) comments on religious lifestyle branding she calls into question what is authentic about religious writings and beliefs as they are purposely stylised in the media. Her example of a fashion bible demonstrates how a new form of magazine style publication articulates Christian doctrines in very different ways from original religious writings. Within this context, authenticity is understood as both a replica of an original and something that is authenticated by a recognised institution. The context of representations and commercial considerations complicates matters of authenticity and religion.

In popular culture, the nature of paranormal ideas adapts and is adapted to new forms and contexts of articulation. One participant said: 'our media culture makes us more sceptical' (22-year-old male student). Any discussion of hauntings or extrasensory perception as represented on television and the web includes a large dose of scepticism. Critical analysis of representations of paranormal phenomena is common amongst participants in this study. There is awareness about manipulation of images through digital technologies and software, or the control of televised ghost hunts through careful editing and selective casting of characters. This is partly explained by media literacy skills such as genre knowledge, awareness of representation and production techniques, and partly by a generally cynical approach to the media as commercial industries. It would be unusual if participants were uncritical of paranormal claims within the context of television or the web as there is an awareness of a crisis of evidence in the media in general.

News and journalism are in a professional crisis. There are problems with ownership and editorial direction, a decrease in advertising and revenues, and an overall decline in readership. Alongside this professional context are public debates about the quality of news, lack of impartiality, the credibility of news sources, and a perceived tabloid agenda to news coverage (see Thussu 2007). Debates about news amongst audiences includes concern about a crisis of evidence, and how to trust journalists, their sources, and news accounts of national and world events (see Hill 2007). A related set of concerns accompanies documentary, both in terms of a decline in production, training and quality standards, and in trust in the truth claims made by documentary makers (see Winston 2001). High-profile scandals of fakery and the use of stylised techniques that borrow from drama or soap opera have become part of audience discussions of documentary and its evidentiary status (see Hill 2007 and Ellis 2005 amongst others). Debates about photography and image manipulation highlight a crisis of trust in visual evidence (Ellis 2009). Professional photographers are held to account in online social forums where the public question the truth claims of a photographer and their intentions when taking photographs (Corner 2009).

The rise of reality entertainment as a hybrid genre of fact and fiction expands the context of a crisis of evidence to a host of other non-fiction genres, including investigative journalism, current affairs, lifestyle and entertainment. Reality TV is like a magic trick in that it is not what it claims to be (Hill 2005). Modes of engagement with non-fiction media content highlight various ways audiences deal with uncertainty about truth claims within the media and trust in information and testimony.

The role of the media in bearing witness is one that carries great weight in contemporary research on journalism or photography. Barbie Zelizer has written of media representations of death and dying in events in recent history and argued that bearing witness through news pictures of war, or amateur footage of 9/11, has altered our understanding of witnessing and visual evidence (2005). Stewart Hoover writes of the media's role in witnessing 9/11 as a major source of experience of the terrorist attacks on the twin towers of the World Trade Center. These news images were graphically visual and instantaneous for audiences and publics bearing witness to this traumatic event (2006: 237–38). The problems of news journalism, or the reality status of documentary or photography are not so great, or so institutionally endemic, that audiences and publics reject outright the role of the media as a witness. But within the context of paranormal claims, the media have little authority in bearing witness. It opens a door to discussions of paranormal claims, but it is not the basis from which beliefs are maintained. Widespread distrust in institutions within religion, science, medicine, politics and the media is a feature of paranormal matters. The most trusted source is the self and even with regard to personal experience there is a measure of uncertainty.

The issue of paranormal claims in the media indicates how matters of authenticity and evidence are debated. A participant commented:

> The problem is we are so used to seeing things on television having been carefully orchestrated beforehand, you think about what is true or what isn't. But if you are actually in a real live situation which is happening then it is pretty fantastic, and you come away thinking 'wow'! But, it just doesn't come across on television because everyone is thinking 'well, somebody is pushing the table with a magnet.' But I've been there, and I've been in several table turning exercises run by people who are very renowned mediums. And I have seen stuff I never thought possible. When you actually experience it yourself, you see somebody, they've just got two fingers on the table and someone is sitting on the table and it's moving around the room rapidly, then you understand the energy involved.
>
> (36-year-old male)

Authenticity is stage managed within a media environment, and truth becomes something manipulated for commercial and entertainment purposes. Alternatively, in a 'real live' environment authenticity is like an electrical charge jolting someone into experiences never 'thought possible.'

In a different context the media can be interpreted as tangible and credible sources of evidence. This participant explained:

> I think that one of the reasons why I went along to that investigation was to try to have a personal experience … I'm going to do it, I was right into it. I was locked in a wine cellar with a video camera and audio recording. I was locked in, physically locked in this room … I listened to the sound and suddenly there were little things … I am looking for experiences, hoping for something to happen.
>
> (26-year-old male vision mixer)

Here, authenticity is a matter that must be explored in isolation with technical resources. There is a double articulation of authenticity in the media. As Silverstone (1994) argued, the media are both material and symbolic. Media objects are material evidence within personal testimonials. And the media also symbolise problems of trust in the evidentiary claims made within television or the web.

Discursive analysis of witnesses and personal accounts of alleged paranormal phenomena suggest people come from a position of distrust. The modes of communication between a medium, or psychic and their audience are based on recognising and negotiating scepticism and addressing matters of authenticity, authority and expertise (Wooffitt 2006). High-profile scandals of fraud are common within psychic professions. Wooffitt argues that psychic-sitter interactions highlight non-formal institutional discourses. The psychic professions constitute an alternative institution of sorts, with professional associations, guidelines and codes of conduct, and laws regarding psychic claims. If a law demands that a psychic or medium must state they are working for entertainment purposes only, then the consumer comes with a degree of distrust towards paranormal claims. It is one of the most revealing aspects of communication between a medium or psychic and their audience that this distrust is negotiated and indeed utilised as a basis from which evidence and authentic accounts are drawn. Uncertainty becomes the basis from which evidence is assessed and accepted or rejected.

The ways people engage with a crisis of evidence can be seen in their strategies for communicating personal experiences. For example: 'until something has happened to you, you will always doubt it really' (20-year-old male student). Or 'It's a very personal thing what people believe' (22-year-old beauty therapist). The ideology of the individual dominates reflections on authenticity: 'I am really sceptical of other people's accounts. It is a personal thing. You hear other stories and you would like to believe, but I find it hard to believe other people' (female participant at a ghost hunting event). Evidence and bearing witness can become such an uncertain process that even no evidence and nothing to see can be interpreted as authentic. One male participant on a ghost hunting event explained: 'I would be much more happy knowing I left in the morning and hadn't found a thing than knowing I left in the morning and someone was shaking the table.'

The stigma of gullibility is strong in communication about paranormal claims. Authenticity becomes an interior, psychological and emotional issue, as well as a cognitive and empirical problem. Plausible deception includes fraud and conscious manipulation of evidence, and also self-deception and unconscious selection of evidence (see Wiseman 1997). Unreliable testimony relates to a lack of impartiality, ignorance and blind faith in paranormal claims, and also cognitive traps and human error (see French and Wilson 2006). Debates about evidence of paranormal phenomena are tied to a problem of authoritative sources of knowledge and information. One person explained:

> My knowledge is very limited on a whole load of things and I think even scientists with ten PhDs probably wouldn't be able to explain certain physical things. But that doesn't mean there isn't actually a measure for it. So, for me personally, I've had weird experiences and strange things that I can't necessarily account for, but it still doesn't convince me that anything is paranormal.
>
> (30-year-old female library assistant)

A problem of evidence and reliable testimony becomes bound up with a problem of knowledge.

In Santino's research on accounts of the paranormal amongst airline professionals ghost stories became a part of the professional culture, a non-formal discourse for people in a perceived high risk profession. Their ghost stories were a coping strategy for understanding inexplicable crashes: 'where cognitive holes exist, symbolic and supernatural phenomena appear to plug them up. In this way these stories contribute to a kind of symbolic ecology, which there is both cosmological and cognitive balance' (1988: 217). In terms of psychological explanations for paranormal beliefs Irwin (2009) also suggests paranormal interpretations of strange experiences can give people a feeling of certainty and control over a seemingly inexplicable event. In personal accounts by participants some certainty comes from communicating their experience as evidence of the paranormal. As one woman put it: 'it's comforting to think that there are ghosts and people around you' (42-year-old female office manager). However, other issues around deception and unreliable testimony also show how cognitive holes still exist. A crisis of evidence does not disappear on the strength of trust in personal experience. Popular psychology shows the self can be an unreliable witness. One man explained: 'how many times do you know if you are actually dreaming or not dreaming. When I was little I used to like aliens and ET, and for years, every time I slept I dreamed of aliens. You don't know if it's real or not' (25-year-old auto electrician).

Issues of authenticity follow a circular logic. Within the context of the media and representations of paranormal matters, issues of authenticity are part of a widespread debate about a crisis of evidence and the truth claims made within media institutions. Audiences are cynical of the media as a commercial and entertainment enterprise and therefore sceptical of the role of the media in bearing witness to allegedly real paranormal phenomena. One strategy is to distrust second-order experiences of alleged paranormal phenomena and trust in first-order experiences. However, awareness that people can deceive themselves or be an unreliable witness complicates things. If even your own mind cannot be trusted, then authenticity is an elusive ideal. It is within this circular logic that audiences jolt themselves out of uncertainty by putting faith in their own extraordinary experiences and using these as a basis for producing beliefs.

Personal experiences

Within paranormal beliefs, authenticity is less associated with a formal institution or authorised body of knowledge, and more connected to non-formal institutions and alternative information and sources. Within this context, authenticity is often articulated as true to the self and personal experience. This understanding is part of psychological explanations of paranormal beliefs as instinctive interpretations of inexplicable phenomena. Psychological studies indicate that 'cognitive foundations of belief generation and evaluation' show a reliance on 'intuitive-experiential interpretation' (Irwin 2009: 117). Irwin explains:

> the involvement of a psi or magical process is endorsed primarily because this is how the anomalous incident initially felt and not so much because the information is consistent with independent knowledge or with opinions of mainstream scientists.
>
> (ibid)

In this way, the paranormal becomes associated with solipsism, a form of scepticism that denies the possibility of any knowledge other than personal existence. Irwin notes that 'belief generation and evaluation of a highly analytical kind' is less common in the general population than paranormal beliefs grounded in personal experience that appears 'intuitively obvious' to the experient (116–18). Although Irwin doesn't rule out critical analysis, he tends to see believers more likely to 'suspend such analysis in relation to beliefs attested by experience and to apply critical analysis more routinely only to other types of belief' (118).

Robin Wooffitt uses a discursive approach to parapsychology in *Telling Tales of the Unexpected* (1992) and *The Language of Mediums and Psychics: the Social Organisation of Everyday Miracles* (2006). Wooffitt's discursive approach adds another dimension to understanding intuitive-experiential interpretation. He argues the social organisation of communication provides examples of how people manage matters of authority, authenticity and expertise (2006: 186).

For example, a medium and sitter negotiate and manage issues of authenticity together in a complex series of communicative acts. The details a medium provides are signs of authenticity, and if these details are accepted by the sitter then matters of authority and expertise come into play in the ensuing interactions. In people's personal accounts of extraordinary experiences authenticity is explored and negotiated through the telling of the tale. How we understand the meaning of the tale shows how matters of authenticity connect with authority. As Andrew Martin notes in *Ghoul Britannia* (2009):

> Nobody wants to listen to someone who begins 'And the 16th time I saw a ghost … ' or to read a ghost story narrated by a character who, like the Satanist in *My Black Mirror* by Wilkie Collins (1856), gleefully declares: 'I have not one morsel of rationality about me.'[1]

People use a number of narrative techniques to establish themselves as credible sources of knowledge.

In this section participants narrate their experiences of what they understand as paranormal phenomena. Many of these narratives are by women. Research in paranormal beliefs is inconclusive on whether gender is a factor in the formation of beliefs, with some researchers suggesting women are more likely to hold beliefs in spirits or divination, and men more likely to hold beliefs in aliens, for example, whilst other researchers have found no significant differences. Irwin concludes that the techniques used in surveys are flawed and methodological differences are a reason for inconclusive evidence on gender in psychological studies (2009). In the qualitative research on cultural practices in this study a different methodological approach is used, that of popular cultural ethnography. What emerged in terms of gender was a perception on behalf of men and women that there was a difference in their beliefs, with women having a more intuitive, emotional style than that of men in their discussion of beliefs. It was the case that more men adopted a scientific style of narration where evidence and facts were debated more explicitly than the women in this study. But, at the same time, men would speak intuitively and emotionally about their experiences, and women would speak in a matter of fact way about evidence, so perceptions amongst participants did change during group discussions. Nevertheless, when it came to narrating personal experiences more women did so with a natural style for storytelling and a good rapport with their audience. Given the emphasis on intuition, emotion and social interaction in discourses of paranormal beliefs and representations in popular culture it is perhaps not so surprising that women in this study told good ghost stories.

There are a range of resources which help people communicate their sense of the extraordinary. Warner (2006) notes spirit forms reappear in history and culture partly because they are familiar. For example, crossroads are a geographical place of some significance in histories of hauntings, where local parishes removed the bodies of suicides to crossroads so that troubled spirits could not return to their place of death (Davies 2007).Ghost road stories are compelling and familiar examples of extraordinary experiences:

> I am going to tell you a ghost story ... oh my god, my god. We were in Mexico driving one day, and suddenly I watched a guy in the back of my car, the guy was covered with blood and had a cut on his neck. I panicked and told my boyfriend I had seen this guy in the back of the car. I just cried. My boyfriend said 'listen, my best friend died in a car crash, I've never told you this before but my friend died on this road.' I described the guy and he said 'oh my god!'
>
> (23-year-old female student)

This ghost road story has all the elements of a classic haunting, a tragedy, return of the victim to the site of violence, and the memory of a dead friend disrupting present time. In this example, matters of authenticity can be understood as the telling of a ghost story as an authentic copy of an original. It is a real experience for this person and it seems real to an audience partly because it is familiar.

In the histories of ghosts, haunted houses have strong emotional purchase as they represent unseen forces and unsettling experiences in ordinary household spaces. The following example is from a childhood experience of a haunted house:

> To be honest with you, I don't think there was one spirit in the house. I could feel more than one. I think there were different things happening ... At the very top of the house, I know there was a lady, probably from the turn of the century because you could hear by the dress. There was a woman upstairs and she talked to us at night in bed. The downstairs, there was a man, definitely a man there. There was something, to be honest with you, all the times I lived in the house. I was so scared. We used to sing hymns and things just to distract us.
>
> (49-year-old female teacher)

This woman's personal memories of the family home showed her fear of living with 'different things happening.' She draws on a set of resources from history and culture to communicate her unique experience within a recognisable form. In this case, matters of authenticity can also be understood as integrity, where the repetition of 'to be honest with you' signals personal disclosure and the sharing of a haunting experience.

Wooffitt identifies a strategy of normalising the paranormal in personal accounts. One way of communicating a unique experience is to juxtapose it within an everyday context. One man explained his haunted house experience:

> As soon as we walked in the house, we felt cold. And even in the middle of summer, you felt cold. I was sitting there one night with my friend and we

were eating, and there was a fruit bowl between us, and fruit was just rolling off. Just like that. Just rolled off from the table, all fruits were rolling, and in the kitchen the doors are opening and closing on their own … I saw a sort of shadow there.

(48-year-old male train driver)

The ordinary setting of the kitchen, the fruit rolling off the kitchen table, is juxtaposed with a strange, shadowy presence. In this example what is authentic about this experience is the detail of the fruit which makes it appear real to the teller and to his audience who are asked to trust his interpretation of a haunting.

Authentic experiences of paranormal phenomena connect with ideas of true facts and evidence. Everyday objects become significant to the performance of paranormal beliefs, used as props in the telling of extraordinary tales. One person recounted their experience after a funeral:

A good friend of ours who loved to drink, he drank for England, he died and we'd been to his funeral. We were in a pub afterwards with his brother and cousins … We ordered three drinks and a glass hopped up from a shelf onto all three drinks, smashed and ruined all the drinks. We all looked at each other and said, 'that's him.'

(51-year-old female secretary)

This woman spoke of her mother's messages from the other side:

I am convinced I have seen it. That is why I believe. I have a teacup that no one is allowed to touch. It is my mum's shrine … the most recent thing happened to the teacup. I did the dishes, put everything away, no water in my bowl, got up in the morning and as I go to put the kettle on there was water half way in the bowl and my mum's tea cup was in the bowl. … I lost her three years ago. I don't know if I like to think it is your mum, it is comforting to think that. Come on mum, if this is you I need a sign. I need to know. Give me a sign so I know it is you.

(39-year-old female)

This woman's account shows how one strategy can be combined with another in recounting personal experiences. There is a statement of belief, a reflection on how to interpret this sign, and an awareness experiences are open to interpretation and misinterpretation. Her final plea 'I need to know' is one echoed by others in their telling of extraordinary experiences.

There are examples of communication technologies acting strangely in paranormal stories. In the nineteenth century, new technologies took on psychic powers, for example the photograph became a device through which spirits could communicate with the living (see Sconce 2000 amongst others). This mobile phone ghost story uses an object as evidence of spirit communication:

> I got a message three minutes after I arranged my husband's funeral from his phone ... we were walking back from the churchyard and my message thing went and I picked up the phone and his name came up. I couldn't read it. I thought 'oh my god.' I opened the message which was nothing ... how could it happen? It's a really weird message ... I tried to delete it but I can't.
>
> (56-year-old female homemaker)

In a different context, the media can be used as a documented source of information:

> One night, I sat on the bed and had a horrible sense, I just knew, there was a plane crash. I couldn't breathe and suddenly I found myself on this plane. I was pregnant and thought I was nuts. The next morning, front page news, the plane landed first and burst into flames. I experienced it, I was on the plane.
>
> (55-year-old female entrepreneur)

Both of these women have extraordinary experiences which are perceived by them as evidence of spirits and extrasensory perception. The media, as a conduit or a source of information, adds authority to interpretations of evidence. Media technologies can be used as strategies for verifying paranormal beliefs.

Wooffitt (1992) notes how intersubjectivities are part of personal accounts of the paranormal, where experiences are witnessed and verified by the reactions of others. A woman's childhood experience was recounted through her own and a friend's response to a strange presence:

> My best friend and I were sleeping and we felt this thing. It was cold. It was evil and dense, it had weight to it. I was terrified. Terrified. I said to my friend, 'what's that?' She said, 'I don't know,' but she knew what I was talking about. She put the light on. She was too scared to move. She was paralysed by it. Me, the biggest cynic, makes the sign of the cross. Do you know it left, it never ever came back. It was tangible. It was terrifying.
>
> (55-year-old female entrepreneur)

Her memory of this experience is made all the more tangible because of the physical reactions of both children to this terrifying appearance. In another account, a haunting is verified through another person's similar experience:

> It was a Saturday or Sunday morning. I was thinking, 'oh I'm getting up in a minute,' and then by the side of my bed appeared a lady. She was white, everything about her was white. I could see her face, nose, eyes ... and I wasn't scared at all ... I pinched myself a few times, really, really hard. I wasn't scared. She was still there. I put my hands out to touch her and she disappeared. Well, as I got older I doubted myself, because I was a

child. ... A guy who lived in the same block of flats, who was a similar age to me, told me exactly the same story. Exactly! Now I was freaked because I never discussed it. I'd never told anyone, not even my sisters. He told me exactly the same story. And it did really make me feel cold ... So I do believe it because I saw it.

(51-year-old female secretary)

A familiar story of a white lady, one that recurs in histories of hauntings, takes on added significance because of its re-appearance to someone else. There is a narrative arc through the intersubjective positions where the haunting is perceived as real, then doubted, then reinstated as evidence of paranormal belief.

Discursive strategies mix together in compelling narratives of paranormal experiences. This woman told of her childhood experience of a haunting as authentic evidence of spirits:

It was the first day of the Christmas holidays. It was snowing and we were very excited, so we all ran down to the garden. This is four children, we never thought about ghosts or anything like that. We were playing and building a snowman and we heard the front door slam. 'Oh mum's back.' So we started running down the garden to see what was in her shopping bag, and all of sudden we heard someone coming into the house, walking through the passage and going upstairs. We looked up to the building where there was a window and there was a man standing looking at us playing in the garden. 'Who's that?' Nobody was in the house ... We were really crying and scared because we thought someone was in the house, but there wasn't ... The way we described him later on was the description of a man who used to live downstairs. Brown suit and long coat.

(49-year-old female teacher)

There is the strategy of normalising the paranormal in the children playing in the snow. There is the witnessing of a haunting in the collective experience of all the children together. Verification comes from historical sources which connect the male spirit to a former tenant of the house. And the details help locate the narrative in a discourse of realism – 'brown suit and long coat.'

Peter Lamont (2005) notes an avowal of prior scepticism is another discursive strategy for establishing paranormal beliefs. One woman explained how she transformed from a sceptic to believer:

I was completely sceptical, never believed in anything at all. Eight years ago I was staying in a hotel. I suddenly woke up in the middle of night and there was someone in my room. I knew the door was locked and turned around. It was a man. I feel so silly saying this, because it sounds kind of strange, I know. But there was a man in sort of full military uniform standing in the door way, just standing still, and looking straight ahead. I froze. I knew that

I could see something. I wasn't imagining the whole thing. It was weird. I turned away, and then turned back again, he'd gone. It just scared me ... just completely freaked me out, it was weird. I never had an experience like that before, I never had one since. It was very, very strange. I was the most sceptical person ... I definitely believe it, having kind of seen that, definitely something, someone there. Very strange, so definitely I believe now. I was much more comfortable when I didn't believe that ... It did change my life. I still feel kind of silly speaking about ghosts. I did see something. I think, maybe, I was always sort of black and white, that it doesn't exist, you can't see it, that's it. Actually, knowing I was sceptical and knowing that I saw the ghost that night, it did make me aware of the potential of the world out there. So it did change me to be open minded.

(33-year-old female analyst)

In this case, authenticity is understood as witnessing the truth – 'I did see something.' This is a story that is less about ghosts and more about a transformative identity experience – 'it did change my life.' Her story implicitly connects paranormal beliefs with ideas of empowerment – 'aware of the potential of the world out there.' The experience is meaningful for her, not only as evidence of paranormal phenomena, but as an example of human potential.

Narratives of extraordinary identity experiences can be about empowerment. Experience is understood as self-knowledge. One woman reflected on a spiritual identity experience:

People experience God in all different ways. I wanted to feel what they were feeling. I closed my eyes and asked to be shown a way. Nothing ever happened. And on this occasion, I did the same thing and I felt my body pulled back. I stood straight, 'I am awake, I am not doing it by myself.' I opened my eyes and my arms were up like this and slowly came down, and the sensation of waves. I closed my eyes and the sensation came back again ... I was really questioning what was going on. I felt my entire body was literally moving ... then I thought wow, because I was in the house of Christ. I felt very heavy, you know to the point where I actually felt like I kneeled down ... I feel, I asked God to show himself to me, that was what happened to me. That was my first and only experience. I really wanted and wanted it and it happened. I know I was conscious of it and really wanted to know the experience.

(41-year-old female dancer/choreographer)

Following Goffman's idea of the performance of the self in everyday life, this woman's performance of her spiritual self is presented as an enlightening experience. Matters of authenticity are framed as true to the self, where instinctive, emotional and sensory engagement is centre stage.

Following Wooffitt and his analysis of communication, the personal experiences presented here are understood within the context of social relations.

Whether people's experiences can be interpreted as anomalous or not the process of telling their experiences is a powerful and shared moment of communication. It also highlights a pragmatic strategy which puts human experience centre stage (Lunt 2009: 134). When these experiences are recounted, there are various strategies people use to show they are being true to themselves. And they ask their audience to recognise they are the authority of their own experiences and what it means to them. Interpretations of their stories of paranormal phenomena are inextricably linked to matters of authenticity and trust in the self. One woman said of her experience of a terrifying presence 'it was tangible.' Her experience carries weight. Although she describes herself as the biggest cynic of all, this single moment has an impact on her perception of the world. It shapes her beliefs. The next section reflects on how cultural industries respond to personal experience as a foundation for paranormal beliefs.

Mind, body and spirit

In her novel *Beyond Black* Hilary Mantel wrote: 'the punters all think they are talented now, gifted. They've been told so often that everyone has dormant psychic powers that they're only waiting for the opportunity for theirs to wake up, preferably in public' (2005: 362). There is a growing market for people who want extraordinary identity experiences. In mind, body and spirit publications, the emphasis is on how people can wake up their dormant powers. In this regard, secular moral and spiritual beliefs are restyled as self-help where the emphasis is on the psychology of human potential. These cultural forms are another resource in the performance of paranormal beliefs.

Mind, body and spirit is a description of an alternative movement and a cultural category for secular spiritual practices. Paranormal beliefs associated with spiritism, divinatory arts, Eastern and Western religions and philosophies, pagan and new age practices come under the heading of mind, body and spirit in books, audio guides, magazines, websites, and related products. Examples include metaphysical thinking that focuses on healing through the power of the mind; angel communication where guides help in matters of romance, money, and the home; psychic predictions and ways of improving the sixth sense; spirit messages from loved ones; or holistic healing and alternative therapies. Social attitudes towards mind, body and spirit signal a common understanding of these practices. Sancho (2001: 11) found a general acceptance: 'people were comfortable with a very large set of alternative physical and mental health processes, such as hypnotherapy, psychotherapy, transcendental meditation, regression etc. They were regarded as accessible and familiar.' She also wrote: 'psychic practices such as horoscopes, reading auras, chakra healing and crystals were seen as relatively harmless. Most thought much of it, for example horoscopes, palmistry etc was about the acquisition of positive, comforting information and generic advice' (12).

Alternative moral and spiritual beliefs and practices are connected to the psychology of self-empowerment. In the specialist magazine *Kindred Spirit* a celebration of its hundredth issue showed a change in the presentation of mind, body and spirit. The editor wrote 'an awful lot of what was considered "kooky", or too New Age has now been accepted by the mainstream as valid healing methods, or sound scientific ideas.'[2] The CEO of The Mind Body and Spirit Experience wrote 'the field of personal empowerment' will be 'intoxicating and delicious', 'it won't be whacky, shabby and off the wall, it will be accessible, slick and acceptable.' His words reflect how alternative religious and metaphysical thinking are now perceived as personal empowerment practices. Barefoot Doctor, an alternative health and well being practitioner and author wrote that mind, body and spirit 'will be establishment rather than fringe.' He is not only referring to health and well being but also how ideas of empowerment connect with wider issues in alternative and new age movements related to health, environmentalism, anti-globalisation, and non-governmental organisations.

A hybrid of mind, body and spirit and the psychology of self-empowerment is a dominant form in books, audio guides, training and development. One of the most successful examples of this hybrid form is the 1988 bestseller *You Can Heal Yourself* by Louise Hay, which topped the *New York Times* Bestseller list and has since sold over 35 million copies worldwide. Hay House books and related merchandise are international hits, with motivational speakers, positive thinkers, psychics, angel therapists, water therapists, and psychic healers. Motivational guru Wayne Dyer's self-help guide *Change Your Thoughts – Change Your Life: Living the Wisdom of the Tao* is one of many books published by Hay which shows their metaphysical and psychological approach to life. Hay House authors work across several media, promoting their secular spiritual beliefs and advising the public on how to tap into their potential. Dyer appears regularly on chat shows in America. Marianne Williamson teaches a course in miracles on Oprah and Friends, the radio network, as well as publishing books, guides and running training events. Angel communicator Doreen Virtue writes columns in popular women's magazines alongside selling her angel advice cards and accompanying books. Heidi Sawyer is the official advisor to the Sci Fi Channel and author of psychic development books, offering advise on how to tap into a sixth and seventh sense. All of these authors come under the publishing category of mind, body and spirit.

Another successful example of the psychology of human potential is that of hypnotherapy and neuro linguistic programming (NLP). The hypnotist Paul McKenna became a celebrity with his television series *The Hypnotic World of Paul McKenna* (1993–95) reaching 12 million viewers at its peak in Britain, and sold internationally to 42 countries with an estimated 200 million viewers worldwide.[3] After making *Paul McKenna's Paranormal World* (1997), he went on to establish himself as Britain's bestselling non-fiction author, publishing books on the psychology of human potential in 23 different languages. NLP sees the brain as similar to a computer and teaches people to re-programme the brain to overcome mental barriers and achieve success in life. Its American co-founder Richard Bandler teamed up with McKenna to create Paul McKenna Training, which claims to be the largest hypnosis and NLP training centre in the world.

The partnership highlights the modern mixing of psychology and hypnotism. McKenna signed a deal with Discovery in 2008 for *I Can Make You Thin*, a series of programmes based on his bestselling book. The deal is worth around £23 million; Discovery hopes to make him a US diet guru, along the lines of Dr Phil, meeting members of the public and tackling the obesity problem in America. His book *Instant Confidence* was published in 2006 and that year saw his sales reach £3.5 million. His website boasts six million customers worldwide. British journalist Jon Ronson wrote a profile of McKenna in the *Guardian*, 'Don't worry, get therapy', where he attended a seven-day course run by McKenna and Bandler which he estimated made the company £1 million. Ronson was critical of the course, wary of the controversial Bandler (acquitted of the murder of a drug baron's girlfriend) and disturbed by the 'weirdness' of NLP. He also admitted McKenna helped him with personal fears, explaining 'people shouldn't judge gurus until they need one.'[4]

In *Religion in the Media Age* Stuart Hoover investigated 'metaphysical believers and seekers' who had an 'intuitive sense of religion and spirituality' (2006: 80). These kinds of believers have a strong sense of self, searching for individual experiences on their personal spiritual quests. They are connected to the baby boom generation, and appeal to men and women. Mind, body and spirit publications appeal to believers and seekers. Messages of personal empowerment and human potential encourage readers to try for themselves. For example, an article in *Soul and Spirit:* 'Your Spiritual Life Coach' is called 'change your thoughts to change your life.' It echoes self-help author Wayne Dyer. Advice includes taking control of your future, connecting to something greater, such as nature. Drawing on NLP and hypnotherapy this article is all about mind over matter and creating a new, more positive you. There are similar articles on how to change your life through your sixth sense, or with crystals, or through angelic dream visitations. The references to psychology and self-help are explicit, showing how mind, body and spirit is a hybrid of paranormal beliefs and popular psychology.

Although mind, body and spirit appeals to men and women, there are more publications devoted to women in popular culture with an easy fit between mind, body and spirit as self-help and lifestyle magazines. In the women's magazine *Spirit and Destiny* there is a twenty-page section devoted to mind, body and spirit matters which covers holistic health, emotional well being, and mystical guidance. These are all presented as accessible, familiar, comforting and above all positive. There are articles on adrenal fatigue and crystal healing. There is a first-person account of learning the power of flowers at the Psychic Café. An angel communicator shows readers how to connect with their guardian angels. The spirit whisperer helps readers speak with loved ones from the other side. There is an astro agony column with celestial solutions to relationship issues. A problem page has advice from a shamanic healer, a life coach and a people whisperer. These experts offer advice based on shamanism, reality rebalancing, or NLP, in accessible messages such as 'create a better reality', 'visualise and imagine', and 'listen to your heart.' There are connections with new age thinking, nature and environmentalism, feminism, multiculturalism and human and animal rights. These connections are loosely woven into the main messages of self-empowerment. For example, a column in *Spirit and Destiny* called *Bewitched* focuses on Goddess practices, meditation and alternative remedies, spells, chants and magical tips. There are messages of alternative ideologies in white witchcraft, Goddess and pagan practices. These connect with philosophies towards nature and environmentalism, and new age practices around health and well being. There are also messages of self-empowerment. Readers are asked to write in for a 'magical makeover'. Spells of the month cover relationship issues, beauty routines, increasing self-esteem. One single mother wrote asking for advice about an affair, and was told to find someone new, including a spell for a new pink bra with the chant 'bad men I want none/heartache be gone!'

Lynn Schofield Clark (2003: 227–28) researched attitudes towards super-naturalism amongst young adults. She found religious pluralism and openness to the possibility of spiritual matters. Young adults in her study had fluid ideas of the supernatural. For the adults in this study an 'exploration of uncertainty, openness to possibility' (229) is important to the way they communicate their experiences. The phrase 'being open minded' is especially related to mind, body and spirit because the category carries so many different kinds of paranormal beliefs, philosophies, writings, and practices. Being open minded can mean balancing opinions, evidence, and interpretations. One man described his experience on a ghost hunting event:

> everyone ideally wants a ghost to come right up to you. New people jump at the least little thing, but after a while you become accustomed to all the noises and you do have to question everything. You have to be open minded.
>
> (28-year-old male)

It can also mean opening up to the possibility of the mind, body and spirit. It is this meaning that connects the paranormal with self-empowerment. One man commented:

> We all have a sixth sense, but over the years, people have lost the tuning. So everybody can tune into it. I normally dream of situations like déjà vu … I always dream ahead … Those spiritual things, whatever you want to call it, all those things come through meditation. I meditate through prayer, and prayer is an invitation, makes you more open to those things.
>
> (36-year-old male regional business manager)

Within the psychology of self-help personal experiences are the bedrock to a better life. When this ideology of the individual merges with paranormal ideas then personal experience becomes evidence for beliefs.

Graham Murdoch (2008) wrote of a 'culture of re-enchantment' which 'introduces elements of the mystical, intangible and sacred' into popular imagination and secular society. He argues the conditions of modernity have created an environment for re-enchantment through systems of capitalism and cultural industries. Murdoch signals an alternative approach to morality and spiritual issues in environmentalism and global justice movements which react against systems of capitalism. There is a strong association of mind, body and spirit with new age movements, environmentalism, anti-globalisation, alternative health and lifestyle. However, mind, body and spirit arises from the conditions of modernity and is not free from the marketplace. Such alternative moral and spiritual beliefs flourish in cultural industries. Lynn Schofield Clark's (2007: 27) notion of 'religious lifestyle branding' is apparent in mind, body and spirit matters where a hybrid of beliefs and trends are the norm.

Rather than perceive cultural industries as creating the conditions for re-enchantment, it is the case that industries opportunistically respond to the conditions of modernity as encompassing mainstream and alternative identity experiences. One historical study of occultism in Germany indicates that these practices arose from the ambiguities of modernity in the late nineteenth and early twentieth centuries (Treitel 2004). Mass culture helped to market occultism for a wider audience by capitalising on these existing trends in alternative modernities. Similarly, contemporary paranormal cultural practices arise from a wider interest in alternative modernities. Polls data on paranormal beliefs connect with the World Values Survey and increasing interests in alternative lifestyles, religions, ecology and green politics. Lynch (2007: 20) notes how in Western societies there has been a 'development of new religious identities, groups and networks' who are also involved in 'campaigns on various issues from debt in the developing world, gay rights, global warming.' A market quickly responds with a range of products and practices which speak to existing trends in alternative modernities.

Landy and Saler (2009) speak of the re-enchantment of the world. They perceive modernity as both enchanted and disenchanted at the same time, rather than a common idea of modernity as one or the other. Modernity is therefore understood as having ambiguous associations with rationality and reason, and irrationality and a sense of wonder. Landy and Saler explore secular religion, or magic, as examples of these ambiguous associations in mass culture. Mind, body and spirit is one of several markets that draw on seemingly incompatible types of knowledge – that which is perceived as real and part of a rational understanding of the world is mixed up with that which is beyond the immediate reality and connected to paranormal and spiritual matters. Such a culture of re-enchantment gathers momentum at this historical juncture because it is part of the new age movement, feminism, or eco politics and environmentalism.

The return of religious thinking connects with a culture of re-enchantment. There are similarities to paranormal cultural practices in that beliefs are founded on something that is commonly understood as scientifically inexplicable. There are leaders within mind, body and spirit, called gurus, who have followers just as there are leaders in religious organisations. As work on media and religion suggests, people's beliefs in the paranormal or religion are intricately bound up with market forces and the articulation of beliefs on television, the web or print forms. But there are differences between religious and paranormal cultural practices. Irwin notes the inclusion of traditional Judeo-Christian religious beliefs in a definition of paranormal beliefs (2009) is contentious. Religious beliefs don't exhibit the same properties as paranormal beliefs, although they share a superficial connection with supernaturalism, such as the existence of angels or miracles (5–6). The paranormal is an area that aligns itself with the unorthodox, such as alternative movements in health and well being, or ecologies. It is a set of eclectic beliefs that are not based on any one doctrine or way of thinking. In mind, body and spirit there are few established churches, although there are many ways people come together as consumers or people with shared interests. Paranormal beliefs arise from the ambiguities of modernity and within the market place are framed as alternative modernities, something different from tradition.

Perhaps most significantly, there is an instinctive-experiential interpretation of the paranormal which has made the individual a bedrock to the formation and maintenance of beliefs. Such a focus on personal experience suggests pragmatism is part of paranormal beliefs. As Peter Lunt notes there is an 'intellectual legacy of William James' radical empiricism and his contribution to the development of pragmatism as a philosophical position.' He argues 'the contestation of the idea of truth as an inherent property of ideas and the adoption of the idea that truth resides in events or process is an important part of pragmatism' (2009: 133). Faced with the problem of authenticity and evidence, people judge the character of individuals and themselves through their actions and experiences. In this way, people's strategies for narrating their extraordinary stories put human experience at the centre. And they regard the truth of the existence of paranormal phenomena as revealed through their experience. The issue of authenticity becomes part of a social process where uncertainty and trust in truth claims become the very basis from which alternative identity experiences emerge. These strategies of pragmatism surrounding paranormal beliefs based on experience are rich resources for alternative modernities.

Conclusion

One woman said: 'at the end of the day, people have got their own opinions and they want to believe what they want to believe. If it is true, it's true to them, isn't it?' (34-year-old female). This question is one that gets to the heart of paranormal beliefs and representations in popular culture. The question of truth unites two seemingly incompatible issues of evidence and experience. The issue of evidence connects with concerns about a crisis of authenticity in media and society. The issue of experience connects with concerns about the centrality of the individual in Western societies. Whilst in a media context people instinctively distrust representations of allegedly paranormal phenomena, in the context of their own lives they instinctively trust their paranormal interpretations.

Different strategies for dealing with matters of authenticity point to different kinds of knowledge amongst audiences. There is the knowledge of the media, commercialisation and concerns about deception as a basis for rationalism and critical thinking. There is also a form of solipsism where experience, instinct and intuition are a basis for belief formation. These styles of knowledge are used in complex ways by cultural industries to sell ambiguous experiences. There is a growing market for people who distrust mainstream science, or religion. Instead, they want alternative ways of thinking and identity experiences that go against the grain. Mind, body and spirit is one such market that has quickly responded to a rise in paranormal beliefs and related new age and alternative practices. People who engage with mind, body and spirit practices are part of a cycle of culture where their search for alternative identity experiences is directed towards a market place designed specifically for them. To return to the question of truth, what is true about people's experiences of the paranormal becomes caught up in a bigger question of what is true about narratives of the self in Western society and culture.

Notes

1 Cited in an article by Sam Leith 'Are you sitting comfortably … ' the *Daily Mail*, accessed online at www.dailymail.co.uk/home/books/article-1218524/Are-sitting-uncomfortably-old-house-candlelight-Then-Ill-begin–GHOUL-BRITANNIA-BY-ANDREW-MARTIN.html#ixzz0mDkkYjD9 26 April 2010.
2 All references *Kindred Spirit* Issue 11, September, October 2009: pp 21–23.
3 See interview with McKenna in the *Independent on Sunday*, 16 July 2006, accessed online at www.times.co.uk 1 February 2009.
4 Ronson, Jon. 'Don't Worry, Get Therapy', the *Guardian*, 20 May 2006, accessed online at www.theguardian.co.uk 1 February 2009.

Chapter 7

Beyond magic

'Beyond the concept of magic.'

Magicians are performers who need audiences to help create magical entertainment. A magician and their audience are a double act where the performer reveals and conceals and the audience allows themselves to be led in the act. Magic is based on deception, but if a magician appears to be deceiving their audience they will seem like a second hand car salesman. In order to disguise deception, magicians use a variety of skills and draw on the everyday practices, values and beliefs of their audience, using such knowledge in their act. Magic is an example of how the cultural practices of an audience are incorporated into the construction of live entertainment.

Derren Brown combines psychology, magic and showmanship. He focuses on scepticism and belief in the paranormal or supernaturalism, drawing on the historical tradition of mentalism, which is a form of magic that has the appearance of psychic powers. He explains how conjuring tricks such as table levitation or mind reading can be achieved by psychological manipulation. A live show such as 'An Evening of Wonders' blurs boundaries between rational explanation for conjuring acts, and metaphysical explanation that Brown is capable of mind control. People jokingly refer to him as a Jedi Master. For such conjuring acts to work, Brown utilises audience preconceptions, understandings and misunderstandings of paranormal ideas, psychology and the power of the mind, and magic and misdirection. Brown is so successful in his use of psychology that his performances 'go beyond the concept of magic', as one person described it. In such a way, Brown anticipates, manages and exploits how his audience thinks about psychology, magic and the paranormal.

Magical thinking

In *Religion and the Decline of Magic*, Keith Thomas (1971) analysed early modern European magical and religious beliefs within the social and intellectual conditions of the time. Life expectancy was low, disease was rife, food

Figure 7.1 Stage show advertisement *An Evening of Wonders*, courtesy of Derren
    Brown

was scarce, and doctors were unable to diagnose or treat most illnesses:
'poverty, sickness and sudden disaster were thus familiar features of the
social environment of this period' (Thomas 1971: 20). Thomas argued belief
in magical healing, astronomy, prophecies and witchcraft arose to meet a social
need: 'one of the central features was a preoccupation with the explanation
and relief of human misfortune. There can be no doubt that this concern

reflected the hazards of an intensely insecure environment' (1971: 5). During these times:

> popular magicians went under a variety of names – 'cunning men', 'wise women', 'charmers', 'blessers', 'conjurers', 'sorcerers', 'witches' – and they offered a variety of services, which ranged from healing the sick and finding lost goods to fortune telling and divination of all kinds.
>
> (1971: 210)

A range of services were important as several types of practices would be used to address one problem. For example, magical healing offered a 'spell, the medicine and the special condition of the performer' (215). There was no coherent theory underlying these practices but rather a mix of 'natural remedies and supernatural and symbolic ones', such as semi-religious incantations, charms, medicinal use of objects like 'pigeons, gold-rings or snakeskins', healing by touch, and herbal medicine (215–24). The eclecticism of magical healing practices was in response to people vulnerable to many illnesses and diseases that were undiagnosed. Conjurers, wise women, and charmers were much in demand: 'if anything is clear in the history of this difficult subject it is that sorcery arose to meet a need' (298).

Scientists and philosophers were influenced by popular practices, looking to study and rationalise established folk procedures derived from Anglo-Saxon and classical customs. Magical practices 'did not reflect a single coherent cosmology or scheme of classification, but were made up out of the debris of many different systems of thought' (Thomas 1971: 219). During the Middle Ages scientists and philosophers speculated the world was elemental and influenced by heavenly bodies in the cosmos. Intellectuals of Renaissance Europe were influenced by Neoplatonism. This was a school of ancient philosophy which 'fostered a disposition to blur the difference between matter and spirit' (265). Neoplatonic theory influenced the intellectual study of magic through the classical writings of Paracelsus and Agrippa. This magic constructed the cosmos as 'an organic unity in which every part bore a sympathetic relationship to the rest' (ibid). The philosopher and magician practised 'natural magic, concerned to exploit the occult properties of the elemental world; celestial magic, involving the influence of the stars; and ceremonial magic, an appeal for aid to spiritual beings' (ibid). Such an approach also emphasised the importance of 'the imagination upon the body, mind upon matter' (ibid).

In a history of secular magic, Simon During notes 'from about 1700 magic slowly became disconnected from supernature' (2002: 14). Reasons why this transition occurred are more to do with major political, economic and social changes than attitudes to magic as such. As Peter Burke writes in his history of popular culture in the early modern period 'changes do not always take place because someone wants them' (2009: 335). Between 1500 and 1800 the major changes of population growth, and a commercial and communications revolution, altered European popular culture 'in ways no one intended and in ways no contemporary could have forseen' (ibid). Popular culture was, and still is, closely related to its environment, and adapted accordingly (Burke 2009). For Thomas the transition in magical thinking was related to the 'triumph of mechanical philosophy':

> The notion that the universe was subject to immutable laws killed the concept of miracles, weakened belief in the physical efficacy of prayer ... the Cartesian concept of matter relegated spirits, whether good or bad, to the purely mental world.
>
> (1971: 769–70)

This kind of science demanded truths should be demonstrated. Knowledge came from direct experience. The classical writings of Hippocrates, Aristotle and Cicero repudiated superstition and helped to foster a rationalist attitude that became the foundation of the enlightenment. 'In enlightened thought ... when the credulous faced inexplicable, unpredictable events, they imagined false cause of their terror and depression' (During 2002: 15). Thomas points to an increase in technical and empirical knowledge which meant people were better able to defend themselves from their physical and social environment. For example, agricultural improvement increased food production and helped to make people more self-sufficient. The development of mathematics included statistical laws and rational predictions, where an 'awareness of patterns in apparently random behaviour' superseded previous 'speculation about the causes of good and bad fortune' (785). The appearance of the word 'coincidence' to mean causally unrelated events was one example of a rationalist approach to life. As During notes early enlightenment attacks on magic 'developed a conspiracy theory of superstition' (2002: 15). The growth of rationalism and science helped to change attitudes towards magic in popular culture.

By the nineteenth century, magic as illusion was a major part of the development of popular culture. During calls this 'magic's moment', where 'conjuring was being integrated into a show business' (2002: 97). This was a period of rapid invention where physical or mechanical conjuring was created alongside optical and cognitive illusions. The famous French magician Robert-Houdin was a successful watchmaker renowned for his mechanical illusions. For example, automatons like 'The Orange Tree' produced elegant effects in his Parisian theatre Palais Royal. Magicians such as Englishmen John Nevil Maskelyne and David Devant, or Americans Harry Kellar and Howard Thurston, were 'practical men of the theatre who wrestled with their techniques to surprise their audiences with something new' (Steinmeyer 2003: xxi). These theatre men utilised new scientific discoveries to shape their stage acts. For example, Maskelyne established daily magic shows at the Egyptian Hall in London using automatons as part of the performance. 'Psycho, the whist playing automaton, was a particular favourite and appeared in over 4000 consecutive performances' (Steinmeyer 2003: 110).

The secret of Psycho – air pressure – was guarded by Maskelyne throughout his lifetime by elaborate smokescreens and misleading patents (ibid).

At the Polytechnic in Regent Street, London, John Henry Pepper and Thomas Tobin showcased the illusion 'Proteus, or We are Here but not Here' as optical curiosities demonstrated by a scientist and inventor. Some magicians performed conjuring in comedy plays, or ghost shows. The Maskelyne family produced the play 'Will, the Witch and Watchman' which used superstition as a theme to showcase the latest in conjuring tricks, including a magic trunk and levitation illusion. The play ran for 40 years with 11,000 performances in London and around Britain (Steinmeyer 2003: 110). Some magicians became stars capable of attracting large international audiences. Later in the late nineteenth and early twentieth centuries Harry Houdini was an escape artist whose conjuring tricks were constructed as amazing dares – 'the little man taking on the bonds of society.' The Chinese Water Torture Cell was an act which he performed twice a night in America and on international tour for 13 years (Steinmeyer 2003: 9). Magicians entertained audiences with spectacular illusions. The Hippodrome in New York City was so large it covered a city block, seating 5200 people, 'more of an amusement park than a theatre' (Steinmeyer 2003: 261). The opening production in 1902 'A Yankee Circus on Mars' 'conveniently allowed a three ring circus on the stage, a full sized tent, flying spaceships, and a view of the Martian Court, inhabited by hundreds of dancers' (262). It was on this stage that Houdini made Jennie the elephant disappear.

According to Jim Steinmeyer 'everything in magic changed with the ghosts, who quickly rapped and rattled apart the great traditions of Victorian conjuring' (2003: 75). Significant inventions related to ghosts influenced Victorian magicians. The Corsican Trap was a stagecraft that allowed audiences to see a ghost glide across the stage. This invention was joined by Pepper's Ghost, which used angled mirrors to create a misty moving figure. Pepper's Ghost attracted crowds of up to a quarter of a million to see short plays like 'The Ghost of Hamlet' at the Regent Street Polytechnic. Around the same time the Davenport Brothers toured with their live public séance. They claimed to communicate with spirits inside a wooden cabinet all the while apparently tied up with ropes on stage. Steinmeyer notes the Davenports 'successfully painted a "grey area" between superstition and conjuring and deftly straddled it through their career' (2003: 66). They created 'a much rawer and more elemental magic, not the pleasant society conjuring which was then in fashion' (ibid). The combination of these inventions meant 'just as magicians found an entirely new type of presentation based on the Davenport séance, they were presented with an entirely new range of secrets based on Pepper's Ghost' (75).

Lamont and Bates (2007) point out the significance of Indian jugglers to the performances of nineteenth-century magicians. In the early Victorian period Indian jugglers, called conjurors today, performed illusions that would be copied and adapted by European and American magicians. For example, Indian jugglers performed cup and ball conjuring, sword swallowing, fire ordeals such as walking across hot coals, and levitation illusions. The girl in a basket illusion included a sword which was thrust through the basket with bloody effect. Indian jugglers also performed extraordinary feats such as being buried alive. The nineteenth century 'saw the appearance of a variety of past and contemporary accounts of extraordinary feats reportedly having taken place in India' (2007: 315). These feats were attributed in the mainstream press as examples of manual dexterity and the deceptive skills of Indian jugglers. The press speculated about the impact of such skills on audiences and attributed their influence to mesmerism, mass hypnotism and Indian mysticism. Lamont and Bates note the significance of these discussions in nineteenth-century society:

> ambivalent associations with psychic and supernatural forces were to be reinforced with the emergence of modern spiritualism and the growing debate about the cause of the phenomena associated with it.
>
> (2007: 315)

The spiritualist press referred to Indian occultism to explain séance phenomena as part of supernatural forces long practised in the East. The celebrity medium Daniel Dunglas Home used levitation and fire ordeals as part of his séances. Lamont and Bates suggest celebrity mediums like the Davenports were probably inspired by Indian jugglers in their use of rope tricks, which would later influence Houdini and the development of escapology.

Nineteenth-century magicians set out to debunk the elemental magic of pseudo-psychics and mediums. They recreated séances, with flying musical instruments, disappearing and reappearing people, in order to show these pseudo-psychics as charlatans. In doing so, they created a presentational style of magic that benefited from the supernatural elements used in a séance. Mind reading, levitation, fortune telling, invisibility, all became part of magic performances. Lamont and Bates (2007: 321) claim 'Western impressions were always safely framed as trickery (by performers who publicly claimed that spiritualist mediums were nothing more than tricksters).' At the same time these magicians borrowed from jugglers, using Indian symbolism to construct an idea of enchantment and supernatural powers. The performances of Western magicians as Indian Fakirs opened up other spaces for interpretation. As fake Fakirs, these performers introduced the latest illusions as examples of Eastern magic. This created ambivalent associations with supernatural forces as 'Indian juggling itself was increasingly being viewed as something beyond mere legerdemain' (2007: 321). As Lamont and Bates note the founding of the Theosophical Society in 1875, which combined aspects of spiritualism with Buddhism and Indian occultism, added to this construction of India as the land of magic and the idea of a mystical East. Such a mix of magic as trickery and ambiguous associations with paranormal and mystical matters would influence contemporary magicians.

Derren Brown

Derren Brown is a type of magician who focuses on psychic matters. According to Brown he is 'Europe's most controversial Ming-bearded mind-botherer' (2006: back cover). He explains:

> The type of performance I upsettingly force on you has its roots in a craft called mentalism, which in turn is rooted in magic and conjuring. Many mentalists (such as me, though I never use the term) started out as magicians before turning, as it almost amusingly were, mental. However while most magicians are fairly recognizable and conform to a limited set of types, mentalists are fewer and further between and can be radically different. The skills are harder to acquire, and personality is paramount. Many cross what to me is an ethical line and become tarot readers and 'psychics'. Some talk to the dead. Some work in churches, both Spiritualist and mainstream. Some remain entertainers but routinely claim real psychic abilities. Some debunk those that do.
>
> (18–19)

Brown's performance is deliberately ambiguous, mixing magic and mentalism with a charismatic personality. TV critic Charlie Brooker wrote Brown is 'either a balls-out con artist or the scariest man in Britain.'[1] The ambiguity of his approach is what makes him so popular with audiences. One person said: 'he plays with what you are thinking' (33-year-old female analyst). Another commented 'he is a genius. I think he is just very clever ... I don't think I'd like to meet him because I just don't know what he's capable of doing – stealing your mind' (26-year-old male vision mixer).

In the stage show 'An Evening of Wonders' (2008), Brown performed conjuring acts that exposed mind readers and psychics as charlatans. The advertisement for the show depicted Brown as a mind reader wearing a turban. This image playfully references Indian jugglers and Victorian magicians who helped to construct an image of magic as part of Eastern mysticism (Lamont and Bates 2007). The evening included a séance act. The *Guardian* newspaper critic wrote:

> "That is clearly some sort of conjuring trick," says Derren Brown. But we are not listening. We are busy gibbering at the sight of the wooden table, which he has just used for a séance, now floating freely around the stage. It is part of Brown's shtick to pooh-pooh psychic explanations for his tricks. But that just twists the knife into the dumbfounded onlookers – because, for such feats, metaphysical explanations actually seem more credible than physical ones.[2]

Brown's performances blur boundaries between rational explanation and amazement at the illusion itself. Another act included mind reading amongst the audience. Again the critic commented:

My gobsmack fatigue reared up; popular US mindbender Marc Salem has been doing the Oracle trick for years. But Brown, who never stints on showmanship, added several new dimensions to this routine. Blindfolded, feigning mental distress and accompanied by eerie music, he divines biographical details seemingly from audience members' voices alone. Stella, he guesses, wants to know if she should live in Greece again. Lucy is the owner of 36 gerbils. "Your dog's name is Gizmo, and your phobia is tinned peas." Some sort of conjuring trick, maybe. But to pull it off this convincingly, and with such flair, is as freaky as telepathy.

(ibid)

Brown manages the impossible – a trick so convincing that it is beyond explanation. This kind of ambiguous association with psychic and mystical matters is part of the success of his illusions.

Houdini was thought to possess a superhuman force and charged by some spiritualists in concealing his psychic abilities. Brown is also rumoured to be psychic. Journalist William Little asked Brown about this rumour, referring to amazing feats of telepathy:

It's a tricky one … Debunking is usually witless and bitter and ends up being rather bloodless and negative. I try to avoid doing that. I want to incorporate the magic of what psychics do, but leave people guessing how I do it. I think it's more entertaining. I don't want to simply say I can show you how I do it, I don't want to give viewers the safety of an easy answer. It's more powerful. It appeals to the imagination, whereas straightforward debunking does not.

(Brown in Little 2009: 232)

What is appealing to the imagination of his audience is the way he takes magic and transforms it into something else. As this person said:

I think that he moves beyond the concept of magic because he is talking about manipulation. It's completely changing the way people think, changing their behaviour, so it's not magic any more, it's completely beyond that.

(30-year-old female)

Although Brown is not psychic he is neither a magician in the eyes of his audience.

One of the ways Derren Brown moves beyond the concept of magic is in differentiating himself from his contemporaries. His performances challenge audiences about their preconceptions of what is magical entertainment. For example:

Derren Brown goes, 'you are an intelligent person, you know this is magic and you can work it out.' Normally, with these things I think it's rubbish, but actually I enjoy it. ... It's a different audience as well ... I've seen others as idiots, and I watch them and laugh. But, I watch Derren Brown and it's really exciting and I'm scared like a child ... But also I can still see I am a bit intelligent.

(28-year-female volunteer manager)

He speaks to a generation of audiences that are not interested in older styles of magic, their tastes are for a novel twist on magical entertainment. That Brown performs his televised events on Channel Four signals the kind of audiences he appeals to, mainly the 16–34-year-old age group looking for entertainment with a difference.

Significantly, Brown treats his audience as intelligent people. Steinmeyer comments on the difficulty magicians face if they focus on deception as the essence of their skills: 'it's an attitude often re-enforced by audiences, who have learned to expect very little from magic acts ... With expectations set so low, most magicians are perfectly happy to descend to them' (2003: 93). Brown explains:

The issue of honesty ties in with an inherent problem with any form of magical entertainment. Unless the performer is an out-and-out fraud, claiming to be absolutely for real, there exists in the bulk of any audience an acceptance that some form of jiggery-pokery must be at work. Now this experience of being fooled by a magician should be made pleasurable and captivating by the performer, otherwise he has failed as an entertainer. However, he is entering into an odd relationship with his audience: he is saying in effect, 'I am going to act as if this were all very real; but you know, and I know that you know that I know, that it's really a game.'

(2006: 19)

Another person commented on the game of magic and lies:

The magic format is sort of old really, and for lots of people just not convincing, so it's just a next level of that ... I know he entertains people like you and me because we understand that things like that don't just happen through magic, or things that we can't explain. We want to know what's going on ... He is not telling you exactly how he does all the stuff. The fact that you don't really know what's going on, he does surprise stuff, makes it an illusion, a kind of magic. It's not like a rabbit out of a hat, that's why it's interesting.

(25-year-old male marketing assistant)

Audiences know there is no such thing as magic, but they know that he knows they want 'a kind of magic.' In the next section, the psychology of magic is explored in relation to audience responses to Brown's performances as psychological entertainment.

The psychology of magic

There is a strong connection between psychology and magic. Lamont and Wiseman in *Magic in Theory* (1999: ix) explain:

> Psychologists have long recognized that they may have much to learn from the techniques used by magicians to fool their audiences. Magicians are able to persuade an audience to look in a certain direction, misperceive actions and objects, misremember key aspects of performances. As such magic has proved of interest to psychologists researching attention, perception and memory, as well as those with a more general interest in deception.

The premise of a magic trick consists of an effect and a method. Within the construction of a trick there is a basic design where the audience sees the effect without realising the method behind it. Magic relies on something happening which is outside a normal understanding of how the world works (1999: x). 'There are a range of physical and psychological ploys that the magician may use to help enhance the effect and conceal the method' (1999: xi). An audience often attempts to work out the method behind the effect and there are many ways magicians influence the reconstruction process. Lamont and Wiseman note 'magic, properly performed, is a complex and skilful art, and is capable of deceiving anyone' (xvi).

As a magician who focuses on the appearance of psychic powers Derren Brown uses a wide range of conjuring effects that can be traced through the history of Indian jugglers, magicians and mentalists. For example, Brown performs extraordinary feats such as walking across broken glass, or over hot coals, which come from Indian jugglers who influenced Victorian magicians. Lamont and Wiseman classify physical feats as 'the appearance of extraordinary strength or invulnerability to ostensibly harmful effects' (1999: 5). Other feats include 'the appearance of extraordinary mental ability' (ibid). In a recorded live show with a celebrity audience Brown managed to memorise the entire A-Z of London, whilst also performing rapid mathematical calculations using numbers selected by the audience.[3] Another feat is telekinesis, 'the apparent ability to control movement of objects without physical contact' (1999: 6). In 'An Evening of Wonders' a floating table is a good example of this effect. The history of Victorian magicians and mentalists signals the crossovers between magical entertainment and pseudo psychics and mediums. This includes clairvoyance, defined by Lamont and Wiseman as 'the acquirement of information not known to others apparently via extrasensory means' (1999: 6), telepathy, which is 'the acquirement of information from others apparently via extrasensory means', and precognition, which is 'the apparent acquirement of information from the future'. Brown's 'Oracle' act in 'An Evening of Wonders' is an example of a mind reading effect. Another speciality is mental control, 'the apparent control over another's mind' (ibid). Many of his performances are based on this effect, with the title of his early TV series *Mind Control* (Channel 4, UK) signalling to the audience his distinctive style of magic.

'Russian Roulette' was a stunt televised live to the British public in 2003. The stunt involved a nationwide search for a member of the public who was asked to load a real gun with one bullet. Brown then worked out what chamber contained the live bullet whilst holding the gun to his head. The DVD back cover for this stunt included the question 'will his skills give him the power to dodge the bullet?' The magical effect is created from his extraordinary ability to 'dodge the bullet' through his prediction of the loaded chamber. Any number of methods could be used to achieve this effect, from the action of the gun influenced by unseen internal or external connections (mechanisms, lighting), to a way of discovering the loaded chamber of the gun through limited choice forcing, sound or lip reading, pumping for information, or straightforward guessing (Lamont and Wiseman 1999: 16–24). Brown's skill as a performer is in keeping the audience guessing as to the methods behind the effects. Two viewers described watching the stunt:

SUSAN: When he did the Russian Roulette with a gun, one bullet was in there, and he had to fire it, that was just amazing. He'd actually done it. It's not a trick, he'd actually done it, by whatever method he'd done it. (23-year-old female sales assistant)

JAMIE: It is a trick. (27-year-old male games tester)

SUSAN: Of course it is a trick.

JAMIE: It's not a trick, in a sense. There is no fake trap, no bunch of flowers in sleeves like magic tricks. It's so clever, not like the others. It's just him. It's just him.

SUSAN: The ability to read people and use people, if you like, and how they are going to think. That's why it's fascinating.

It was reported in the newspapers the day after the live stunt that Brown used rubber bullets rather than live ammunition. But, 'Russian Roulette' doesn't seem like a trick according to expectations of magic as a fake trap. Brown creates mind traps with his audience where he appears to go beyond the concept of magic – 'it's not a trick', 'it's just him.'

From the beginning Brown established a psychological frame for conjuring effects. On the back cover of the DVD 'Inside Your Mind' the advert claimed Brown 'can seemingly predict and control human behaviour' by using 'a mixture of psychology, misdirection and showmanship.' The key word missing is magic. A quote from *Empire* magazine reinforced the mind control frame – 'the closest our galaxy can boast to a Jedi Master.' Lamont and Wiseman (1999: 142) say 'many magicians ... want to be seen as skilful manipulators and some deliberately promote this image. In doing so, of course, they offer the spectator a general explanation for what he sees.' As part of his style Brown offers the audience various explanations for the methods behind conjuring effects. In his book

Tricks of the Mind (2006) some of these methods are explained for the general reader. These include perception and suggestion. For example, ideomotor movement is where 'if you focus on the idea of making a movement, you will likely end up making a similar tiny movement without realising it' (2006: 45). Brown explains how use of an Ouija board during his live shows relies on tricks with suggestion. Another is memory systems, like a linking system which places a visual link next to words. These are explanations to mental feats such as memorising the London A-Z. Hypnotic phenomena are connected to suggestive techniques rather than trance states. He explains the hypnotic experience 'in terms of quite ordinary "task motivators" such as focused attention, role playing, imagination, response expectancy, social conformity, compliance, belief in the hypnotist, response to charisma, relaxation, rapport, suggestion' (142). For Brown, this form of stage hypnotism is a co-performance between the hypnotist and members of the audience. Various aspects of unconscious communication are used as explanations for his tricks, including psychological tests for deception and awareness of body language in communicative acts. Cognitive traps include misunderstandings regarding science, mathematics and probability reasoning, as well as the confirmation bias in strong belief systems.

It is significant that magicians rely on the way audiences think to create successful illusions. Steinmeyer writes: 'great magicians don't leave the audience thought patterns to chance; they depend on the audience's bringing something to the table – preconceptions or assumptions that can be naturally exploited' (2003: 117). Magical entertainment is rooted in an understanding of contemporary cultural and social practices. Steinmeyer describes how many magic tricks of the past relied on everyday cultural practices. For example, paper cones used to store sugar or coffee in the greengrocers: 'there were dozens of fascinating magic tricks from the start of the twentieth century, deceptions using specially prepared paper cones, which are virtually useless today because of the fashions in greengrocers' shops' (2003: 118). Brown understands the way his audience thinks. What audiences bring to the table are preconceptions, misconceptions and assumptions about human behaviour, social psychology, and cognitive patterns. For example, the popularity of neurolinguistic programming in psychology books, self-help guides and weekend training courses is apparent in some of the tricks Brown uses. Or the idea of the power of suggestion is another preconception utilised in his hypnotism act. That many people have used hypnotism to lose weight, stop smoking, or cope with stress is part of what audiences bring to the table during his performances. One viewer noted: 'the techniques he uses are quite in fashion as well, like hypnotherapy. All things people do in the real world. Sometimes they go for treatment, they use it, so they can relate to it' (28-year-old male civil servant). The popular idea of unconscious communication revealing the inner thoughts of others – spotting a cheat, lie detector tests, or successful dating techniques – is also used by Brown in explanations for his tricks. As a magician, Brown can rely on a majority of his audience knowing ideas within popular psychology. Indeed it is a sign of how prevalent psychology is in everyday cultural practices that Brown can perform so many tricks based on a general understanding and misunderstanding of psychology today.

For example, the effect of the trick 'Don't Kill the Kitten' is based on audiences bringing to the table a preconception of negative suggestion (*Trick or Treat* series two, Channel 4, May 2008). The sequence was described by *The Times* TV critic as:

> He takes a dear sweet little fluffy kitten and puts it inside a glass tank on a metal floor that is attached to the mains. Then, with a little extra hocus-pocus, he tells a student, "You can win £500 if you don't, repeat don't, kill the poor little kitty." Essential viewing for animal rights activists.[4]

The Cat's Protection League complained about the show because the student did appear to kill the kitty. With seconds to go she did the unthinkable. In the closing statement Brown asked the audience: would you kill the kitten? Reactions to the show included the *Mirror's* headline 'Fury at Derren Brown "cat killer" TV show.'[5] In response, Brown claimed 'I'm no cat killer.' The box was not wired up, the kitten unharmed: it was an experiment. He explained the woman's experience was a cognitive trap 'whereby we focus so much on trying to avoid being or doing a certain thing that we end up being or doing that thing because we focus so much on it.' This student had a high level of self-criticism and he constructed an experiment to highlight the destructive power of negative thinking: 'we created a horrible conflict for her ... she was psychologically cornered into doing it.'[6] He told her 'every time in the future that you find yourself focusing negatively, your brain will take you back to this powerful and emotional experience and will zap you into a more positive and constructive state.'[7]

The following discussion of 'Don't kill the kitten' highlights the way this illusion can be interpreted in multiple ways:

> I think he is fake anyway. It is very convincing, but I just think he is fake. He knows how to play people. He knows exactly what it is. He is very good on psychology stuff. It's not magic at all, it's pure psychology. I don't know if anyone saw they had a kitten in a cage. It was like, if you press the button, you execute the kitten. Don't do it, don't do it, and he played around her mind, and about thirty seconds before the time – bang! And she killed the kitten. And it wasn't because you had mind control, simply he knew the type of things to say to her to change her point of view. He's just – (38-year-old male supporting artist)
>
> Actually evil. (33-year-old female youth worker)
>
> Really. (34-year-old female senior youth worker)
>
> I watched it, and I was really upset. But you knew that kitten was not going to die. But it's just proving the point, what some psychologists call the banality of evil. And the experiment they did, you get people, just normal people

to do really horrific things. But I don't think that was magic. (38-year-old female consultant)

The stuff of psychology is the skill in the negative suggestion, awareness of personality types, and the construction of an extreme experiment. The seemingly contradictory responses of genuine emotions associated with watching the kitten appear to die, and yet knowing this is TV stagecraft, points to tensions within the psychology of magic. The illusion constructed to entertain audiences also informs them of the self-knowledge that normal people can do horrific things. The closing statement: 'would you kill the kitten?' shows how this illusion becomes something beyond magic.

On the front cover of his book *Tricks of the Mind* is a picture of Brown with a red devil, a classic image used by the American magician Harry Kellar in his stage advertisements. Brown explains 'when I am working, I mix psychology with conjuring, either often masquerading as the other' (2006: 226). The psychological explanations are part of the performance, where there are elements of truth, but also elements of deceit in the claims he makes. According to Richard Wiseman Derren Brown's magic is a 'mystery because there are several explanations you won't be able to know because you weren't there.' In this sense 'you are part of the illusion.'[8] A blogger wrote of his stage shows:

> One of Derren's brilliant achievements is to feed just the right amount of psychology to the TV audience so that they forget that he is also a magician and so they always work from the starting point of it being a psychology trick and often miss any physical aspects of it at all! My favourite comment I overheard from one couple after the show whilst waiting at the stage door (they were talking about the Oracle act) was 'There's no way that you can tell that just from the way someone says 'Yes' – that's convinced me that they must have all been paid stooges!'. They were gutted that the whole thing had been 'staged', yet when the logistics of paying for thirty actors every night for a tour was pointed out to them by their partner the realisation sank in and they were fooled again. All thanks to the misdirection that everything is purely mental.[9]

In the magic of Derren Brown psychology is part of the misdirection. Anomolistic psychologist Chris French says Brown is 'misleading sceptics, misleading believers' by claiming 'this is all based on non verbal communication' which is 'just tosh'.[10] He notes Brown altered his performance after criticism on this issue in the press. Brown explains (2006: 343): 'I am often dishonest in my techniques, but always honest about my dishonesty.'

Misdirection is 'that which directs the audience towards the effect and away from the method' (Lamont and Wiseman 1999: 31). Physical misdirection is used to 'direct what is seen and noticed' by the audience. Psychological misdirection is used to direct what the audience is thinking, shaping the interpretation of what they see in order to reduce and divert their suspicion and attention (1999: 80–81). Techniques can include passive diversion such as movement or contrast, an active diversion through the use of eyes, voice and body language. Such skills can be seen in Brown's live performances where his use of voice is very effective. Psychological misdirection includes reducing the suspicion of the audience by maximising the naturalness of the magic act, or increasing the conviction of the audience in the effect. This kind of misdirection is apparent in the use of psychological explanations which appear convincing to his audience. Another technique is establishing charisma and authority through the performance of the magician, and reinforcing the beliefs of the audience (Lamont and Wiseman 1999). Brown is highly skilled in this regard. Misdirection is an art in itself and 'effective misdirection can misdirect anyone' (Lamont and Wiseman 1999: 81).

Some people are aware of misdirection used by Brown in his performances. One person commented:

> He was cast as a psychological person which convinces me of the fact he is using tricks that all other illusionists would use, but it's just a little package that nobody else is packaging that way. And if he says, 'oh it's all about the power of suggestion' and, you know, tricks of mind or whatever. It's not really. It's the same as everyone else has done, but in a new way, packaging people to think 'ah, so that's how he does that, maybe I can learn how to control people's minds', you know. But actually, it is what it is.
>
> (30-year-old female library assistant)

Other viewers suggested:

> He uses mind tricks and diversion and deceives. Basically, you have to accept some of things he is doing, being deceitful, is like street magic. You can't be sure the subjects are entirely genuine because it's an illusion. You accept that what you are watching is potentially stage craft ...
>
> (27-year-old male media producer)

> He's an illusionist. I think he leads people on to believe that what he is doing has some sort of psychological basis, or some sort of mind control. But I think he is simply doing what illusionists have been doing forever. Making us believe what he is doing. But actually it's simply trickery ...
>
> (25-year-old female teacher)

A magician's job is to influence the reconstruction process. Lamont and Wiseman (1999) explain some of the techniques based on lack of knowledge. First there is the lack of knowledge of magic, a profession famous for its secrecy. There are many complex methods used by magicians alongside psychological approaches. These include the use of '"gimmicks", which are secret devices, and "fekes", which are secretly prepared props that simulate normal objects' – these magic 'secrets are almost unimaginable' (1999: 85). Another technique is that of the psychology of multiple outs. This is an approach that 'relies on the use of alternative endings to an effect, by the use of more than one potential method. Depending on how the effect proceeds, the appropriate ending is chosen and the necessary method is employed' (1999: 85–86). Brown's tricks rely on a high degree of audience participation. The use of multiple outs means he can shape the effects of his conjuring tricks through the choices made by his participants. This is why his charisma on stage is so important to the way he utilises alternative endings, as people are rarely aware of such techniques during the performance. His audiences are baffled by the methodological diversity of his conjuring tricks and have great difficulty in the reconstruction process. There is no easy trap door, but rather a series of elaborate mind traps. Brown directs the reconstruction process to such an extent that people are confused in even recalling the trick itself. In a televised live show Brown informed his audience he would trick them into not remembering much of his act, and as promised at the end of the performance few could recall what they had witnessed on stage.[11] He keeps people guessing: 'you just can't work out what he is doing, so that's good. ... it's like thinking you did work it out, but you didn't ... I know it's not magic. I like that, how he's done that, I want to work it out' (32-year-old female interpreter).

Brown also influences the reconstruction process through lack of scientific knowledge. Lamont and Wiseman (1999) explain:

> Many physical feats rely on the audience being unaware of physiological or chemical processes ... mathematical magic tricks regularly rely on the spectator being unaware of certain mathematical procedures ... Many mediums have relied on ideomotor actions to produce apparent spiritualistic phenomena with Ouija boards and pendulums ... Cold readers rely on population stereotypes in their readings, and on the fact that few people are aware of how common certain characteristics are.
>
> (84–85)

Brown appeals to people's general sense of psychology whilst drawing on their misunderstanding of many aspects of clinical and social psychology and parapsychology. As this person said:

> There are so many things I can't explain, I don't know about science and stopped studying it when I was sixteen. There are not many things I can explain in the world, if I am pressed on it. You know, what do I actually know? If I don't think something is particularly believable, I couldn't actually discredit it because I don't know. I just don't have the scientific skills and knowledge to really know whether it's really true or not ...
>
> (25-year-old female student)

One of Brown's conjuring tricks involves the appearance of table levitation, or table tipping, effects also used by pseudo psychics in séances. There is a picture of

Brown amazing the scientist Dr Robert Smith with a three-legged table levitating above them: Smith 'sat quietly for a few moments afterwards and then said "Fuck me, I have no idea"' (Brown 2006: 'Modern Table Levitation', centre insert). He directs the reconstruction process through drawing on belief systems. With a general audience Brown can mix lack of conjuring knowledge with pre-conceptions and misunderstandings of psychology. In the following example, a viewer commented on a trick that involved members of the audience apparently moving a table:

> He knows that everything he does is based on the power of suggestion. That's why people are moving the table but they aren't aware that they are doing it. The way he talks to people, he puts things in their mind. What he was saying, word by word, slowly, there are messages in there – 'you are going to push it.' It's all about psychology and the power of suggestion. I don't believe the table is moving itself. To me, I found it even more fascinating that he could get people to do that without knowing that they were doing it.
>
> (27-year-old male games tester)

The power of suggestion is one of several explanations for the method behind the effect. His audience ends up exactly where he wants them in the reconstruction process.

Steinmeyer writes: 'when magicians are good at their jobs, it is because they anticipate the way an audience thinks' (2003: 117). An audience with Derren Brown is one familiar with debates about paranormal beliefs and fakery scandals. They are familiar with the practices of hypnotists, fortune tellers, or psychics because they have direct or second hand experience. Brown includes himself with his audience, using an avowal of prior belief – 'coming out of Christianity' – to re-enforce his approach of questioning belief systems (Lamont 2005). Although he relies on lack of knowledge to create magical entertainment, he doesn't treat his audience as stupid. For example, one viewer commented on his ability to under-stand the way an audience thinks: 'he is just an incredibly intelligent man ... he is not making them feel stupid if they believe. "This is a trick, this is what I've done, you know, it is possible to do it, but I am not marking you as stupid by believing in them"' (24-year-old female online marketer). Or as another viewer explained: 'I think he chooses audiences, he does appeal to certain types ... when he is doing his show live, the way he does it he is not patronising people, he is cool. People go "wow"!' (35-year-old female administrator). A good understanding of his audience includes an awareness of their intelligence, their contemporary practices, and their pleasure in participating in magical entertainment.

Multiple realities

Steinmeyer in *Hiding the Elephant* (2003) describes the alternative explanations for an illusion where what the audience sees is only one reality whilst another is created by the illusionist. The magician Howard Thurston performed a levitation illusion where an Indian Princess floated above the stage. He would tell the audience how he had 'discovered the secrets of levitation from an Indian fakir', recite a mystic incantation, pass a seamless metal hoop over the princess draped in silk, and then invite a small boy from the audience onto the stage: 'taking the boy by the hand, Thurston walked him completely around the floating lady, then lifted him so that he could touch the golden ring on her finger for good luck' (2003: 4–15). Steinmeyer explains how Thurston created an elaborate fantasy of Eastern mysticism on stage and he depended on the invited members of the audience being confused by what they saw. His skill of cueing meant he whispered instructions to the volunteers under his breath: 'his novel presentation focused on the thousand people in the audience who did not step onstage, calculating that by quietly exposing the trick to a few, he was creating a miracle for everyone else' (210). One volunteer described how as a small boy he had been onstage: 'I saw more damn wires than I have ever seen in my life! As Thurston lifted me up, he whispered, "if you touch any of those blankety-blank wires ... "At that moment, I opened my eyes and my mouth wide, which made everyone in the audience think that I was amazed at what I was seeing' (210–11).

In a blog by magicians at the James Randi website, discussion of Brown's act 'Don't kill the kitten' focused on the 'dual reality trick'. Explanations included the supposition that off camera Brown told the participant there were ten kittens in another room and they would all die if she didn't press the button. Thus, a terrible dilemma was created and this explained her actions. Another suggestion was that anyone involved in that trick would anticipate the producers would not kill a kitten on national TV so they would press the button to participate in the act, wanting to please Brown and influenced by the power of his personality. In viewers' discussions of this trick there was an awareness that the TV producers would be unlikely to kill a kitten, but this was due to knowledge of the media, not of magic.

In the stage show 'Something Wicked Comes This Way' (2006) Brown performed 'Blockhead', which involved him apparently hammering a nail all the way up inside his nose. He was assisted by a member of the audience who testified to the authenticity of the nail and hammer. The conjuring trick was deliberately ambiguous, simply performed in virtual silence to a stunned audience who were directed to make up their own minds as to what they had witnessed live on stage. There was no explanation given by Brown, instead he drew on audience preconceptions, knowledge and misunderstandings of magic, mysticism and psychology to influence the reconstruction process.

People responded to this extraordinary feat by looking for both rational and non-rational explanations. A few examples highlight how people reconstructed the feat as illusion:

> It's a trick. No, just no way, you are seriously bleeding if that was real. You can't get it past a certain point, surely, no.
>
> (28-year-old female public relations person)

I think it's false. I've seen other magicians doing these things ... I am not a medical expert, but how it has to be, yeah, it's a trick.

(30-year-old male financier)

Maybe the angle was slightly moving so you sort of put the nail up there somewhere else, but I don't think it's a real nail.

(24-year-old female online marketer)

Others wavered between different explanations, unsure how to reconstruct the feat:

I don't know if it is possible. Can you hammer the nail, if it is real, like that long? That's going to hurt, or something is going to, you know ... And a couple of things that I thought were, you know, there was a camera on the back, which meant it could be pre-recorded. She could be part of the actors as well ... If it is real, then, it's wonderful, wow. But, you know, just as you saw him near the end, when he was about to hammer it in, a camera man was just in the way. I don't know, too many thoughts. I don't know, maybe from a medical point of view it can possibly be done, maybe another nail was switched. I don't know.

(28-year-old male computer programmer)

Others referred to the act as an extraordinary feat:

I say it is definitely possible. You see actual documentaries about, like, piercing stuff in strange places. It's to do with tradition. It's possible. Why not do it live on stage?

(21-year-old male student)

I believe the nail went in, but still it's not relevant like magic. That wasn't to me magic. That was stupid. All way up through the nose, honestly, who does that ... It's not like magic.

(33-year-old female youth worker)

These responses illustrate the way magic can turn things upside down so that what appears to one person an illusion is to another not like magic at all.

One woman reflected on the natural and supernatural in her response to this extraordinary feat:

It wasn't magic, though, was it? Because magic, you should say how to do that. That's purely physical, 'this is what I can do.' Lots of mystics do that sort of feat, to go beyond the pain threshold. He's obviously mastered the ability to do that ... I saw a mystic, and the things the man was doing, quite frankly I don't want to see again. He got a nail and he popped out his eye ball. Now it was absolutely not all the way, but after he put it back again, I thought, no, why do they do that? As a form of religious practice when they get themselves into a high status of awareness, that's what they do, and they push themselves to go further and further ... I personally think that he has got ability, he just calls it something else. Some people call it medium-ship and they specifically train themselves to connect with a particular level of sprits. Other people are healers. Lots of people who have these abilities say they don't call it that, they call it reading body language, or they will be a particularly good psychologist, and they can read people that way. But it's still there, however you look at it, still a similar kind of energy. It's just different people calling it by different names.

(38-year-old female consultant)

The reference to Eastern mysticism, alternative spiritual practices, supernatural abilities based on a 'high state of awareness', are all part of common under-standing of extraordinary feats as examples of phenomena beyond explanation. The ambiguous associations of magic and mysticism frame her interpretation of this act as beyond magic.

One woman said:

He shows you how powerful your mind is. You only use a tiny percentage of your brain anyway, so, you are not a hundred per cent sure what he's capable of ... I do believe he is doing that. And you know, people are affected by it, and it's just really fascinating finding out, you know, what he is capable of. ... I want to know what he is doing is kind of genuine. You know, if it's all made up, then there's no point in watching that.

(23-year-old female art technician)

Such thinking on the power of the mind was common to participants in this study. This person reflected: 'It might be true. There is huge amount of our brain that is not used, we only use a small percentage of the potential capability' (49-year-old female teacher).

In audience responses to this type of magic, popular ideas of psychology move into an ambiguous area of unexplainable phenomena. These cultural practices highlight a myth of psychology as all powerful. When people discussed Brown's performances they provided examples of the psychology of human potential:

I think we have different dimensions of minds, you know, like supernatural, when you sense things are going happen to you.

(24-year-old female sales executive)

I think instinct comes to play a lot, like gut feelings. I've been in situations that have made me sort of jump. I've been in situations as well where I have actually felt things, and you know I do trust my instincts on things like that.

(28-year-old male civil servant)

Instincts are within you. It's like a subtle emotion, or some kind of trigger. People are talking about instinct which is completely separate from sprits or something, it's part of your brain.

(23-year-old male student)

The types of conjuring tricks that Brown specialises in – extraordinary feats, extrasensory perception – can become the topic of discussion amongst some members of his audience, offering a way for people to explore their own ideas and experiences about the power of the mind.

Nineteenth-century accounts of fake Indian Fakirs (Lamont and Bates 2007) suggest seemingly incompatible ways of thinking about magic as an illusion to be rationally explained and magic as a mystical power that is beyond explanation. It is also possible to see a myth of psychology as all powerful as one which allows Derren Brown to perform conjuring tricks within a rationalist framework whilst drawing on the imaginary of the power of the mind. This construction of psychology is apparent in popular self-help books and training on neurolinguistic programming and hypnosis to stop smoking or lose weight. It is apparent in self-empowerment books and training on mind, body and spirit matters. There are many examples of health and well being practices and literature which emphasise metaphysical thinking and the power of the mind to heal the body of illness. Successful guides to cosmic ordering rely on the idea of mind over matter to improve business, find relationships, and make a million. Various experts, books, audio guides and training sessions all promote ideas of psychology and self-empowerment, self-help and human potential. Audiences know about these ideas, and indeed many will have experienced them at first or second hand.

Lamont and Bates (2006) argue the myth of India as the land of magic was a Western myth which allowed magicians within a rationalist framework to draw on the imaginary of Eastern mysticism. The mysteries of the East had a role to play in the construction of Europe as the birth of the modern. In a disenchanted West there was the possibility of the enchantments of an exotic, other world (2006: 324). In Simon During's discussion of magic and modern enchantments, the imagination and by extension illusion are crucial to modern society's construction of itself (2002). For During, enchantment continues as a feature of the development of modernity as both enchanted and disenchanted at the same time. Psychology also has an impact on this argument about the imagination and modern enchantments. The myth of psychology as all powerful connects with the previous chapter and an exploration of matters of authenticity in human experiences. In the magic of Derren Brown and audience responses to his performances, psychology is an explanation for both rational interpretations of unusual experiences and intuitive accounts of extraordinary feats. Conjuring and illusion are not the primary features of this performance of magic. Instead, there is an emphasis on multiple truths to human experiences which depend on the context within which they are framed. Psychological entertainment is an excellent example of how the individual is centre stage in modern Western societies. It is a cultural form that gives people 'a joy of the mystery of playing with minds' (28-year-old female public relations person).

Conclusion

The social history of magic highlights how magical entertainment combined rational explanation with ambiguous associations of metaphysical thinking, mysticism and psychic phenomena. For example, magicians of the late nineteenth and early twentieth centuries created illusions based on levitation, mind reading, or spirit communication which promised to expose the tricks of the trade amongst pseudo psychics and mediums. At the same time, these magicians borrowed from Indian jugglers in constructing illusions that referenced India as a land of magic and drew on Eastern mysticism. In this way, magicians exploited the beliefs of their audiences in their creation and performance of entertainment.

Derren Brown is a type of magician who has the appearance of psychic powers. His conjuring tricks are based on extraordinary feats, such as walking across broken glass, table levitation and mind reading. His audience believes he is more than a magician. Playfully referred to as a Jedi Master, audiences see him as skilled in mind control. In the construction of his entertainment Brown uses a range of methods to make it difficult for audiences to work out how he does it. He offers explanations such as hypnotism, unconscious communication, or memory systems, but these explanations whilst partly true are also deceptive. Brown uses multiple conjuring methods and a wide range of physical and psychological misdirection to make it difficult for people to detect the truth behind the effects of the tricks. His style of entertainment highlights the framing of popular psychology as both a rational explanation for human behaviour and the mysteries of the mind. It indicates the dominance of cultural practices associated with self-help, self-empowerment, human potential and alternative health and well being. In the same way that nineteenth-century magicians used a myth of the East to suggest ambiguous associations with magic and mysticism, so too does Brown use the myth of psychology as all powerful to great effect.

Notes

1 Back cover of Derren Brown *Tricks of the Mind*, Channel Four Publishing 2006.
2 Brian Logan 'Derren Brown: Mind Reader' the *Guardian*, Tuesday, 13 May 2008, accessed online at www.guardianunlimited.com 15 August 2008.
3 Derren Brown: 'The Gathering', Channel Four, broadcast, 18 February 2010, 11 pm, repeat.
4 *The Times* online accessed at http://entertainment.timesonline.co.uk/tol/arts_ and_entertainment/tv_and_radio/article3895863.ece 26 May 2009.
5 *Mirror*, Richard Smith 12/05/2008, accessed online at http://www.mirror.co. uk/celebs/news/2008/05/12/fury-at-derren-brown-cat-killer-tv-show-115875-20415125/ 26 May 2009.
6 *Metro*, 20 May 2008, accessed online at www.metro.co.uk/fame/interviews/ article.html?in_article_id=148689&in_page_id = 11 26 May 2009.

7 Channel Four website, accessed online at www.channel4.com/entertainment/
   tv/microsites/D/derrenbrown/pictures/trickortreat2/episode2/gallery_7_
   index.html 16 May 2009.
8 Interview with author 17 June 2008.
9 Blogger posted 12 May 2007, accessed online at www.talkmagic.co.uk/
   sutra169362.php&highlight=15 August 2009.
10 Interview with author 11 June 2008.
11 See Derren Brown: 'The Gathering', note 3.

Chapter 8

The audience is the show

'People produce beliefs.'

Researchers face a challenge in capturing the variety of people's relationships with a range of media and communications technologies. The concept of audience participation is useful in exploring connections between production, content and reception in multimedia environments. In a talk show members of the public participate in the production itself, as guests interviewed by the host, as a studio audience, and watching, listening, interacting with the show on TV, radio, mobile and web. This concept also captures the way new communication technologies give people opportunities for making and sharing their own media content, such as documentaries created and produced by members of the public and uploaded to the web where they can be downloaded to personal computers, mobiles and iPods. Audience participation addresses the complex dynamics of cultural practices.

Being an audience can be like participating in a show. A public performance, exhibition, or event shows people's cultural practices. At an agricultural show, for example, people make jams, or grow vegetables to compete in prizes. A public demonstration can be a platform for people's professional or amateur interests in cars or airplanes. At a variety show there are a range of performance styles from dance routines, songs, or comedy acts, to physical feats like juggling or acrobatics. A show includes the production of performances, sometimes by the performers themselves, more often by others working backstage, such as the producers of television or radio programmes. A show can go on without an audience, for example there are full dress rehearsals which help performers and producers to perfect a production. But a show is designed to work best with an audience, showcasing talent, skills and interests, to the public, family and friends, who in turn show their reactions through appreciation, criticism and interaction.

There is a style of entertainment and communication where the performer and audience create the show together. In an analysis of qualitative audience research the idea of the audience as the show is explored in relation to historical and

Figure 8.1 'An Audience with Derren Brown', courtesy of Derren Brown

contemporary examples from public entertainment, in particular stage magic and medium demonstrations which involve a high degree of audience participation. A medium, or psychic, who performs in public needs an audience not only to watch or listen, but to actually make the performance happen. A magician or medium performs entertainment that is based on audience participation. Most singers or actors can still perform even if there is no audience, but a magician or medium must have an audience because their form of communication and entertainment is created with a high degree of public participation. As this woman said: 'people produce beliefs' (51-year-old female secretary). An audience with a medium co-produces belief in spirit communication; an audience with a magician co-produces a sense of wonder. In a very real sense the audience is the show.

The attentive audience

An audience that listens, watches, and engages closely with a performance has emerged over time. The word 'auditorium' came into the English language after 1727 (Winston 2005: 225). Contemporary understanding of an auditorium as a place for appreciation of a performance is quite different from early examples of audiences at the opera or theatre. Brian Winston comments:

> It was by no means the case at either theatrical or musical public entertain-ments that people were silent during the performance. In fact, aristocrats seemed to regard quiet attentiveness as an unforgivably bourgeois trait. Performances were social gatherings and the done thing was to circulate – exactly as is still done at modern parties.
>
> (2005: 224)

Donald Sassoon (2006: 233) describes opera goers as anything but attentive to the music:

> Before the 1800s, in popular theatres and in taverns some attention was paid to the action on the stage, but in the opera houses patronised by the upper

classes bedlam reigned. At the Paris Opera, the system made the subscribers, in fact, tenants of the theatre box, where they could do as they saw fit. Punctuality and silence were not thought to be necessary, or even desirable ... Attentiveness was a social *faux pas* ... The opera house was like a twentieth-century nightclub: people dropped in when it suited them, and would come and go during the performance.

The most sought after seats in theatres were the ones on, or near, the stage. This was not because of the good view; in fact it was worse in these seats as people were blinded by oil lamps, but because the rest of the audience could see them. 'Visibility to others was crucial. The audience was the show' (Sassoon 2006: 234).

Towards the end of the eighteenth century 'the more attentive behaviour which was characteristic of audiences at private performances of chamber music began to be adopted in the public arena' (Sassoon 2006: 235). 'As theatres become more market-dependent ... watching the aristocracy provided only limited entertainment for the middle classes. When all was said and done, the bourgeois ethos consisted in getting value for money' (239). The magic-lantern show was an example of a transition from the inattentive to attentive audience. Early lantern shows took place in an informal, domestic environment, with no fixed seating, where people circulated, chatted and interacted with each other, paying little attention to the lantern show itself (Winston 2005). During the end of the eighteenth and early nineteenth centuries lantern shows shifted from the private soirée to the public theatre. Robertson's *Fantasmagorie* were lantern shows where audiences sat in fixed rows in a public space. The design of these shows drew the audience into a macabre narrative, mixing single images or effects of ghosts and ghouls with stories. The *Fantasmagorie* were an early example of 'narrative and non-narrative spectacle' (Winston 2005: 226). They signalled a style of entertainment that involved an audience at a public show.

By the mid nineteenth century magic-lantern shows were overtaken by the popularity of 'attractions' which came to mean a mix of performance styles, including animal or aquatic dramas, panoramas and dioramas, or burlesque. These attractions were similar to what now would be called variety shows. They mixed images and sounds with stories. Attractions were part of a repertoire of family-friendly theatres. Managers had changed their policies to increase the comfort and safety of theatre space by replacing the pit with civilised reserved seats. These theatres appealed to women by eliminating drink, tobacco and prostitution. In the 1840s managers like P. T. Barnum introduced museum theatres, 'adopting the manners of the middle class parlours and assuring a moral climate on and off stage' (Butsch 2008: 64). Barnum was one of the first to showcase the Fox sisters, public mediums who performed spirit rapping for a paying audience. As part of Victorian attractions, magicians, mediums and lecturers showcased new visual and aural modes of experience – the telegraph, the photograph, panoramas, stereoramas. Many new attractions relied on fixed seating, for example, Pepper's Ghost. Steinmeyer (2003) notes the invention of optical illusions used in theatrical dramas influenced the way mediums and magicians performed in public, directing the audience to see specific images through complex use of lighting, sightlines, mirrors and mechanics.

Richard Butsch points out theatre spaces, policies and performances worked together in the emergence of nineteenth-century ideas of cultural appreciation. Etiquette manuals advised people on how to present themselves in public and private, with many cautions against spontaneous displays of emotion, or physical acts. These bourgeois theatregoers avoided rowdy working class venues, favouring respectable places in newly developed areas. Etiquette rules on how to be a theatregoer emphasised 'the duty of the audience to give full attention to the performance, in order to cultivate oneself' (Butsch 2008: 65). The right of audiences to speak and act out was considered working class behaviour and 'an outrage against both performers and other members of the audience' (ibid). Manuals warned against talking during the performance as ticket holders had a right to enjoy entertainment uninterrupted. Theatregoers were schooled to stay in their seats, not to eat peanuts, to refrain from loud gestures or sounds (65–66). A children's etiquette book exemplified late Victorian attitudes to cultural appreciation and respectability: 'perhaps nowhere are bad manners more disagreeable than in public places of amusement ... [where people] are defrauded of the pleasure they have paid for by the conduct of those about them' (ibid).

Butsch argues Victorian theatregoers represented different visions of audiences as crowds and publics. In early American theatre 'revolutionary discourse framed audiences as engaging in legitimate actions in their roles as citizens, both exercising rights and participating in political debate' (2008: 24). Depictions of working class men in the city theatres of the 1830s and 40s showed a vocal, boisterous crowd. This image changed with concerns about the incivility of the working classes. Nineteenth-century crowd psychology synthesised intellectual views about the 'emotionality and suggestibility of subordinate groups' (33). These theatregoers were thought to be lacking in reason, quickly capable of becoming a dangerous mob. The influential writings of Gustave Le Bon (1875) and Boris Sidis (1899) on crowd psychology drew upon ideas of mesmerism and hypnosis, both of which were popular in theatres as part of lecture tours or stage acts (see Melechi 2008). Early writings conceived the crowd as mobs: 'the speaker or focus of the crowd was simply the trigger to unify it into one mind, making it more powerful; its emotionality and volatility then made it an agent of chaos and destruction' (Butsch 2008: 36–37). Later writings represented 'the crowd as dependent upon and under the control of the speaker' (37). These were different constructions of an audience in Victorian theatres, one that was unruly and inattentive, and another that was too attentive to the manipulation of the speaker or performer.

The historical context of the attentive audience helps to explain the work of mediums and magicians. In the case of nineteenth-century mediums many started out conducting private sittings in their own homes. The style of the séance provided an element of the experience of watching and listening to a private performance. The class distinctions of Victorian audiences and crowds were apparent in the different venues for demonstrations of séance phenomena. Prominent patrons of spiritualism organised private séances in their homes. Some mediums only worked in such spaces, never charging for their demonstrations but instead relying on patronage. Others worked in public theatres to a paying audience. In both types of performance spaces the attention of the audience was crucial – these séances happened in the dark, with fixed seating, where the medium could control their performance and the participation of the audience. People had to pay attention, whether to catch fraudulent mediums in the act, as their critics suggested, or to witness proof of an afterlife. The scientist W. D. Carpenter coined the term 'expectant attention' as an explanation for people's unconscious acts of movement or thought which helped to create séance phenomena (Lamont 2005: 41). For example, in the act of table tipping the questions posed by a medium were unconsciously answered by other participants in their effort to make the 'table talk'. Today this is commonly referred to as ideomotor movement and is one of the explanations used for trickery associated with pseudo psychics.

The vision of Victorian audiences of mediums as victims of a delusion fitted into crowd psychology of the time. It also suggested concerns about female audiences and performers, as many women were associated with public and private demonstrations of mediumship. The magician John Henry Anderson denounced spiritualism in a pamphlet which he sold for a shilling at his shows. He stated this delusion had driven 10,000 people mad, causing them to 'become lunatics ... and thousands of poor infatuated victims ... have become melancholy misanthropes and imbecile tormentors' (cited in Lamont 2005: 62). In his London shows, performed to a full house, he revealed the secrets of spiritualism – 'The Homological Evaporation', 'the Aqua-avial Paradox', 'The Mesmeric Couch' – to all be the product of mechanical methods. Anderson with grave tone 'expatiated on the mischief done by pretended spirit media' and his performance was 'received with applause equally serious' (cited in Lamont 2005: 63). The construction of audiences of mediums as dupes and imbeciles worked alongside the image of sceptical audiences as critical and sane. Lamont writes: 'most of the public did not need convincing, their view of spiritualism being instinctively dismissive, and they were quite happy to accept the rhetoric and pseudo-explanations of the Wizard' (2005: 65).

Such ideas of mediums and their audiences failed to capture the complexity of their performances and public responses. Fake mediums Charles Forster, Henry Slade and the Davenports performed in public to a paying audience and their 'speciality feats ... entered the repertoires of mainstream magicians' (Lamont 2006: 22). For example, Foster's speciality was to involve an audience member in billet reading, where the names of the recently departed would be mysteriously spelt out through spirit raps, or dramatically written in red on his body. Slade's speciality of slate writing directed the audience to look closely at a blank slate for the appearance of messages, drawing attention away from any hidden mechanisms. The Davenports would invite audience members to tie the ropes that secured them in their spirit cabinet, thus ensuring focus on the stage. These performances were close to those of conjurers but 'it was essential that ... their feats were seen as genuinely supernatural' (Lamont 2006: 22). As such, 'fake mediums had to fabricate both the phenomena and the performance as a whole' (26). The strategies employed by fraudulent mediums enabled audiences to feel they were witnessing authentic séance phenomena. These included the use of novel effects not known as conjuring tricks by their audience. They added spiritual significance to these effects, for example asking audience members for the names of recently departed loved ones, rather than simply to pick a random word. Unlike magicians who performed conjuring with ease, mediums drew attention to their labour as spirit messengers:

> By fabricating both a desirable purpose and a lack of control, the medium was able to align himself with the audience and distance himself from the phenomena (both the implied source and the real source). Thus medium and sitter were in it together, neither in control of events yet both seeking success. (27)

Lamont's analysis indicates how mediums and their audiences produced alternative frames of interpretation that made fake spirit communication seem real.

The history of an attentive audience highlights how a specific style of live entertainment and communication emerged during the nineteenth century. The private experience of the salon transformed into public entertainment. Theatre managers changed policies and business practices, installing fixed seating in theatres, electricity and lighting, producing narrative and non-narrative spectacles, attractions, dramas and public demonstrations. New styles of listening and watching performances emerged, with the appreciation of a performance characterised by attentiveness and respectability. In this environment, mediums and magicians created a type of live entertainment that relied on audience participation. They used seating and lighting plans to their advantage, increasing control of audience reactions and concealing the means of producing these reactions. In magical entertainment and medium demonstrations the audience was the show in a different sense than a century before. Rather than ignore the performance, an audience made the performance possible.

Producing beliefs

Magical entertainment is about audience participation. Take as an example the art of misdirection. This begins from the basis that an audience is attentive to the performer and therefore can be directed towards the magic effects and away from the methods behind them. Lamont and Wiseman (1999) explain physical misdirection is all about directing the attention of the audience to what they see (the space, person, object) and when they see it (timing, placement, movement). Magicians have multiple methods of physical misdirection. They use passive diversion which directs the audience to look at areas of interest which appear natural (contrasting colours or light); active diversion draws the audience to specially created areas of interest (deliberate use of eyes, or voice in the performance). Another diversion involves reducing or increasing attention at a specific moment in the performance (at the point of effect). A skilled magician regulates audience attention through focus and timing.

Psychological misdirection is about how a magician controls audience interpretation of a magic effect. This can be done by using natural actions that appear appropriate within the context of a performance (shuffling cards in the same manner each time during a card trick). Or a magician can make an inconsistent action appear consistent by using familiar actions (producing a false shuffle amongst many similar card shuffles). A ruse involves the false justification of an action as necessary to the performance (coughing to cover hand palming in a card trick). A convincing performer can divert suspicion by misrepresentation, using false solutions and expectations, or 'sucker effects' (1999: 75). This approach utilises audience expectations about false traps, or the power of suggestion, to direct them to misinterpret a conjuring act.

To create a magical experience involves an understanding of audience participation as more than misdirection. Magician and mentalist Derren Brown says 'magic isn't about fakes and switches and dropping coins in your lap. It's about entering into a relationship with a person whereby you can lead him, economically and deftly, to experience an event as magical' (2006: 36). The novelist Hilary Mantel (2006: 3) explains:

> When a trick is performed, the harder you watch, the more you may miss. You become committed to its process; you are complicit, and your attention moves as directed. It is natural, when we are surprised, to exaggerate the oddity and wonder of our experience.

Mentalist Paul Stockman uses terms like 'audience handler' to signal the close relationship between performer and audience. He explains:

> Psychological entertainment for me is 90 per cent performance and 10 per cent method. It's all about the entertainment, and holding the attention of a large audience needs a lot of preparation as far as script and audience management techniques are concerned.
>
> (Hey 2009: 13)

An audience with a mentalist knows that their participation is crucial. For example, 'Derren Brown always has somebody with him, somebody from the audience, just kind of randomly picked, that makes it more believable as well' (28-year-old male computer programmer). Brown makes his audience feel special: 'it's like you want to believe it, you want to be the one' (26-year-old male student). 'The joy is that, "oh that could happen to me" And he is kind of playing with the unknown parts of yourself – "will I be able to do that?"' (28-year-old female public relations person). To experience an event as magical involves an audience investing in the process of playing with their minds.

In this discussion, participants debated the process of participating in a magical experience:

JOHN: It's a kind of enlightenment experience … If you look at it, we are kind of sceptical … the magic format is sort of old really, and for lots of people just not convincing. So this is just kind of the next level of that. (25-year-old male marketing assistant)

MARK: 'Russian Roulette'. (20-year-old unemployed male)

CLARE: Also, he tricks minds. (28-year-old female volunteer manager)

GAVIN: Recently magic became really sexy. Everyone is into magic. My mate started getting into it, and he works at a bar and he does stuff like that. (19-year-old male student)

CHRIS: And people really like it. Really, yeah it's become sexy. It's just become very popular. (28-year-old male civil servant)

CLARE: I don't think Derren Brown and David Blaine are anything to do with magic though. Really, truly …

GAVIN: It's illusion.

CLARE: But magic to me is like, I don't know, I can't explain it, but not to do with tricking someone's mind. The trick itself wouldn't be magic, but the person who watched it.

CHRIS: I was watching Derren, I like using my own imagination more rather than trying to give scientific proof.

JohN: He tries to explain things, how they could possibly happen.

CHRIS: I don't rely on science to explain things to me, though.

JOHN: I don't understand, if science doesn't explain it …

CHRIS: Well, to prove different things, the science of the mind, to sort of prove how people are doing it, I don't need exactly to know how hypnotherapy and alternative therapy works. I don't need any proof.

JACKIE: I found, in a kind of way, it spoils it to know how they do it. Whenever I see a magic show, I guess it's interesting to see how they do it, but that's not how I watch it. I want to see what they can do, really.

CLARE: I just found it's really disappointing. I really would want to know the answer, but when I did I wasn't really interested in it anymore. That's why I like Derren Brown because he doesn't give you answers, but he wants you to try to work it out, and that's part of it. And so you can have a bit, but you can't have all of it.

The context of magic is important. It has to be fresh and contemporary, to tap into what an audience thinks, drawing on shared expectations, practices and beliefs. The kind of magic that is popular amongst this group is deliberately ambiguous, a form of psychological entertainment rather than what they perceive as a conjuring trick. Popular psychology, alternative therapies, and pseudo-science form the backdrop to the construction of magic as psychological entertainment. A magician and mentalist such as Brown assumes a level of scepticism from his audience, not only about magic but also about related issues such as hypnotherapy. Rational thinking is the basis from which the magical experience is constructed, 'a kind of enlightenment experience.' This is why his style of performance focuses so much on explanations behind the magic effects, for example hypnotism works because of the power of suggestion. But these explanations are part of psychological misdirection. An audience follows twists and turns so that their own logical thinking leads them down the garden path. There is an understanding that the construction of a magic effect involves audience participation – 'you try to work it out, and that's part of it.' To achieve a sense of wonder in the magic effect is difficult to explain. And that is the point – a magical experience is beyond explanation.

The relationship between the production of beliefs in magic and the paranormal is of significance. In the case of magic tricks, the performer and audience work together to create an experience that lasts for as long as the act. Once outside the entertainment frame, the magic has gone. A medium is demonstrating what is thought to exist outside of the performance itself. Lamont comments that even though a medium constructs a performance on the basis of paranormal beliefs, it is not necessarily the case that audiences believe in them. Indeed an audience with a medium brings their own scepticism to the performance: 'ostensibly psychic phenomena are not only unusual and surprising, but inherently anomalous. Few people view such events without suspicion and many reject them as highly unlikely if not impossible' (Lamont 2006: 25). The problems of belief in psychic phenomena signal one of the ways paranormal experiences are created by a medium and their audience. The difficulties, contradictions, and unusual nature of the phenomena, are a basis for the construction of the performance and experience. There is a shared understanding of the inherently anomalous nature of the phenomena.

There is a lot of detailed advice as to how to be the audience of a medium. One woman described psychics as dodgy plumbers. People offer advice routinely – prepare in advance, do your research, ask around, and when you meet the medium give nothing away, be non-responsive, but also be alert and active. For example:

> Good mediums don't ask you questions. If you go into a medium, and say, I've got John here, you know a John, well, everyone knows a John somehow … then you say, no, no. Basically you don't feed them anything. Then they tell you. You don't tell them anything … And a good medium doesn't tell you someone close to you is going to die. It could be your mum, or child, oh my god, someone is going to die, and it really makes you

paranoid ... Word of mouth is the best way to get good mediums. If you know people have been to a medium and verified them.

(46-year-old female care worker)

All the advice is about being self-aware – looking at emotional, psychological and spiritual responses. The problem of belief directs the attention of the audience towards themselves.

In her novel *Beyond Black* Hilary Mantel (2005: 26) writes of the relationship between a medium and their audience. The character Alison explains:

This is how you handle them; you tell them the small things, the personal things, the things no one else could really know. By this means you make them drop their guard: only then will the dead begin to speak. On a good night, you can hear the scepticism leaking from their minds, with a low hiss like a tyre deflating.

Often when a medium performs in public they make reference to the audience in the warm-up explaining that they would like yes or no answers because it is important to give accurate readings, and at the same time explaining without audience participation nothing will happen. Thus, an audience with a medium is on double duty giving out the energy and openness to spirits they are told is necessary for spirit communication to work and also keeping a tight reign on their responses so as not to give too much away. It is a curious open and closed feeling where audiences regulate their level of participation. As Mantel notes, the punters for a medium 'entertain any number of conflicting opinions. They could believe ... and not believe ... , both at once' (2005: 31).

The medium Gordon Smith describes the experience of a live performance:

Every event is absolutely unique and I don't really know what's going to happen any more than the audience does. It's a real act of faith ... my name may be on the bill, but it's not my show. The word 'medium' comes from the same root as 'media'. I am a messenger, a carrier of messages.

(2007: 78)

Audiences also carry messages, in their own responses, the collective responses from the crowd, and the responses of absent others brought to life by an audience and medium together. Although people attend a public demonstration of a medium's skills, it is also a demonstration of the skills of a live audience, alert to their emotions, psychological processes, critical of themselves and others, and at the same time open to experiences, producing beliefs.

Participation

Audience participation signals the merging of ideas around an active audience with production research, and social and cultural theory. The active audience model promotes a complex understanding of how people think, feel and act. For example, studies on soap operas or households explored issues of gender, power and ideology (see Hobson 1982, Allen 1985, Lull 1990, Morley 1986, amongst others). The relations between audiences and everyday life highlighted the way the media was part of broader cultural and social practices (see Silverstone 1994, Gauntlett and Hill 1999, amongst others). Researchers studied media reception at home, in the workplace, on trains, in waiting rooms; they looked at individuals, households, crowds (see Hermes 2005, McArthy 2001, amongst others). As the active model developed, multiple methods were used, from interviews, focus groups, or participant observation, to surveys or conversation analysis. Multiple approaches were adopted, from a basis in social science, to work in cultural anthropology and geography, visual sociology or social psychology. Participation is a natural progression in understanding audiences today.

Participation can mean different things. One approach can mean participation as citizenship and consumer rights, drawing on broader notions of the public knowledge project (see Hill 2007). Participation is framed by social and cultural theories regarding the normative concept of the public sphere, and subsequent variations of this theory as public spheres and alternative publics. Cultural citizenship includes a connection between the individual, audience and public and their participation or avoidance of political matters within public and private spheres (see Hermes 2005). This puts the citizen at the heart of understanding audience participation, within the broader framework of the media and democracy (see Dahlgren 2009). Another related approach considers the individual, audience and public as an agent of change, engaged in dynamic practices (see Bird 2003 amongst others). The promise of web environments as participatory can be a tool for empowerment, and different styles of cultural production can offer multiple modes of engagement (see Gauntlett 2007 amongst others). This sees participation as practices that evolve within media and cultural environments.

Live performances are powerful moments of participation. There is participation on several levels, such as sitting, standing, clapping or going on stage. There is participation through thinking, feeling, looking and listening. Architect and designer Frederick Kiesler wanted his theatre audiences to 'recognise the act of seeing, or receiving, as participation in the creative process no less essential than the artist's own' (cited in Pringle 2002: 344). In the case of a magician or medium, the performer and audience commit to participation in the creative process. Their relationship is like a conductor and orchestra. A magician conducts their audience as if they are members of an orchestra. They create the performance together. When a magician is good at what they do there is a collective pleasure in their skills to conduct the audience; some participants perform solos, some perform as part of an orchestral section, and at key moments the entire audience performs together. There are tonal qualities to audience experiences of a live performance with a magician where they are participating in major and minor moments in the show. A magician wants their audience to tune into the magic of the moment. A live demonstration with a medium involves a similar relationship. An audience comes to a demonstration alternating between scepticism in paranormal claims and belief in what they personally see as evidence of life after death. A medium conducts the audience as they orchestrate their own scepticism and belief. Their participation shows great investment in the process. An audience with a medium is committed to performing or playing out their beliefs both within and outside of the live show.

Here is an example of a conductor and orchestra in action:

Location – darkened room in apparently haunted building in London. Group of ten men and women around a Ouija board, with a glass and letters of the alphabet positioned on the table.

GROUP LEADER: Don't be shy, come forward and use our energy to move the glass.

Silence.

[Whispers amongst the group]

PARTICIPANT: If you are standing you tend to sway in the dark.

[Silence.]

GROUP LEADER: Is anybody here? Spirit, or astral being, please come forward. Show us you are here. Make a sign by moving this glass.

[Silence.]

PARTICIPANT: What's that?

GROUP LEADER: Is anybody here? Give us a sign, by moving the glass please.

[Silence.]

PARTICIPANT: Do you know what.?

PARTICIPANT: There it goes, look!

PARTICIPANT: It is moving

PARTICIPANT: Show it to me

GROUP LEADER: Go on, move it to yes

PARTICIPANT: It is moving

PARTICIPANT: That is moving

PARTICIPANT: Can you move it some more please

PARTICIPANT: It is moving.

PARTICIPANT: It is moving very slightly.

PARTICIPANT: We are very light fingered, just barely touching.

PARTICIPANT: We just want to know a little more about you.

[Silence.]

[Whispers amongst the group.]

PARTICIPANT: Just give us a sign that you are here, do what you did before.

PARTICIPANT: Can you communicate with us in another way?

[Whispers.]

GROUP LEADER: It seems to be moving very slowly.

PARTICIPANT: There it is! It moved! It moved, it moved, it moved!

GROUP INVESTIGATOR: Do you feel it has moved?
GROUP LEADER: Yes, it has. Has it?
GROUP INVESTIGATOR: No, not at all.
PARTICIPANT: You do feel it.

This is participation in a social experience where people collectively play a part in the production of beliefs.

In different contexts the audience as show highlights the power of live or seemingly live performances and events. Tele-evangelists are charismatic leaders. From the stage they conduct the audience as an orchestra, with a theatrical performance of emotions and religious beliefs. A regular part of their stage show includes the dramatic transformation of the sceptic to believer. Rather like a solo act, one participant comes on stage and performs in tandem with the tele-evangelist. Together they co-produce the transformative act of sceptic to believer and in doing so re-enforce a collective experience of religious belief. The tele-evangelist cannot do this alone; their performance is based on audience participation. There are similarities with the psychology of mediums and their audiences. There is a demonstration of skills and a live audience produces the belief that makes possible an interpretation of such skills as genuine. High-profile fakery scandals indicate some tele-evangelists are frauds. To say that audiences of tele-evangelists are gullible misses the power of the live performance of the charismatic leader and their audience. Derren Brown's television show *Messiah* (Channel Four, UK 2005) specifically addressed the ways in which a magician can masquerade as a charismatic leader, using the professional skills of mentalism to produce the appearance of a spiritual experience. When Brown explains how magicians enter into a relationship with a person or audience, whereby they can lead them, economically and deftly, to experience an event as magical (2006: 36) this is also true of certain types of charismatic leaders and the relationship with their audience.

Another example is that of politics. A politician in Britain or America con-structs their performance on the basis that audiences do not trust them. They address their audience as sceptics, disillusioned by the modern style of Western politics, by high-profile scandals involving corruption in money or sex, by the slick ways politicians spin issues to their advantage. Rather like a medium, most people assume a lot of politicians are frauds, even criminals, and come with a prior degree of scepticism in the claims of a politician to act on the public's behalf for the public good. Also, rather like a magician, people expect a politician to deceive them. The difference between a good and bad politician can be in the way they use these expectations of deception to their advantage. A politician can use the scepticism of their audience in the construction of political performances. For example, when a politician attempts to reduce public suspicion they can do so by controlling the interpretation of a political act. Some use false explanations as psychological misdirection. Some use charisma and a personal style to regulate and control the public's attention. Research by Peter Dahlgren (2009), or John

Corner and Dick Pels (2003), shows how ideas of performance are part of understanding modern politics. Work by Couldry et al (2007) highlights how audiences critically engage with celebrity politics in the wider political arena. A successful politician understands the psychology of their audience and constructs a performance based on a high degree of public participation. In order to win votes, a politician has to lead the public, economically and deftly, to experience an event as democratic even when that same public is suspicious of politicians. It is a transformative act where even in the most hostile of environments people can produce beliefs.

In the case of media experiences, the audience as show works in different ways, depending on the degree of participation both in terms of a collective, live audience, and the participative frame used by producers. As Livingstone and Lunt (1994) suggested in their research on talk shows, certain styles of production invite participation by the studio and television audience. The type of talk shows that include ordinary people and their stories are filmed as live, and include a participative frame that invites a studio audience to vocally and emotionally engage with the performances; indeed it is a co-performance carefully produced by the programme makers and host. In turn, but to a lesser degree, television audiences are invited to participate with the studio audience, what Daniel Dayan describes as 'collective attention' or 'watching with', where 'audiences embody a fundamental dimension of social experience' (2005: 55). In a similar way to the early experience of opera goers, there is a rowdy, noisy audience in these talk-shows that are just as much a part of the performance as anybody else. But, this is an audience as show where the incivilities of a live crowd are orchestrated by the talk show host and producers to shape a collective cultural experience. The audience as show works best on television when a live show is transformed into participatory acts.

Dayan argues that publics emerge through co-production: 'to go public in our societies means going on air, or in print, more often than taking to the streets' and this 'involves being allowed or encouraged to do so' (2005: 63). In the case of web environments, publics emerge through the participative frame of digital media which encourages people to perform, participate and produce content to be shared by a few or many around the world. David Gauntlett comments that the web 2.0 environment encourages users to be the show.[1] If aristocratic audiences of early opera acted like tenants because of the theatre policies of the time, now web users act like the performers, crowds, managers, owners and architects of the show. The idea of attention is ever more important in a web environment, where bloggers actively encourage specific links to increase the flow of users to their sites. Whilst the web is known for its always, anytime, anywhere function, where content is available for people when they want it, there are elements which relate to live participatory acts. For example, web discussions are scheduled live after a TV show, with actors or journalists going online to participate in a live debate. Flash mob experiences, such as dancing at a crowded train station in London at a particular moment, are organised beforehand through the use of web and mobile communications, but the point is to create a live event with a high degree of participation where the audience is the show.

Reality entertainment formats involve both live television performances and web engagement which encourages participatory acts for audiences and users. The broadcasting success story of the past decade is shows like *Pop Idol, X Factor, Britain's Got Talent,* or *Strictly Come Dancing* (also known as *Dancing with the Stars*). All of these shows are filmed live with a studio audience. The show consists of variety acts, professionals and non-professionals singing, dancing, or performing comedy, acrobatics, or magic acts. A panel of expert judges rates the performances and invites the public to vote for their favourite performers. The show could be filmed without a live audience in the studio but this would miss the point. The producers want to create a show that involves audience participation. To do so they must invite the audience to co-produce the outcome of the show through their votes. What is so successful about these reality formats is the way the excitement of the live performance and the close involvement of the studio audience are communicated to the broadcast audience. This is a moment of televised entertainment where the public participate in an extraordinary way. At a time of dwindling shares and fragmented audiences, these shows get the attention of the nation. With record shares of over 50 per cent of broadcast audiences, shows like *Idol* or *X Factor* outperform their rivals because they capture the feeling of being in the moment at a live performance. The studio audience is a stand-in for the public and their reactions are important to the televised event, but the power is reserved for the audience at large, participating via their telephones, TVs, computers and mobiles. The relationship between the producers of *X Factor* and their audience is not the same as a conductor and their orchestra. The YouTube Orchestra was produced by Google to promote digital media and creative collaboration. A leading composer wrote a new piece 'Internet Symphony No 1' and a selection of YouTube users were chosen to perform the symphony at Carnegie Hall in New York, broadcast live across world wide web. The producers of reality entertainment shows have found a way to make live entertainment feel like a creative collaboration between performers and audiences. It is the next generation in the production of entertainment experiences.

Conclusion

The idea of audience as show relates to notions of participation. For example, elite audiences at the opera in the eighteenth century were inattentive to entertainment performances. When Sassoon (2006) says 'the audience was the show' he is referring to the framing of the upper classes as the focus of attention at the opera. This was an early example of audience management where an elite few directed the majority view. It was also an example of audience participation in a cultural experience where sociability was more important than appreciation of a performance. Another notion of the audience as the show utilised the attentive audience as part of the performance. Etiquette rules on how to be an attentive audience were an example of audience management, where a middle class crowd co-produced an environment for cultural appreciation. During the nineteenth century the profession of magicians and mediums developed in tandem with the idea of an attentive audience. Magic acts were constructed around an understanding of audience participation and management. Public demonstrations of mediums were shaped around an attentive audience that helped to produce beliefs in the skills of the performer. The nineteenth century saw a particular type of live entertainment and communication experience emerge where the audience was the show.

Ways of understanding audiences with magicians or mediums have included psychology and mass communication theories concerning media influences and effects. Nineteenth-century crowd psychology explicitly referenced mesmerism and mass hypnosis as explanations for the reactions of working class audiences in theatres or at public events. Suggestion and emotion, irrationality and uncritical thinking: these would become hallmarks of some early ideas of mass audiences. Another way of understanding audiences is that of participation. Magicians are audience handlers with a high degree of knowledge and skills in participatory experiences. In turn, audiences know their participation is crucial to the production of a magic show.

There are several key issues that arise from the idea of the audience is the show. The first is the power of live performances as moments where performers and audiences produce a memorable experience. In the case of some professions, magicians, mediums, or for example tele-vangelists and politicians, the live performance is a powerful moment where the charismatic leader on stage attempts to transform the scepticism of their audience into the production of beliefs. In this way an audience becomes committed to the process of their own experience. As ways of participating in live events, televised live shows and multimedia environments develop, audiences evolve. Through various acts of participation people breathe life into a show. In so doing audiences embody the culture they experience.

Note

1 Email to author 12 December 2009.

Chapter 9

Transformative acts

'With the paranormal "why" is the key word.'

The paranormal is unexplored territory, like deep space. It is the dark matter of popular culture. Yet at the same time in this environment participation is central. You don't have to be an astronaut, you don't need special permission or masses of money. You can be a plumber by day and ghost hunter by night. Television, tourism, images and audio, web and print forms, theatre and live events, shape the paranormal as the final frontier. Products, services and experiences are opportunities for great explorers. The search for explanations to paranormal phenomena is a driving force in people's cultural practices. We are 'constantly looking for explanations' (26-year-old male vision mixer). For those who claim some form of paranormal belief, the search is a process by which their beliefs are made and remade. For those who don't know what to believe, the search is an exploratory process with open-ended results. People who profess to be sceptics are part of the search process, investigating and debunking claims. People search for explanations and in the process participate in the shaping of beliefs, practices and experiences.

There are several sociological explanations as to why people engage with the phenomenon of the paranormal at this juncture in time. Some of these explanations are about our engagement with life and death. All of us use various cultural practices to process our own mortality. In *Nothing to be Frightened Of* Julian Barnes wrote of death: 'there are so many possibilities to choose from – to have chosen for us; so many different doors, even if they are all marked exit' (2008: 122). Popular culture provides possibilities for exploring many doors marked exit. One person summed up: 'nobody knows when you die, so everyone wants to know' (18-year-old female sales assistant). The flip side of fear of death is the feeling of being alive. Cultural engagement with the paranormal can be a moving experience. As one participant on a live ghost hunting event explained: 'I felt a wash of emotions. My eyes were streaming, it was a great kind of sadness.' These explanations about fear of death and feeling alive work together in the various

Figure 9.1 Ghost hunting at London Dungeon, photograph by Lizzie Jackson

ways people explore themselves. Where there is a door marked exit there is also one marked entrance.

Audiences

Seamus Heaney in *Seeing Things* (1991) wrote poetry is 'true to the grain of things'. Poems re-imagine experiences – 'freshening your outlook beyond the range you thought you settled for' (1991: 99). A recurring question in this book is what happens to our theoretical understanding of audiences if we are 'true to the grain of things', true to people's experiences? Through looking at audiences, speaking with viewers, participating in events, this research hopes to offer fresh perspectives on understanding popular culture. With something so complicated as audiences new perspectives rarely offer clear insights. At best, they extend a range of outlooks. Any attempt to analyse people's experiences fails to fully capture the intensity and emotionality of the moment. Nevertheless it is the role of audience research to bring people to life in order to better understand them. To that end, the research in this book can be characterised as a whole lives approach to audiences.[1] Such an approach involves exploring human experience. The whole lives of audiences looks at experiences in the round, where text, artefact, live events, and practices fit within a spectrum of cultural engagement. It is about how people embody the culture they experience.

In a summary of the research in this book there is an overarching theme of audience participation in cultural experiences. The research is about the stories of people who may or may not believe in the paranormal. Their voices, thoughts, feelings and experiences guide the audience analysis. Their cultural practices provide a rich resource for critical and social theories. This is an understanding of paranormal beliefs less as religion and more as lifestyle practices. Although representations of spirits and magic hark back to historical contexts, paranormal beliefs are now part of a media age and as such are connected to mainstream cultural, social and lifestyle trends. It is an idea of the paranormal deliberately shaped by industries and audiences as unique cultural experiences. These are also ambiguous experiences. The central themes of authenticity and evidence, scepticism and belief, entertainment and illusion, suggest multiple realities. What follows is an overview of the findings from the chapters and reflections on how and why people produce beliefs within an entertainment environment.

Ordinary and extraordinary

The paranormal asks us to question what we think of as normal in popular culture. It shows culture is both ordinary and extraordinary. As such, paranormal matters are part of what Avery Gordon (1997, 2008 reprint) describes as the intricate connections that characterise social life. The statement 'life is complicated' is one that sums up social experience. It is applicable to paranormal matters where a common definition includes 'things which are beyond explanation.' One person described the paranormal as 'a phenomenon we don't understand.' Viviana Zelizer (2005) argues that reason and emotion work together in social relations. Cultural practices suggest we think and feel with our head and hearts. When people engage with paranormal matters they show a web of personal, emotional, psychological and physical connections and contradictions. People show how extraordinary experiences are a part of what we like to think of as our ordinary lives.

Multiple meanings

Owen Davies (2007) argues the history of ghosts over the past 500 years is a remarkable story of the survival of spirit belief. It is also a story of change and uncertainty. People turned to spirit beliefs as one means of managing socio-economic and political changes, alongside moral and cultural imbalance. The nineteenth century is rich in histories of spirits as they move from a religious to secular realm. William James characterised his approach to psychical research as a state of uncertainty. This state of uncertainty was emblematic of spirit forms and beliefs and the ways people engaged with them. The multiple meaning of spirit forms and new technologies was incorporated into the construction of live performances in public séances, magic acts and variety shows where things were not quite what they appeared to be. In this way, the production and reception of ghost shows, spirit photographs, trick ghost films, and theatrical illusions during the nineteenth century illuminates the selling of an ambiguous cultural experience to mass audiences. The ambiguity established during this historical juncture is one that continued throughout the twentieth century and is a central feature of paranormal media today.

Paranormal as lifestyle

The paranormal is part of mainstream contemporary culture. Paranormal drama, reality TV, film, photography and the web, magazines, books, tourism and health and well being, are no longer at the outer limits of the media. The move from the margins to mainstream is connected to a rise in paranormal beliefs, where polls around the world indicate 50 per cent of the global population believe in at least one paranormal phenomenon, such as extrasensory experiences, hauntings, or witchcraft. The paranormal covers a wide range of eclectic beliefs and practices that are associated with the scientifically inexplicable. Entertainment, leisure and tourism industries have turned paranormal beliefs into revenue streams. The porous meaning of paranormal beliefs renders it a rich resource for varied products, representations and experiences. Many of these examples draw on familiar spirit forms of the past, re-imagined in contemporary settings. Donald Sassoon's (2006) history of popular culture indicates recurring themes, in particular the selling of a cultural experience, a desire to see the unique, and a fascination with the living and the dead. A new development is that of the paranormal as lifestyle practices, where beliefs are transformed into personal empowerment and ways of living before and after death. As the paranormal goes mainstream it begins to change meaning, blurring boundaries between what is ordinary and extra-ordinary, what are beliefs and lifestyles, in popular culture.

Disquieting experiences

In Patrick McGrath's *Ghost Town*, set in the past and present of New York City, he explores 'disquieting experiences' – unsettling and inexplicable moments associated with death and the terror of death. People's experiences of the para-normal can be disquieting. There is a physical intensity which is crucial to cultural experiences, for example going on a ghost hunt can make you jump or scream. There is an emotional intensity, for example when someone recently bereaved visits a medium in the hope of messages from a relative or loved one. Common feelings of coldness, dark spaces and strange energies are part of these experiences. Psychological dimensions include issues of fear and trauma, the power of the imagination, self-deception, sympathy and empathy, all of which shape an experience. Historical dimensions include personal and family history, social injustice, haunted spaces where history and memory become intertwined in unsettling forms. There is a social dimension where performance and participation are part of a collective experience, for example a live public demonstration with a medium. Disquieting experiences can engender new perspectives on the self and the social. They can also be about the moment and offer few insights beyond that of the experience itself.

The centrality of ambiguity

'The Shawl' by David Mamet is a play about psychic fraud. Within a game of deception, a medium and client test the boundaries of spirit beliefs. The drama transports an audience through a revolving door of scepticism and belief. You never really know what is happening within the performance of the paranormal.

Watching and interacting with reality ghost hunting TV offers ambiguous perspectives. There is a high degree of scepticism in such staged realities as televised ghost hunts, and at the same time the shows open doors to the possibility of the paranormal. *Most Haunted* is a good example of a factual entertainment programme where the audience is an armchair ghost hunter. Audiences are transported through a revolving door of scepticism in paranormal claims and mediated realities, and at the same time consider the possibility of belief in spiritism, mediums and hauntings. One woman described her experience of watching the show as 'waiting for a haunting to happen.' Ghost hunting TV offers audiences a space within which to explore paranormal beliefs in a performative environment. These shows induce a state of uncertainty where the spaces in between scepticism and belief are explored. As such, the media is a resource for identity work and a playful experimentation with paranormal beliefs.

Sensory journeys

Within tourism, ghost hunting offers unique cultural experiences. All night events in haunted historical locations include individual and group investigations into alleged paranormal phenomena. They combine interests in the paranormal with history, memory and emotions. Most of what goes on in a ghost hunt is not paranormal. However, many participants hope for an extraordinary experience. There is great personal investment in paranormal phenomena because for most participants seeing is believing. Going on a ghost hunt is a sensory journey. Although it is about the dead, the experience makes people feel very much alive. Hearts beat faster, senses are heightened, there is intense emotional and social bonding. The sensory journeys on a ghost hunt are an example of what Raymond Williams (1977) described as a structure of feeling, where within an organised event participants create and re-create personal and social experiences. People develop what Avery Gordon calls a sensuous knowledge in the visible and invisible in social relations. The cultural practices of a ghost hunting event show some of the ways people produce beliefs in something that exists beyond their immediate reality.

Experiences

The novelist Kate Atkinson (2008: 343–44) wrote 'just because you were a rational and sceptical atheist didn't mean that you didn't have to get through everyday the best way you could. There were no rules.' In popular culture, the paranormal opens doors for people who explore a range of identity experiences. These experiences connect with what has been called a culture of re-enchantment, where reason and emotion work together in a complex interplay of thinking and feeling. Strategies for re-enchantment are based on a sense of ambiguity in modern life. Such strategies include being distrustful of paranormal claims and at the same time searching for paranormal experiences. When people narrate their own experiences of hauntings, or extrasensory perception, they show a pragmatism to notions of truth and trust in the authenticity of paranormal phenomena. This pragmatic approach foregrounds the individual as the means by which to judge the truth of human experience. Trends in mind, body and spirit, or alternative health and well being, are examples of markets springing to action. These markets draw on a mix of paranormal beliefs, alternative politics and spiritual thinking, and the psychology of self-empowerment. This is an example of the selling of ambiguous cultural experiences to people who do not want to follow rules.

Psychological entertainment

In magic, a dual reality trick is a type of illusion where an audience sees a partial explanation for the method behind the effect. The psychology of magic plays on the way an audience thinks, anticipating their thoughts, feelings and actions and incorporating these into the magic act itself. The magician Derren Brown is a performer who specialises in the appearance of psychic abilities, such as mind reading. His magic is a mix of showmanship, psychology and conjuring. For his audience, Brown symbolises what one person described as 'beyond the concept of magic.' He anticipates the way an audience thinks about popular psychology, using it as a basis for conjuring and a source of misdirection. An audience with Derren Brown responds to their own understandings and misunderstandings about psychology and magic, such as the power of the mind, or cognitive traps. Audiences construct partial explanations based on what they think they know. These cultural practices highlight the myth of psychology as all powerful. Popular psychology is both a rational explanation for human behaviour and the mysteries of the mind. Such a myth is connected to the dominance of self-help, self-empowerment and the imaginary of the human potential in popular culture.

The audience is the show

To understand the paranormal as it is experienced within popular culture involves seeing an audience not as spectators, or viewers, but as participants in the process of entertainment and communication. People co-perform and co-produce their experiences. An audience with a medium or magician is a creative force. They work closely with their audience, anticipating responses, showcasing skills, leading a collective performance. There is a historical resonance to the audience as show, with examples from early opera, or nineteenth-century theatre. In contemporary media environments, the audience as show is most visible in live events, such as magical entertainment, medium demonstrations, tele-evangelism or political rallies. In other ways, participation and the power of a live collective experience is a part of reality talent shows or web environments. The audience as show highlights how production and performance practices can create and shape cultural experiences.

Reflections on these findings suggest three narrative threads. The first is the notion that culture is ordinary and extraordinary. Drawing on Raymond William's original statement that culture is ordinary, this is a call to media and cultural studies to extend research on common experiences and everyday life to encompass the extraordinary. Paddy Scannell (2007) has noted the culture of everyday life has been a dominant story in the narrative of media and communication as disciplines of academic study. It is time to expand this narrative. In *Varieties of Anomalous Experiences* (Cardeña et al 2000) the editors present a contemporary account of psychological research in uncommon experiences, such as extrasensory perception. The title of the book refers to William James and his early research on religion and psychology. When writing *From Angels to Aliens*, Lynn Schofield Clark (2003) comments on the importance of uncommon experiences in research on media and religion. There are few examples in media and cultural studies that extend the range of outlooks beyond that of the every day. We are missing a vital part of the human condition in focusing only on culture as ordinary. Warner's research on phantasmagoria suggests spirit forms are intrinsic to culture; indeed they are so common these forms have become invisible. Durham Peters notes 'the concept of communication was developed in a culture that routinely sought communication with the dead' (1999: 147). He wonders if our modern sensibility to death and dying 'bespeaks a disturbance in that most crucial of all relationships, our relation to the dead.' The concept of communication continues to be developed in spirit forms, and paranormal beliefs and practices, which are a direct response to our relationship with mortality. The paranormal turn in popular culture provides ample evidence of our fascination with death, other entities, and alternative realities.

When Avery Gordon (1997) wrote hauntings were a part of social life she made an intervention in sociology to study ghosts. She argued ghosts mattered in making the invisible visible, in providing a sensuous knowledge that enriched a sociological imagination. The statement culture is ordinary and extraordinary is an attempt to respond to her ghostly call to arms. From a different perspective, the research here offers an understanding of paranormal matters as lived experiences. The relevance of Raymond Williams' idea of a structure of feeling to ghostly matters is also a feature of the paranormal. For Gordon 'a structure of feeling gives notice to the necessarily social nature of what we call the subjective; it gives notice to the texture and skin of the *this, here, now, alive, active* contemporaneity of our lives' (199). This research has focused on the here and now of cultural practices which are ordinary and extraordinary, objective and subjective. This is an alive and active audience processing feelings in such a powerful way they produce beliefs. The knowledge that most paranormal experiences in popular culture are probably normal doesn't lessen the power of these experiences. It only serves to show how 'popular culture matters' (Stuart Hall 1981) in the ways we engage with it.

The second narrative to emerge from this research is the idea of the audience is the show. It is one that dominates the book through a series of case studies that culminate in an understanding of paranormal cultural practices in an entertainment environment. Armchair ghost hunters, psychic tourists, mind, body and spirit practices, psychological entertainment are all examples of how people participate in paranormal matters. These are case studies which show the irreducible complexity of cultural forms and our engagement with them (Robert C Allen 1991). Each of these examples suggests in different ways people produce beliefs. For example, people produce beliefs through the centrality of ambiguity in paranormal forms, where an absence of evidence becomes filled with multiple meanings. The sensory journeys people take on ghost hunting events create disquieting experiences which are interpreted as paranormal encounters. The ways people manage matters of authenticity in personal accounts of hauntings indicate how experience is evidence of paranormal phenomena and truth is subjective. In magical entertainment, the myth of the power of psychology gives people an opportunity to play with their minds and toy with rational explanations and things which are beyond explanation. People are drawing on their own skills to create collective cultural experiences.

The audience as show is an idea inspired by Robert C Allen's history of movie going in North Carolina 'Going to the Show' (2008). His research highlights the sociality and spatiality of movie going and raises issues about the study of cinema as both text and social and cultural experience. Similarly, this research on the paranormal within popular culture involves seeing an audience not only as spectators or viewers of a text or genre, but also as participants in the shaping of entertainment and communication. This popular cultural ethnography asks what is a paranormal or magical experience? The answers to these questions lead to a neglected area in audience research. Novel cultural formations such as paranormal or magic entertainment go beyond the immediate reality of text or artefact to a more collective self-conscious engagement with varieties of experiences.

The third narrative thread is that of transformation. In Joke Hermes' (2005) discussion of popular culture she draws on the process of working through in psychoanalysis to consider cultural practices as ongoing communal relations. Previous research on audiences of news, documentary and reality TV saw a similar idea of working through as discussed by John Ellis and Hermes connected to double modes of engagement where audiences watched television and reflected on their experience in the process (Hill 2007). In the idea of the audience is the show people transform their sensory, emotional, and psychological engagement with cultural forms into beliefs that are part of ongoing personal and communal relations. For example, there is a personal transition from fears of death to life affirmative messages of the existence of spirits. Narratives of the self and identity as individual and rooted in one reality are transformed through performance practices into ideas of other entities and multiple realities. There are social transitions where discourses of science and Western medicine are transformed into alternative thinking on metaphysics and health and well being. Within popular culture, people perform and play with their fears and anxieties of death and dying, of uncontrollable events, of phenomena that make no sense. What sometimes happens when people perform these acts is they can produce beliefs.

The narrative threads of culture are as ordinary and extraordinary, the audience is the show, and transformation helps us to understand how people encounter the paranormal and magic in popular culture. The final section of this book reflects on why people produce beliefs in this recreational environment. The sociological and cultural argument presented here is rooted in the historical context that since the mid 1800s, if not earlier in time, major changes in ways we think about and process death and dying have led to transitions in how we engage with human experience. The rise of popular culture in the mid nineteenth century highlights the opportunism of cultural industries that respond to these developments in fascination with death and unique experiences. Contemporary cultural engagement with the paranormal and magical entertainment suggests negotiating awareness and fear of death is a dynamic that works alongside varieties of identity experiences in modern life.

Multiple explanations

The porous meaning of the paranormal as 'things you can't explain' makes it a rich subject with many lines of enquiry. Two related enquiries into fear of death and feeling alive explore the whole lives of people. This approach draws on overlapping areas of interest in historical accounts of the paranormal and magic as connected to social and cultural transitions, psychological reasons based on cognitive and affective dynamics, sociological and literary enquiries in re-enchantment and imagination, and media research in producers and audiences.

Fear of death

'Trying to explore all possibilities.'

The social and historical contexts within which cultural practices take place help to explain why the paranormal is so visible now. Joanna Bourke in *Fear: A Cultural History* characterises the twentieth century as an age of anxiety. Fear of the unknown, invisible risks, faceless threats, make an anxious society. She notes in the research for her book 'people everywhere seemed very apprehensive' (2005: ix). We have become a trauma society where fears are ubiquitous:

> Death and disaster; nightmares and phobias; new killing techniques and dangerous technologies; treacherous bodies – a seemingly endless range of terrifying trials and tribulations seemed to face people of the twentieth century. Worse: there were times when all of history seemed to be reciting a traumatic script, devoid of answers or 'sense'.
>
> (ibid)

This age of anxiety is one characterised by seemingly contradictory events: advances in health and increased life expectancy, and at the same time anxieties about ageing and dying alone; an increase in religious beliefs and metaphysical thinking and also an era of violence and trauma of war and terrorism; a digital age where scientists have mapped the DNA of the human body and yet trust in scientists and scientific literacy is at an all time low. Social theories of risk have considered how perception of environmental or health risks and the way we manage our anxieties is part of modern life (see Krimsky and Golding 1992 amongst others)

Warner writes 'the return of religious thinking – and intense conflict – has been one of the strongest surprises of the twenty-first century' (2006: 337). Different ways of understanding the impact of 9/11 and the 'war on terror' draw on connections between historical contexts, psychological responses, and media environments. Michael Burleigh in *Sacred Causes* (2006) argues religion has had an enormous influence on twentieth-century politics and conflict. The terrorist attacks in America on the eleventh of September 2001 are described by Burleigh as 'the day that changed the world' (2006: 450). 9/11, and also subsequent attacks in Bali, Madrid and London, brought about a 'clash of civilisations', where the threat of Islamic terrorists 'has provoked a Western crisis of identity' (2006: 468). The wars in Afghanistan and Iraq have divided people and challenged political and religious thinking. For Bourke, 9/11 was a frightening example of how fear and anxiety become part of state policies and a rationale for war. The impact of the terrorist attacks in America on 9/11 created a 'psychic wound' where religious languages were used alongside psychological ones in terror management (2005: ix).

It is within this context that polls indicate worldwide around 50 per cent of people believe in some form of the paranormal (Wiseman and Watt 2009). The World Values survey also reports an increase in belief in life after death – 81 per cent of Americans and 58 per cent of British people believe in an afterlife.[2] Irwin claims paranormal beliefs act as a 'buffer against anxiety that may be evoked by an awareness of human vulnerability and ultimate mortality' (2009: 106). He explains the value of paranormal beliefs as coping strategies:

> In contemporary Western society it is generally unacceptable to look like a passive fatalist and thus there is an implicit expectation that people should do something about the situations in which they find themselves, even if influence over such situations is not within one's capacity.
>
> (114)

In psychological terms, there is a behavioural consequence to paranormal beliefs. When something happens that provides evidence of the 'uncontrollability of the world' beliefs act as 'reassurance that a degree of control might still be possible, even if only at an intellectual or illusory level' (115). It is a basic human need that drives interpretations of anomalous events and experiences as paranormal in nature (ibid). Irwin calls this an adaptive response where paranormal beliefs attenuate a state of anxiety (122). Other psychological studies support the idea that 'an assurance of order and meaning in the physical and social world is essential for emotional security and psychological adjustment' (115). Fears and anxieties about risks, violence, tragedies and personal trauma are relocated to alternative explanations in a paranormal world.

One participant explained their personal experience on the day of the terrorist attacks in London in 2005:

> The day of July 7th bombings I was supposed to be meeting in Russell Square that day, but I happened to be half an hour late which meant I didn't get on the tube because the tube was already shut down. You could argue that was absolutely coincidence, complete coincidence, but my personal feeling is that wasn't meant to happen to me and I think that was something called destiny, or something … I have never had any religious beliefs. I was brought up to believe what you believe. I've never had any experiences before or since then, but I just feel like, in that context, that one time, rather than putting a logical explanation to it, actually there is more to it … One thing is for me to have a solid experience to convince me anything paranormal is going on. It has to happen to me. Yes, I believe you have to have your own experiences.
>
> (25-year-old female human relations trainer)

This is an example of an interpretation of an anomalous event as paranormal in nature. The question of whether this interpretation is right or wrong is not the issue. The point is to listen to the telling of the experience and try to understand how it is meaningful for this person in their management of terror. It's 'a solid experience' of something beyond 'logical explanation' and contains rational and emotional interpretations of the experience as evidence of 'something called destiny.'

The social process of dying, developments in modern medicine, fear of death are some of the reasons there may be an increase in paranormal beliefs. People live longer in Western societies. Modern healthcare means we can be treated for many illnesses that would have been life threatening in the past. As we get older there are various medical procedures for extending life, even when our heart or lungs have given up and we can no longer breathe. The old fashioned way of pronouncing death by looking for signs of breath had to be revised in line with modern medicine. Today the sign of mortality is brain death (Bourke 2005). In Britain, we can expect to live until we are around 80 years old, seven years more than if we were living in the 1970s (Social Trends 2008). If life expectancy rates are increasing, so too is our anxiety about what is going to happen to us at the point of death. In the nineteenth century fear of death was primarily associated with uncertainty surrounding someone's societal and everlasting status. This changed in the late twentieth century:

> death anxieties were firmly located in bodily experiences. The explosion in anti-aging creams, exercise regimes and cosmetic surgery was a response to

fear of dying. Once at death's portal pain was the dreaded encounter that had to be avoided through the application of increasingly powerful analgesics.

(Bourke 2005: 320)

The focus on 'quality of life' at the point of death has become a topic of medical and moral debate. The 'border between life and death remains unfixed' (50).

Death and dying used to be something that families and communities helped to manage, staying with the dying, listening and talking with each other, performing religious and secular rituals that helped a dying person pass on to the afterlife. In the Victorian period around 70 per cent of British people could expect to die at home with family or friends. In the twenty-first century the reverse is the case – around 70 per cent of people can expect to be in institutions or alone when they die (Bourke 2005). Kellehear in *A Social History of Dying* argues 'the experience of dying has gradually become more private at the same time as its recognition has become more publicly controlled and defined' (2007: 251). Indeed, dying is so privatised that 'the dying person might be the only one aware that he or she is dying' (ibid). This shift from well-managed dying in familiar and personal environments to privatised and institutionalised death severs society from the 'biological, psychological and interpersonal moorings' so important to the process of dying (ibid). Kellehear argues modern society has created a shameful death, where dying people are locked away, silenced and ignored.

One person commented on the border crossings between life and death:

> If I'm really, really upset I can smell my nana. My children and other people can say 'what's that smell?' 'Oh, it's nana, she used to wear that perfume.' I've felt my mum and I know it's her. When my mum died, my son was very close to her and he was waiting at the front door for me, because I had just left her at the hospital to go home and sleep. I got to the door step and I knew, as soon as I got there, I could see my mum. 'What are you doing here'? She had just passed. My son said, 'nanny says she is OK now.' All my children were upset when my mum died. But you are born to die, why worry about it.
>
> (45-year-old female care worker)

Great grandmother, grandmother and mother continued caring for the family by strengthening connections during the death and dying process. These communication acts involve sensory, physical, psychological and social relations.

Bourke points out the less we know about death the more we fear it. As the power of 'exhortations to fear God's omnipresence and omnipotence waned, along with terror of hellfire … what replaced it was no less terrifying. A fear of nothingness replaced the fear of God's judgement' (2005: 49). Fear of the unknown is one of the most dominant fears of the twentieth century.

Julian Barnes reflects on death in *Nothing to Be Frightened Of* (2008). He cites
Jules Renard: 'the word that is most true, most exact, most filled with meaning,
is the word "nothing"' (100). He asks 'how can you be frightened of nothing?'
He places himself in a group of people who fear death:

> Perhaps the important divide is less between the religious and the irrelig-
> ious as between those who fear death and those who don't. We fall thereby
> into four categories, and it's clear which two regard themselves as superior:
> those who do not fear death because they have faith, and those who do
> not fear death despite having no faith. These groups take the high moral
> ground. In third place come those who, despite having faith, cannot rid
> themselves of the old, visceral, rational fear. And then, out of the medals,
> below the salt, up shit creek, come those of us who fear death and have
> no faith.'
>
> (61)

For Barnes 'death is the one appalling fact which defines life; unless
you are constantly aware of it, you cannot begin to understand what life is
about' (126).

One means of understanding life and death is in the personal narratives created
by people. Barnes is suspicious of such stories:

> So, if, as we approach death and look back on our lives, we 'understand our
> narrative' and stamp a final meaning upon it, I suspect we are doing little
> more than confabulating: processing strange, incomprehensible, contra-
> dictory input into some kind, any kind, of believable story – but believable
> mainly to ourselves.
>
> (2008: 189)

And yet, when life and death narratives are performed by people these are no less
meaningful because they are believable mainly to themselves. It suggests narratives of death and dying are about social relations with the living. One woman
spoke of her experience:

> My husband died very suddenly. I was very shattered, hopeless at that time.
> And I found lots of things I was looking for ... I found his christening
> certificate and it was very strange because his certificate was the date of the
> same day he died ... I felt sort of something. I thought him tapping on the
> shoulder telling me where to look ... I had very strong dreams sometimes.
> He was in very nice place. I said 'this is nice, are we going to be here? Are
> we on holiday?' And he said, 'no.' The dream vanished. And he looked
> young and very good. I think that what happened, after someone has died
> they have a sort of period when they are saying goodbye.
>
> (74-year-old retired female)

This narrative highlights what Zelizer (2005) calls 'webs of social relations' where people's 'sense of themselves intertwines closely with the meanings of their relationships to others' (306). The author Justine Picardie wrote in *If the Spirit Moves You* (2001: 167) about a moment when she felt her dead sister's presence. It made her feel close to her family during an intense period of loss: 'we have survived. We are getting there. (Where? It doesn't matter. All that matters is that we are still going.)'

Richard Woolfe, the former producer of *Most Haunted* and Channel Controller of Living, explained:

> September 11th attacks, that moment made people realise there are people who have turned away from religion, and what people are looking for are answers. I think people are individually looking for answers and that is why some people find comfort in the paranormal and mediumship, and that is why there is interest in this area. Maybe in some ways, for some people, it has taken the place of organised religion. It has become more mainstream because of a groundswell of people getting involved. I don't know if mediumship can answer that. I do know that I have seen thousands of people at *Most Haunted* and other shows, and as someone who is an open minded sceptic and has seen how suggestion might be used, I have also seen, time after time after time, mediums and psychics pull something out of the hat and gobsmack me and the audience.[3]

This is an example of a structure of feeling, where the fixity and flow of paranormal matters is a part of a process of social experience. Williams described a structure of feeling as 'affective elements of consciousness and relationships: not feeling against thought, but thought as felt and feeling as thought' (1977: 132). Cultural practices, such as watching *Most Haunted*, going to live ghost hunting events, recording evidence of alleged hauntings on the web, are part of a structure of feeling in the way people respond to human vulnerability and mortality at this historical juncture. These practices create disquieting experiences. They are about being in the moment and then reflecting on your perspective of the world, processing your own sense of mortality.

People who engage with the paranormal in popular culture do so primarily to explore for themselves the answers to questions of mortality. 'Now people question, they research, and look at different sources, they don't just take it, they look it up and make their decisions' (19-year-old male student). Professionals are consulted along the way, understood and misunderstood, listened to and ignored, but the key is personal experience. This leads to the second line of enquiry – that of cultural engagement through feeling. In working through awareness and fear of death people can come full circle in their sense of self and human experience. As one person said 'personal experience is the best thing' (26-year-old advertising standards officer). The final section of the book explores why experience is centre stage.

Feeling alive

'You have to be willing to experience something.'

The idea of audience as show can fit within a model of theatre in the round. It gives the audience an all-encompassing perspective on the performers and action taking place on stage. Such a perspective frames an audience as attentive listeners or spectators of a performance which is produced by professionals, or occasionally amateurs, for their appreciation and criticism. There are many examples in popular culture where this is the perspective of the audience. For example, watching 'The Shawl' by David Mamet involves a theatrical audience listening, watching and feeling the drama during the performance. They are participating in live theatre by being the attentive audience of a show. If they are seated in the round they may, or may not, feel more involved in the drama depending on how the play has been staged and performed with this intended outcome in mind.

In this example, audiences are not on stage themselves. This could mean they are not really participating at all, only partially involved through a distanced perspective of seating arrangements, and controlled by the accepted spaces where they can talk, such as the bar at interval. Zigmunt Bauman (2000) used this perspective of a distanced audience in his notion of 'cloakroom communities' to explain the limits of collectivity within the media. He perceived audiences silently watching media spectacles who may be seated together but ultimately remain alone. Such a sad view of audiences raises the question why would people go to theatre to begin with? Cloakroom communities suggests audiences do so because they are mistaken in believing in the illusion of togetherness that theatre promises. But, as producers and stage designers know, an awareness of the sociality and spatiality of theatre is crucial. There are performers on stage, but audiences are also performing in their own way. When people watch 'The Shawl' the writer, producer, designer, stage manager and actors know their audience is performing through the way they look, listen, think and feel. Indeed, these professionals are partly directing the audience in their performative acts through inviting them to participate in the imagination of the writer, the set designer, or the actors in carefully managed ways. 'The Shawl' is a cultural experience that works best if the audience throws themselves into the drama, figuratively speaking. It works even better when they do this together as a collective, attentive audience. Watching alone may give you some enjoyment, but being part of an audience is a lot more fun.

There are examples in popular culture where audiences not only participate in a show through their attentiveness and imaginative and emotional involvement. In this research an audience with a medium or magician are literally watching and listening to the show and also on stage as well. With a magician, this is most clearly seen when a member of the audience gets up on stage to participate in a theatrical illusion. That person on stage is performing alongside the main audience. Indeed, there are theatrical illusions where the members of the public on stage are used as a ploy to increase and manage the attention of the main audience. In such a case, the performative acts of an audience take on complex dimensions on and off stage. With a medium, this is most clearly seen when the professional reminds the audience at the start of the demonstration that they need to focus and open themselves to the live experience. Sometimes a member of the audience takes the stage, but more often the medium calls out to the crowd and someone responds, making themselves the centre of attention for the medium and everyone else. A vital difference between these two examples is that if a conjuring trick fails the magician may be booed by their audience because they perform within a frame of magic as illusion. A medium can fail to produce messages and still be applauded because they perform within a frame of spiritism as paranormal belief. What is similar though is the high degree of participation by an audience in these live performances that play with ambiguity and multiple realities.

The metaphor of a conductor and orchestra captures the creativity at work by an audience when they are participating in a live cultural experience where they are centre stage. People experience high levels of sensitivity, sympathy, empathy, reflecting back in a synchrony of responses the feelings of themselves as themselves. There are professionals who help to shape these experiences; these are entertainers and magicians, mediums and psychics who conduct an audience as an orchestra. Each member of the orchestra brings talent, skills and interpretation to the way they play their instruments, each musician plays their part in a collective performance, and in turn the orchestra plays with the conductor who leads the performance overall. Communication between the conductor and orchestra is crucial. Each needs the other to make a performance work.

There is a repertoire of performance and management skills in the professional entertainer as conductor. For example, in the case of a medium they conduct their audience in performing and producing paranormal beliefs. Their audience does not start out as believers, so this is an audience who play their sceptical parts early on in the performance, as the medium expects and directs them to do. Later in the live demonstration, if all goes well, the audience play other parts of themselves that believe, or hope to believe, in spirit communication. This collective performance does not work in a vacuum. The medium draws on the cultural practices of their audience, and in turn audiences draw on their expectations, knowledge, and emotional investment in the medium and how they will work with their audience. When one woman said 'there are many dodgy mediums' (56-year-old female care worker), she is not alone in thinking this way. Mediums begin with the assumption the majority of their audience are distrustful of their claims to be genuine. Discursive analysis of the communicative acts between psychics and sitters reveals just how closely a professional works with people's expectations of dodgy mediums by carefully negotiating matters of authenticity and expertise. Thus, a medium uses their own profession as a resource in the performance of paranormal beliefs.

There is a repertoire of responses in the audience as orchestra. There are emotional responses. These are instinctive feelings of shock, fear, apprehension, sadness, relief, laughter, happiness. Emotions are primary to the way audiences play themselves. One woman recounted a strange experience:

> I had an overwhelming feeling that I had a car accident … it wasn't really bad, but nevertheless it was my first car accident. But I knew it before I left home. I knew I was going to have car accident.
>
> (41-year-old female dancer and choreographer)

There is a collective awareness of instinctive feelings as significant to unusual experiences. Another woman said:

> My mum is big on feeling. One time, it sticks in my mind it was quite big, my mum came down one morning and she had a dream about her sister. Her sister's been crying in her dream. She says 'I should ring her, I should ring her, I should ring her.' And I thought, go on then, ring her. She tried to kill herself and was in hospital. That was horrible.
>
> (39-year-old female research consultant)

'Big on feeling' sums up one of the major parts of an audience's repertoire of performative acts.

Closely related to emotions, the five senses of sight, touch, hearing, taste and smell come into relief in live participatory environments. Popular accounts of a sixth, or even seventh, sense in stories of the paranormal or in guides by mind, body and spirit practitioners indicate just how significant the senses are to engagement through feeling. A participant on a ghost hunting event recounted:

> It was the eeriest thing in there … we saw a kind of shadow in a mirror that we could see, a dark shadow coming out and going back in, coming out and going back in. She had her hair pulled, I had a push [demonstrates] like that. It felt like they were leaning on my back. And then two minutes later I felt like I couldn't lift my neck, like someone was holding my hair. I kept seeing things moving down the passage. I think something was a little too scared to come out. But something was definitely in that room, definitely something in there.

This is a good example of a disquieting experience. Something scary is happening which is located in the push and pull of the physical environment and the participant's sensory engagement with that space. Whether their interpretations are right or wrong, they are engaging with an eerie atmosphere through their feelings and emotions. Participants on a ghost hunting event know, expect and are paying for this experience where they are centre stage. Why they are on a ghost hunt may be to do with bereavement, or curiosity with ghosts, but it is also because this is a unique opportunity to bump up against themselves. Another participant explained: 'I was thinking "I can't see anything, nothing can harm me, I am OK." I was scared, very scared. I think if the table would have moved I would have gone ooohhh [intake of breath], "this is too much."'

These performative acts are part of a dynamic process that can, although not always, lead to perspectives of the self, ways of living, and beliefs. For one person their unusual experience led to self-knowledge:

> I was aware that something was in the room, pressing me, pressing down on me, and I couldn't move. I had to focus my mind, at least blink, twitch a little toe or something like that. It only lasted seconds, but seemed to last forever ... It makes you feel terrified ... I had those experiences, off and on, for many, many years. The first time, when I was a child, it was not something I knew about or heard about from anybody else ... As I got older, I became able to make sense of it all ... then you can move on, not be scared. You know what the experiences are going to be and know you can get out of it.
>
> (43-year-old female teaching assistant)

Such a disquieting experience became less terrifying the more perspective this woman gained through her cognitive engagement. It has impacted on her sense of self and influenced her paranormal beliefs.

Feelings and experiences come together in performative acts that can produce beliefs. There are elements of cultural engagement that are hard to define. It is that idea of a soul which is often referred to in a more modern way as the self. This woman commented:

> I felt something in church. I wasn't able to explain it and I thought OK maybe it just sort of happened once, whatever, and I went back again. I had the same feeling there is something more, beyond ... I tried to work out why it's happening, because of the music or singing, but I've been with other people and they felt sort of same thing. Sometimes, I had déjà vu and I know it's déjà vu. I have seen something before and I can remember what happens next. Things like that keep me a bit open.
>
> (26-year-old female receptionist)

There is 'something more' to her sense of self than can only partially be explained by the environment, or emotions and sensations, and so she extends her repertoire, keeping herself open to that which is beyond rational explanation. Another person reflected:

> I just believe there is something there. I am not religious at all. So I don't believe anything like that ... but there are some things you can't really explain. I said I don't believe in anything, I don't mean I don't believe there is nothing there.
>
> (21-year-old male student)

The eclecticism of paranormal beliefs lends itself to a wide-ranging repertoire that pushes people 'beyond ... ' into an ambiguous realm.

Why people believe in paranormal interpretations of unusual identity experiences is a matter debated endlessly by people themselves. This psychological engagement is part of their repertoire of responses. There are people who practise a popular form of solipsism where experience is everything: 'you want to look for something to explain something, but sometimes there isn't anything. What about this? What about that? How do you explain that? And we don't' (49-year-old female teacher). There are people who struggle to make sense of the scientifically inexplicable: 'if you have a paranormal experience, you try to rationalise it. You should be able to and, sometimes, you can't. You don't know whether that's because it can't be rationalised or because you don't have the vocabulary or concepts for it' (25-year-old female teacher). And there are those who take positions on a wide spectrum of scepticism and belief in the paranormal: 'it comes down to how people choose to believe, some people believe through religion, some people try to prove through science, some people ignore it' (32-year-old female accountant).

Hilary Mantel comments 'a group of people praying together, or telling each other ghost stories, are engaged in an emotional bonding exercise of considerable social utility' (2006: 1). Participation in paranormal cultural practices is a social process. One person explained:

> Something may happen to one person and can be interpreted as presence and soul and existence, but interpreted completely differently by somebody else. There isn't the same meaning. So, for me it's all about the representation of our minds, how we represent ourselves to the world.
>
> (39-year-old female research consultant)

The collective experience of producing paranormal beliefs helps people to see themselves and society in action. The idea of collective effervescence in Émile Durkheim's (1912, 2001) study *The Elementary Forms of Religious Life* can be helpful. Durkheim argued 'beliefs work only when they are shared' (320). Religious practices and beliefs are a process by which society experiences itself as itself (xx). He wrote 'society can exist only in individual minds and through them, it must penetrate and become organized inside us; it can become an integral part of our being, and in so doing it elevates and enlarges us' (157).

In *The Re-Enchantment of the World* there are examples taken from philosophy, nineteenth-century magic and spiritualism, and contemporary sporting events, as evidence of secular and conscious strategies for re-enchantment (Landy and Saler 2009). Enchantment refers to a sense of wonder whilst disenchantment refers to rational and scientific explanations. Traditionally it has been common to separate the two in theories of modernity. There is now an 'emergent view that modernity is as enchanted as it is disenchanted' (Saler 2006: 692). Saler (2006: 713) explains 'mass culture is not simply an irrational form of escapism from the rational responsibilities of adulthood' as early theories of modernity expressed by Max Weber and others suggested; nor is mass culture 'a dangerous threat to critical thought' as argued by later critics such as Adorno and Horkheimer. Rather, Saler claims 'disenchanted reason coexists with an enchanted imagination; wonders have become interiorized and are enjoyed with a certain ironic distance.' Re-enchantment therefore includes 'distinctly modern forms of enchantment compatible with modern rationality, secularism, psychologism, and commercial culture' (ibid).

The role of imagination is significant to modern enchantments. Simon During argues in a historical analysis of secular magic that imagination and illusion are part of modern society and its image of itself (2002). Saler suggests strategies for modern enchantment include ironic detachment. For example, when audiences watch magical entertainment they know that the magician knows that they know there is no such thing as magic. Such an understanding of modern enchantments as both about reason and imagination refer to the romantic view of a suspension of disbelief. But, an audience with a magician does not temporarily switch off their scepticism as is implied by a suspension of disbelief.[4] Nor does a magician mesmerise their audience, tricking them into a momentary and false belief in magic, as is implied by critiques of cultural industries. Magical entertainment is based on a complex understanding of the cultural practices of an audience. A relationship exists between the professional magician and their audience where they do not deceive but rather directly invite an audience to play their part. A magician and audience are in it together, collectively shaping a sense of wonder that is the defining feature of magical entertainment.

A sociology of religion or modern enchantments helps in understanding the paranormal turn in popular culture. People's collective acts, their secular strategies, engender experiences which are powerful in the ways people produce beliefs in Western societies. And yet the idea of the audience is the show is not so much about religion and society as about recreation and culture. Perhaps then people take pleasure from their cultural practices showcased in public. There is a rational explanation for the feeling of performing as an orchestra with skills, talent, choice of music and relationship with a conductor. There is also a sense of wonder and being moved by the moment. In this way there are modern enchantments where people perform secular and alternative spiritual and magical beliefs in spaces specially designed for the occasion.

The power dynamics of the audience as show indicates people draw from their repertoire of responses when they are given the opportunity to do so by others. This is not the solitary performer playing alone. Nor is it the professional as puppet master. Rather it is the kind of relationship where professionals and audiences acknowledge the role of the other in shaping a cultural experience. There are positives and negatives to this relationship. As we have seen, entire professions have developed within the psychic industry, theatrical magic, tourism and health and well being, which directly address paranormal beliefs. The regulation of these industries, consumer rights, and professional codes of conduct are areas of tension with a set of unresolved problems to do with the unequal power dynamics between industries and audiences. The case studies in this book have highlighted the tensions in the way a market arises to turn paranormal beliefs into revenue streams. There are examples of audiences worried about the exploitation of themselves and others in their paranormal beliefs, a sure sign these tensions are common knowledge. And yet for all these problems in the unequal power dynamics between industries and audiences, the people in this study are queuing up to be part of the show. Professional magicians or mediums understand the cultural practices of their audience before they begin to produce entertainment and communication. It is this way of thinking that has been absent from much research on popular culture. This person said: 'If there are ghosts, that's amazing. It's incredible to think it. That's an attractive idea, there is something more than we understand in our everyday world' (26-year-old male advertising worker). Professionals in the entertainment and communication industries thrive on this kind of thinking and feeling, finding various ways to capture this excitement and engagement with the idea of the paranormal and turn it into cultural experiences people pay to participate in. As researchers we have dismissed such people as mad, or disillusioned, made them a figure of fun, or ignored them altogether. There is 'something more than we understand in our everyday world' that deserves our attention.

A classical conductor said of their experience of working with an orchestra that together they transported themselves through music to a mystical realm.[5] The participants in this book are players in an orchestral movement about life and death. People perform 'the music of what happens' (Seamus Heaney 'Song' 1979). It is that feeling of being alive you get when performing an ensemble piece. One woman said being part of a ghost hunting team was 'the best thing ever in my whole life. I have been smiling ever since, I am not lying I just love it. I love being part of the team. It sounds corny, but I just love. I love the adrenalin buzz and I like being scared.' Another said: 'we've all got to die. I'd like to tell someone, there is something up there. I'd like to give a message if I could.' (46-year-old female personal assistant). Voices from the greatest show on earth.

Notes

1 My thanks to Peter Lunt for his suggestion of a whole lives approach in discussions of this chapter.
2 World Values Survey 2008, accessed online at www.wordvaluessurvey.org 28 January 2009.
3 Interview with author. Richard Woolfe, Channel controller Five, former controller of Living TV and Sky channels. 1 December 2009.
4 My thanks to Peter Lamont for his views on a suspension of disbelief as an inadequate explanation for magic entertainment.
5 *The Spirit of Music*, *BBC World*, 16 January 2010.

Appendix
Research process

Aims, objectives and general research questions

The study is based on an audience research project conducted by the author and two research assistants, Dr Koko Kondo and Dr Lizzie Jackson. The project included a combination of qualitative research methods. There are 18 focus group interviews with 104 participants (aged 18–65+); and in-depth interviews with 70 participants in 27 households in South East England. Both of these methods allow for semi-structured interviews with a range of people from working to middle class backgrounds who are viewers/users of paranormal media, and related programmes about illusionism, and who held a range of attitudes and beliefs about paranormal phenomena. The project also involved participant observation of ghost hunting events at three selected sites. There were also interviews with a range of experts in the media industry, academic researchers, paranormal professions, and members of psychic and folklore societies, in order to extend contextual knowledge.

The qualitative audience research addressed the following questions:

1 What do adults (aged 18–65+) think about interactive television series such as *Most Haunted*, ghost hunting reality TV and related websites on psychic investigations? What do they think about magic shows such as those by Derren Brown?
2 How do these experiences of contemporary paranormal media and magic connect with attitudes towards other representations of paranormal and extraordinary phenomena?
3 What strategies do participants use to evaluate perceived real and fake paranormal media?
4 What relations are there between attitudes towards these kinds of paranormal media and attitudes towards the paranormal in general?
5 What connections do participants make between paranormal media and the paranormal and psychic industry, such as ghost tourism, or celebrity mediums?

To meet the aims of the project and answer the research questions the following specific objectives were met:

1 A contextualisation of contemporary paranormal media in relation to existing historical and sociological research in phantasmagoria, spirit photography, cinema, theatre, art, and ghosts and folklore in Britain.
2 An overview and critical analysis of the paranormal in popular culture across fiction and non-fiction multiplatform content, and within various popular cultural practices in ghost tourism, celebrity mediums, magic and mentalism, mind, body and spirit publications, in Britain and America.
3 Analysis of selected cultural practices associated with the paranormal in contemporary Western popular culture.
4 Analysis of the relationship between attitudes towards contemporary paranormal media and scepticism and belief in paranormal phenomena.
5 Critical understanding of the role of paranormal media in British society and culture, and social and cultural theories relating to the paranormal and popular cultural practices.

Recruitment and sample

The household in-depth interviews included a sample of 27 households in the South East region. There were 70 people in the sample overall. The breakdown of the sample was as follows. The age range was from 7 to 65 years old, with 20 people aged 7–18 years old, 23 people aged 19–34 years old, and 27 people aged 35–65 years old (one person was 65 and the rest were between 35 and 55). The participants under the age of 18 took part in the in-depth interviews with the permission of their parents; this was not a criterion for the sample, which was to focus on adults aged 18 and over. There were 39 females and 31 males in the sample. Half the sample of households (13) were families with young or teenage children, and the other half (14) were households with couples, friends and flat shares. Nationalities were mainly British (as defined by the participants), with one Jamaican British, American, Australian, South African, and Slovakian, and two people from Italy and two from Zimbabwe in the sample. Occupations ranged from students, teachers, technicians, train drivers, postal workers, nurses, librarians, administrators, chefs, carpenters, counsellors, nannies, soldiers, crane drivers, and people working in the IT, music, fashion and retail industries. Most participants received an annual income in the region of £15–25,000 (24 people), or less than £15,000 (29 people, mostly students, housewives or retired and semi-retired), with 17 people earning more than £25,000 a year.

This sample was part of a broader project on digital media in the home and the researcher Dr Koko Kondo had spent up to two years with these households in a longitudinal ethnographic study. One visit in January to April 2007 was devoted to paranormal media and the type of magic associated with Derren Brown. A series of open questions were designed and piloted, along with clips from

Most Haunted or Derren Brown events. Early on, the interview questions were slightly adjusted along with a range of clips and were shown to work well with a wide range of attitudes and beliefs in the paranormal and representations in popular culture.

The first lesson learned was that the researcher had spent a lot of time with these households over a period of two years observing and participating in their media activities and family dynamics. The issue of their attitudes and beliefs towards the paranormal had not emerged prior to the specific visit for this study. As Santino (1988) has pointed out in his qualitative research of paranormal beliefs amongst airline professionals people carefully chose the context within which to discuss their attitudes and beliefs. These in-depth interviews produced lively data and this would become a hallmark of the research, where individual and focus group interviews would be characterised by passionate, emotional, engaging and animated discussions on the paranormal.

The household interviews showed that many people from a wide range of positions towards the paranormal could be both sceptical and believing at the same time, depending on the context and the type of examples being discussed. An overall theme emerged that people were generally sceptical of representations of the paranormal in popular culture, but more believing of personal experiences and the experiences of family and friends, a finding also supported by other studies in psychology. Research in opinion poll data has indicated education has little impact on attitudes and beliefs in the paranormal (Sjöjin 2002). There was little evidence of education as a factor in different attitudes towards the paranormal in this study. There was a suggestion that younger people (in life stages such as students, early career, parents with young families) tended to have some more sceptical approaches to the paranormal in popular culture, although they could hold personal beliefs in the paranormal. Younger adults tended to like more psychological or pseudo-science themed television programmes, films or websites, such as Derren Brown events, the American drama series *Fringe*, or websites such as badpsychics.com. The interviews also suggested older people (in life stages such as parents with teenagers, mid or late career, semi-retirement) tended to have more personal beliefs in the paranormal, although they were similarly sceptical of the representation of the paranormal in popular culture. Older adults tended to like paranormal drama or reality ghost hunting TV such as *Ghost Whisperer*, or *Most Haunted*, or websites such as Ghostsamongus.

Gender was also an issue, with a general approach by participants that combined both scepticism and belief in the paranormal, but was framed and understood somewhat differently by men and women. Thus, an emergent theme was that males were more sceptical of the paranormal than females (by their own definition), preferring to discuss pseudo-scientific approaches and the use of electrical equipment for ghost hunting, or to rule out paranormal phenomena entirely on the basis of a lack of evidence. However, this did not mean to say that males did not believe in the possibility of the paranormal, but that they framed their scepticism and belief in relation to pseudo-science or parapsychology, and its focus on phenomena such as telepathy. An emergent theme for females was that they were more believing of the paranormal than men (by their own definition), preferring to discuss psychic energy and intuition, and the significance of instinct and openness to paranormal phenomena rather than scientific proof, or an absence of this. However, this did not mean to say females were uncritical of the paranormal, but that they framed their scepticism and belief in relation to personal, emotional and spiritual matters. A point of connection was that males and females relied on personal experience as the ultimate proof of the paranormal rather than professional testimonials or pseudo scientific tests.

The sample for the focus groups included 99 participants. There were 16 semi-structured focus groups. In addition there were two group interviews with five people, which followed the structure of the focus groups. The total sample was 104. The breakdown for the sample was as follows, based on a self-completion questionnaire administered during the interviews. Over half the sample (56 people) were aged 18–34 years old and the rest (48) were aged 35–65+ (seven were retired and aged over 65). Occupations ranged from students, artists, dancers, gardeners, construction workers, care workers, nurses, teachers, consultants, book sellers, administrators, electricians, estate agents, police and security workers, people who worked in the media, music, IT and retail professions, and those retired or semi-retired. Most participants received an annual income in the region of £15–25,000 (34 people), or less than £15,000 (48, mostly students, housewives and retired or semi-retired), with 22 people earning more than £25,000 a year. The majority of participants were British (81), with six British Asians, four Irish, three mixed race, two Australians, two Malaysians, two South Africans, and one person from the West Indies, Italy, Greece and France (all self-defined).

More females than males attended the focus groups, with 74 women and 30 men. This follows the general sense amongst professionals in the paranormal industry, and polls data, that there is a 70–30 split in favour of women and attitudes and beliefs in the paranormal. Some suggest the gender division is more likely 60–40. The sample was designed for mixed-gender focus groups, although fulfilling the quota of men in each group was a challenge and there were more women than men in all the groups. Five of the focus groups were all female, which was mainly a result of the gatekeeper for these groups and their circle of friends. Most of the groups were held at a central London location, but a few were conducted in the homes of gatekeepers in the South East region who had brought together family and friends for the evening. Based on the results of the household in-depth interviews it was possible to group people roughly into two age groups (18–34 and 35–65+). There were exceptions within groups, for example a retired man loved Derren Brown and hated *Most Haunted*, but this clustering of preferences for different themed fiction and non-fiction entertainment worked well in the focus groups overall.

This was a fit for purpose sample using snowball sampling techniques. There was a filter questionnaire conducted by telephone used to ensure a range of people with different attitudes and beliefs towards the paranormal in popular culture.

An inspiration for a spectrum of attitudes and beliefs came from the ITC research *Beyond Entertainment* on psychic and occult television. The research design included a sample of a 'range of people with different attitudes and beliefs towards psychic and occult phenomena' (Sancho 2001: 8). In the qualitative study consisting of in-depth focus groups they categorised the respondents as 'vulnerables' ('those who had experienced a significant life-changing event in the past 12 months'), 'acceptors' ('interest in alternative religious practices, or experience of alternative therapy'), 'rational rejecters' ('disbelief in an afterlife and dislike of thoughts and ideas for which there is no concrete proof'), 'frightened rejecters' ('afraid of things like Ouija board, tarot and clairvoyants'), 'don't knows' ('said that they did not know enough about alternative practices to make a judgement or have an opinion'), and 'experts' ('energy healer, spiritual healer, diocese exorcists, homeopath, parapsychologist academic, psychiatric social workers').

The focus group sample clustered people who defined themselves as moderate sceptics and/or believers, and people who didn't know one way or another about paranormal phenomena. It excluded people who had experienced a recent death or trauma in their lives in the past year. It should be said that people who believed in paranormal phenomena of some kind tended to have been through a personal experience which was thought to be life changing by the experient. Such a finding is also reflected in other studies in psychology on anomalous identity experiences. Thus some participants perceived themselves as having a life-changing experience involving paranormal phenomena. Those with strong attitudes and beliefs for or against the paranormal were interviewed separately in a one-to-one setting (five people). Also experts and professionals were part of individual interviews and included two psychologists, two parapsychologists, one clinical psychologist, two mediums, and two sensitives.

Other factors thought to be relevant to attitudes and beliefs in paranormal phenomena are related to clinical studies in psychology and include fantasy proneness, emotionality, hypnotic susceptibility, amongst others. Such factors were not included in the sample design because this was a media research project. However, the emotionality of attitudes and beliefs in the paranormal is a major theme of this book and a finding of the qualitative data. Whether people who have an emotionally high register (according to clinical studies) tend to believe more in the paranormal or not is open to debate. Participants themselves characterised women as more open to the paranormal than men, and this was often a humorous way of discussing different approaches to scepticism and belief in general. Participants thought many aspects of the paranormal in popular culture were about emotions and sensations and this suggests it is an area that has been shaped by and continues to shape emotional and sensory engagement in personal experiences.

Question design

The semi-structured questions for the household interviews and focus groups were the same. The pilot showed how clustering the questions around four themes worked well with a range of people with different attitudes and beliefs to paranormal phenomena. The themes included paranormal investigations on television and in other media, magic and issues of scepticism, personal attitudes and beliefs in the paranormal, and approaches to the paranormal in general. The question design went from the specific to the more general. Clips were used to prompt discussion when necessary. There was time for open discussion and for new questions as appropriate to the nature of each group and the direction of the discussion.

Introduction

This is a project about why people believe in ghosts and other things you can't explain. I am doing a study on this and will be writing a book on the topic next year. We want to find out everything we can about ghosts and the paranormal on TV, film, the web, and in everyday life. There is no right or wrong answer, what you say will be confidential and we thank you for talking to us.

I Psychic Investigations

Show clip from *Most Haunted*

What do you think to this?

Follow-up questions on: the medium, the presenter, the camera crew, audiences at home.

Have you seen anything like this before?

On TV, the web ... probe representations of ghosts and psychic investigations in general.

2 Illusionism

Show clip from *Derren Brown*

What do you think to this?

Follow-up on questions on: Derren Brown, the participants, the television series, audiences at home.

Have you seen anything like this before? On TV, the web ...

Probe representations of magic and illusionism in general.

3 Beliefs

Have you ever had an experience you can't explain?

Probe ghosts, afterlife, outer body experiences, paranormal activities.

Has anyone you know had an experience they can't explain?

Do you think people can communicate with ghosts?

Probe the two examples from Most Haunted and Derren Brown on real and fake communication with ghosts.

Would you like to be able to get in touch with ghosts?

Probe belief in the afterlife, paranormal experiences, something else out there, feelings ...

4 Paranormal

Open question, prompt as necessary ...

What evidence would you say could prove the existence of the paranormal. Does this matter to you?

Probe instincts, they feel there is nothing out there, there is something else out there, unexplained phenomena ...

Probe scientific proof, hard evidence of ghosts, photos, film, sounds, touch, smell, room temperature dropping, historical facts ...

What do you think are the reasons people believe?

Probe beliefs, evidence, trauma, bereavement.

Probe links with other things we might believe in but have no proof for, from fortune telling, to alternative medicine, to UFOs, to religious beliefs.

Participant observation

A pilot took place at one rural location with an amateur ghost hunting group. Two researchers were at the event, the author and Dr Lizzie Jackson. We observed and participated in the entire event, interviewing, filming, photographing, watching, listening and physically responding to the series of activities throughout the night. We both kept notes and discussed the evening together, comparing data and observations. Audio interviews were conducted on the spot with the team leaders and participants on the ghost hunt.

Two ghost hunting events were selected for the main data. London Paranormal organised both events and were chosen as a reputable company with a regular series of events in the London area. Both researchers were welcomed by the team, and the author conducted several interviews with the owner at separate times from the events. The two events took place at indoor venues, Clerkenwell, and London Dungeon, during May and June of 2007. The same approach was adopted from the pilot, with both of the researchers splitting up into different groups out of a large group of 40 people at each event. The data included film, photographs, audio recordings, field notes over a six-hour event. After both events the researchers compared observations and data and discussed emergent findings. The author also discussed issues with the owner of London Paranormal and the main organiser at both of these events, and a draft of the chapter on these data was sent to them for comment. The richness of the experience and comments from people at the events and by the organisers had a significant impact on understanding the importance of personal experience and how this relates to understanding the paranormal in popular culture.

Data analysis

The main data analysis involved an immersion in the audio recordings, field notes, photographs and moving image data looking for repetition and differences amongst respondents and across themes. The focus groups and individual interviews were fully transcribed. The data were organised both as standalone interviews or notes from the specific time of the data collection to cross-sections of data that worked in emergent themes. The specificity of the data and respondents and its relevance in a more general sense to emergent themes was a constant approach used throughout the data analysis period. The validity of the data was examined in relation to its self-contained sample and also to other relevant data samples in other areas of research. The reliability of the data was examined in relation to repetition and difference within and across the various data sets.

Data were returned to again and again for reading, re-reading, and multiple points of interpretation. The data were coded and recoded over a period of one year alongside the writing of this book. This process of thinking allowed for themes to emerge and be checked in relation to the data and relevant social and cultural theories and research in related areas. The themes included a combination of scepticism and belief by people, issues of evidence and authenticity, emotional and sensual engagement, issues of celebrity status and professional mediums or spiritual leaders, the ordinary and extraordinary as discursive strategies in personal experiences, the importance of personal experiences in paranormal attitudes and beliefs, the issue of popular psychology and the power of the mind, consumer and lifestyle practices and mind, body and spirit practices, and participation in cultural experiences associated with the paranormal in popular culture. These themes have been explored and analysed in various ways using a combination of approaches from disciplines in sociology, media, communication and cultural studies, psychology, cultural geography, and media and religion. Various experts in these areas have kindly offered comments and advice on draft chapters to ensure a basic understanding of ideas and theories in a range of disciplines. Wherever possible data have been used to extend and strengthen understanding of ideas on the paranormal in popular culture. One of the hardest aspects of the data analysis was leaving out so many wonderful accounts and insights by the people in this study.

References

Abercrombie, Nicholas and Longhurst, Brian. (1998) *Audiences: a Sociological Theory of Performance and Imagination*, London: Sage.

Ackerman, Diane. (1995) *A Natural History of the Senses*, London: Vintage Books.

Adare, Lord. (1869) *Experiences in Spiritualism with D.D. Home*, private publication, reprinted by the Society for Psychical Research, London, 1924.

Allen, Robert C. (1985) *Speaking of Soap Operas*, Chapel Hill, NC: North Carolina University Press.

Allen, Robert C. (1991) *Horrible Prettiness: Burlesque and American Culture*, Chapel Hill, NC: UNC University Press.

Allen, Robert C. (2008) 'Going to the Show' conference paper ECREA, November 2008, University of Barcelona. Also see 'Going to the Show' history of moviegoing project at official website www.docsouth.unc.edu/gtts. Accessed 14 December 2009.

Ang, Ien. (1985) *Watching Dallas: Soap Opera and the Melodramatic Imagination*, New York and London: Methuen.

Atherton, John Michael. (2007) 'Philosophy outdoors: first person physical' in McNamee, Mike, J. (ed.) *Philosophy, Risk and Adventure Sports*, London: Routledge: 43–55.

Atkinson, Kate. (2008) *When Will There Be Good News*, London: Random House.

Barker, Martin. (2007) 'The field of audience research', keynote speech at 'Transforming Audiences' conference, September 2007, University of Westminster.

Barnes, Annette. (1998) *Seeing Through Self-deception*, Cambridge: Cambridge University Press.

Barnes, Julian. (2008) *Nothing to Be Frightened Of*, London: Jonathan Cape.

Barrett, William Fletcher. (1882) 'On some phenomena associated with abnormal conditions of mind' (revised paper of 1876) in *Proceedings of the Society for Psychical Research* 1: 238–44.

Bauman, Zigmunt. (2000) *Liquid Modernity*, Cambridge: Polity Press.

Berger, Peter, L., Sacks, Jonathon, Martin, David, Weiming, Tu, Weigel, George, Davie, Grace, Naim and Ahmed Allah Abd (eds.) (1999) *The Desecularisation of the World: Resurgent Religion and World Politics*, Grand Rapids, MI: Wm. B. Eerdmans.

Berger. Peter, L. (1990) *The Sacred Canopy: Elements of a Sociological Theory of Religion*, New York: Anchor.

Bird, Elizabeth. (2003) *The Audience in Everyday Life*, London: Routledge.

Blum, Deborah. (2007) *Ghost Hunters: the Victorians and the Hunt for Proof of Life After Death*, London: Arrow Books.

Bonner, Frances. (2003) *Ordinary Television*, London: Sage.

Bourke, Joanna. (2005) *Fear: A Cultural History*, London: Virago Press.

Briggs, Asa and Burke, Peter. (2006) *A Social History of the Media: from Gutenberg to the Internet*, Cambridge: Polity.

Brooker, Will and Jermyn, Deborah (2002) *The Audience Studies Reader*, London: Routledge.

Brown, Derren. (2006) *Tricks of the Mind*, London: Channel Four Books.

Burke, Peter. (2009) *Popular Culture in Early Modern Europe*, third edition, London: Ashgate.

Burleigh, Michael. (2006) *Sacred Causes: Religion and Politics from the European Dictators to Al Qaeda*, London: Harper Perennial.

Butsch, Richard. (2008) *The Citizen Audience: Crowds, Publics and Individuals*, London and New York: Routledge.

Calhoon, Craig and Sennett, Richard. (eds.) (2007) *Practising Culture*, London: Routledge.

Cardeña, Etzel, Lynn, Steven, Jay and Krippner, Stanley (eds.) (2000) *Varieties of Anomalous Experience: Examining the Scientific Evidence*, Washington: American Psychological Association.

Cardeña, Etzel, Terhune, Devin, B., Lööf, Angelica and Buratti, Sandra. (2009) 'Hypnotic Experience is Related to Emotional Contagion', *International Journal of Clinical and Experimental Hypnosis*, 57 (1): 33–46.

Classen, Constance. (1993) *Worlds of Sense: Exploring the Senses in History and Across Cultures*, London: Routledge.

Collins, Jo and Jervis, John. (2008) *Uncanny Modernity: Cultural Theories, Modern Anxieties*, London: Palgrave Macmillan.

Cook, James, W. (2001) *The Arts of Deception: Playing with Fraud in the Age of Barnum*, Cambridge, MA: Harvard University Press.

Corner, John. (2009) 'Photography' presentation at Digicult conference 'Television and the Public Sphere', University of Bergen, Norway and University of Paris, Paris, France, 22–24 October 2008.

Corner, John. (2007) 'Epilogue: Sense and Perspective', *European Journal of Cultural Studies*, 10: 135–40.

Corner, John and Pels, Dick (eds.) (2003) *Media and the Restyling of Politics*, London: Sage.

Couldry, Nick, Livingstone, Sonia and Markham, Tim. (2007) *Media Consumption and Public Engagement: Beyond the Presumption of Attention*, Basingstoke and New York: Palgrave Macmillan.

Cubitt, Geoffrey. (2008) *History and Memory*, Manchester: Manchester University Press.

Dahlgren, Peter. (2009) *Media and Political Engagement: Citizens, Communication and Democracy*, Cambridge: Cambridge University Press.

Dayan, Daniel. (2005) 'Mothers, Midwives and Abortionists: Genealogy, Obstetrics, Audiences and Publics' in Livingstone, S. (ed.) *Audiences and Publics: When Cultural Engagement Matters for the Public Sphere*, Bristol: Intellect Books: 43–76.

Davies, Owen. (2007) *The Haunted: A Social History of Ghosts*, London: Palgrave Macmillan.

Dawkins, Richard. (2006) *The God Delusion*, London: Black Swan.

De Certeau, Michel, Giard, Luce and Mayol, Pierre (1998) *The Practice of Everyday Life*, Volume 2: Living and Cooking, Minneapolis, MN: University of Minnesota Press.

De Groot, Jerome. (2009) *Consuming History: Historians and Heritage in Contemporary Popular Culture*, London: Routledge.

Durham Peters, John. (1999) *Speaking into the Air*, Chicago, IL: University of Chicago Press.

Durkheim, Émile. (1912, 2001 reprint) *The Elementary Forms of Religious Life*, Oxford: Oxford University Press.

During, Simon. (2002) *Modern Enchantments: the Cultural Power of Secular Magic*, Cambridge, MA: Harvard University Press.

Edensor, Tim. (2008) 'Mundane Hauntings: Commuting Through the Phantasmagoric Working Class Spaces of Manchester, England', *Cultural Geographies*, 15: 313–33.

Ekirch, A. Roger. (2005) *At Day's Close: A History of Nighttime*, London: Orion Books.

Ellis, John. (2005) 'Documentary and Truth on Television: the Crisis of 1999' in Rosenthal, A. and Corner, J. (eds.) *New Challenges for Documentary*, second edition, Manchester: Manchester University Press: 342–62.

Ellis, John. (2009) 'Sceptics' presentation at Digicult conference 'Television and the Public Sphere', University of Bergen, Norway and University of Paris, France, 22–24 October 2008.

Ferris, Alison. (2003) 'Disembodied Spirits: Spirit Photography and Rachel Whiteread's Ghost', *Art Journal*, Vol 62, 2003: 1–5.

Frazier, Kendrik (ed.) (1986) *Science Confronts the Paranormal*, Buffalo, NY: Prometheus Books.

French, Christopher and Wilson, Krissy. (2006) 'Incredible Memories: How Accurate are Reports of Anomalous Events?', *European Journal of Parapsychology*, Vol 21, 2: 166–81.

Fry, Colin. (2007) *Life Before Death*, London: Rider, Random House.

Gauchet, Marcel. (1997) *The Disenchantment of the World: A Political History of Religion*, Princeton, NJ: Princeton University Press.

Gauntlett, David and Hill, Annette (1999) *TV Living: Television, Culture and Everyday Life*, London: Routledge.

Gauntlett, David. (2007) *Creative Explorations: New Approaches to Audiences and Identities*, London: Routledge.

Geraghty, Christine. (2000, reprint 2007) 'Re-examining Stardom: Questions of Texts, Bodies and Performance' in Redmond, S. and Holmes, S. (eds.) *Stardom and Celebrity: a Reader*, London: Sage: 98–110.

Giddens, Anthony. (1991) *Modernity and Self Identity: Self and Society in the Late Modern Age*, Cambridge: Polity.

Gill, Rosalind. (2007) *Gender and the Media*, London: Routledge.

Goffman, Erving (1959) *The Presentation of the Self in Everyday Life*, New York and London: Anchor.

Goldacre, Ben. (2008) *Bad Science*, London: HarperCollins.

Goode, Erich. (1999) *Paranormal Beliefs: A Sociological Introduction*, Prospect Heights, IL: Waveland Press Inc.

Gordon, Avery. (1997) *Ghostly Matters: Hauntings and the Sociological Imagination*, Minneapolis, MN: University of Minnesota Press.

Gregg, Melissa. (2007) 'The Importance of Being Ordinary', *International Journal of Cultural Studies*, 10: 95–104.

Gunning, Tom. (1995) 'Phantom Images and Modern Manifestations: Spirit Photography, Magic Theater, Trick Films, and Photography's Uncanny' in Patrice Petro (ed.) *Fugitive Images: From Photography to Video*, Bloomington, IN: Indiana University Press: 42–68.

Hall, Stuart. (1981) 'Notes on Deconstructing the Popular' in Samuel, R. (ed.) *People's History and Socialist Theory*, London: Routledge: 239.

Harvey, John. (2007) *Photography and Spirit*, London: Reaktion Books.

Heaney, Seamus. (1979) *Fieldwork*, London: Faber and Faber.

Heaney, Seamus. (1991) *Seeing Things*, London: Faber and Faber.

Hermes, Joke. (2005) *Re-reading Popular Culture*, London: Blackwells.

Hess, David, J. (1994) 'Parallel Universes: Anthropology in the World of Technoscience', *Anthropology Today*, Vol 10, No 2: 16–18.

Hess, David. (1993) *Science in the New Age: The Paranormal, Its Defenders and Debunkers, and American Culture*, Madison, WI: University of Wisconsin Press.

Hey, Graham. (2009) 'Paul Stockman: from Drummer to Mentalist on a Roll', *Magicseen*, Vol 5, No 4: 12–15.

Hill, Annette. (2005) *Reality TV: Audiences and Popular Factual Television*, London: Routledge.

Hill, Annette. (2007) *Restyling Factual TV: Audiences and News, Documentary and Reality Genres*, London: Routledge.

Hills, Matt. (2005) *The Pleasures of Horror*, London and New York: Continuum.

Hjarvard, Stig. (2008) 'The Mediatization of Religion: A Theory of the Media as Agents of Religious Change', in *Northern Lights, Vol 6, Issue 1: The Mediatisation of Religion: Enchantment, Media and Popular Culture*, London: Intellect.

Hobson, Dorothy. (1982) *Crossroads: the Drama of a Soap Opera*, London: Methuen.

Holloway, Julian and Kneale, James. (2008) 'Locating Haunting: a Ghost-hunter's Guide', *Cultural Geographies*, 15: 297–312.

Home, Daniel, Dunglas. (1863) *Incidents in My Life*, London: Pitman.

Home, Daniel, Dunglas. (1877) *Lights and Shadows of Spiritualism*, first published in London: Virtue and Co, republished by Kessinger Publishing 2004.

Hoover, Stuart. (2006) *Religion in the Media Age*, New York: Routledge.

Hoover, Stuart. (2007) 'Afterward' in Schofield Clark, Lynn (ed.) *Religion, Media, and the Marketplace*, New Brunswick, NJ: Rutgers University Press.

Irwin, Harvey, J. and Watt, Caroline. (2007) *An Introduction to Parapsychology*, fifth edition, Jefferson, NC: McFarland.

Irwin, Jarvey, J. (2009) *The Psychology of Paranormal Belief: A Researcher's Handbook*, Hertfordshire: University of Hertfordshire Press.

James, William. (1890) *The Principles of Psychology*, two volumes, New York: Henry Holt, republished New York: Cosimo 2007.

James, William. (1896) 'The Will to Believe' address to the Philosophical Clubs of Yale and Brown Universities (published in the *New World*, June 1896).

James, William. (1909) 'The Confidences of a Psychical Researcher', *American Magazine*, 68: 580–89.

Jansson, André and Lagerqvist, Amanda (eds.) (2009) *Strange Spaces: Explorations into Mediated Obscurity*, Oxon: Ashgate.

Jirasek, Ivo. (2007) 'Extreme Sports and the Ontology of Experience' in McNamee, Mike, J. (ed.) *Philosophy, Risk and Adventure Sports*, London: Routledge: 138–40.

Jolly, Martin. (2006) *Faces of the Living Dead: The Belief in Spirit Photography*, London: British Library.

Jones, Caroline A. and Arning, Bill. (2006) *Sensorium: Embodied Experience, Technology, and Contemporary Art*, Cambridge, MA: MIT Press.

Kaplan, Louis. (2008) *The Strange Case of William Mumler Spirit Photographer*, Minneapolis, MN: University of Minnesota Press.

Kieve, Paul. (2007) *Hocus Pocus*, London: Bloomsbury.

Karl, Jason. (2007) *21st Century Ghosts: Encounters with Ghosts in the New Millennium*, London: New Holland Publishers.

Kellehear, Allan. (2007) *A Social History of Dying*, Cambridge: Cambridge University Press.

Kilborn, Richard. (2003) *Staging Reality*, Manchester: Manchester University Press.

Klenk, Rebecca. (2004) 'Seeing Ghosts', *Ethnography*, 5 (2): 229–46.

Kovacs, Lee. (2006) *The Haunted Screen: Ghosts in Literature and Film*, London: McFarland and Company.

Krimsky, S. and Golding, D. (eds) (1992) *Social Theories of Risk*, Westport, CT: Praeger.

Kurtz, Paul. (1986) 'Debunking, Neutrality and Skepticism in Science' in Frazier, K. (ed.) *Science Confronts the Paranormal*, Buffalo, NY: Prometheus Books.

Lamont, Peter and Wiseman, Richard. (1999) *Magic in Theory*, Hertfordshire: University of Hertfordshire Press.

Lamont, Peter and Bates, Crispin. (2007) 'Conjuring Images of India in Nineteenth Century Britain', *Social History*, Vol 32, No 3: 308–24.

Lamont, Peter. (2005) *The First Psychic: the Peculiar Mystery of a Notorious Victorian Wizard*, London: Abacus.

Lamont, Peter. (2006) 'Magician as Conjuror: a Frame Analysis of Victorian Mediums', *Early Popular Visual Culture*, Vol 4, No 1: 21–33.

Lamont, Peter. (2007) 'Paranormal Belief and the Avowal of Prior Scepticism', *Theory and Psychology*, Vol 17 (5): 681–96.

Landy, Joshua and Saler, Michael (eds.) (2009) *The Re-Enchantment of the World: Secular Magic in a Rational Age*, Stanford, CA: Stanford University Press.

Le Bon, Gustave. (1875, 1960) *The Crowd*, New York: Viking Press.

Leeder, Murray. (2010) 'M. Robert-Houdin Goes to Algeria: Spectatorship and Panic in Illusion and Early Cinema', *Early Popular Visual Culture*, Vol 8, No 2: 209–25.

Lennon, John, J. and Foley, Malcolm. (2000) *Dark Tourism: the Attraction of Death and Disaster*, London: Continuum.

Little, William. (2009) *The Psychic Tourist: a Voyage into the Curious World of Predicting the Future*, London: Icon Books.

Livingstone, Sonia and Lunt, Peter. (1994) *Talk on Television: Audience Participation and Public Debate*, London: Routledge.

Livingstone, Sonia, Van Couvering, Elizabeth and Thumim, Nancy. (2005) *Adult Media Literacy: A Review of the Research Literature*. Report commissioned by the Office of Communication, London.

Livingstone, Sonia. (2005) 'On the Relation between Audiences and Publics' in Livingstone, S. (ed.) *Audiences and Publics: When Cultural Engagement Matters for the Public Sphere*, Bristol: Intellect Books: 17–42.

Lull, James. (1990) *Inside Family Viewing: Ethnographic Research on Television Audiences*, London: Routledge.

Lunt, Peter. (2009) *Stanley Milgram: Understanding Obedience and its Implications*, London: Palgrave Macmillan.

Lunt, Peter and Stenner, Paul. (2005) '*The Jerry Springer Show* as Emotional Public Sphere', *Media, Culture and Society*, Vol 27, No 1: 59–81.

Lynch, Gordon. (2007) *New Spirituality: An Introduction to Belief Beyond Religion*, London: I B Taurus.

Mantel, Hilary. (2005) *Beyond Black*, London: Harper Perennial.

Mantel, Hilary. (2006) 'Magical thinking: Hilary Mantel studies the self-deprecating master of debunking: *Tricks of the Mind* by Derren Brown', Saturday Review, Cultural Studies, the *Guardian*, 16 December 2006: 3.

Marks, Laura. (2002) *Touch: Sensuous Theory and Multisensory Media*, Minneapolis, MN: University of Minnesota Press.

Marks, Lawrence, E. (2000) 'Synesthesia' in Cardeña, Etzel, Lynn, Steven, Jay and Krippner, Stanley (eds.) *Varieties of Anomalous Experience: Examining the Scientific Evidence*, Washington: American Psychological Association: 121–50.

Martin, Andrew. (2009) *Ghoul Britannia: Notes from a Haunted Isle*, London: Short Books Ltd.

Mauss, Marcel. (reprint 2007) *A General Theory of Magic*, London: Routledge.

McArthy, Anna (2001) *Ambient Television*, Durham and London: Duke University Press.

McGrath, Patrick. (2005) *Ghost Town: Tales of Manhattan Then and Now*, London: Bloomsbury.

McKusick, Marshall. (1982) 'Psychic Archeology: Theory, Method and Mythology', *Journal of Field Archeology*, Vol 9, No 1: 99–118.

Melechi, Antonio. (2008) *Servants of the Supernatural: The Night Side of the Victorian Mind*, London: William Heinemann.

Mills, Antonia and Lynn, Steven Jay. (2000) 'Past-life Experiences' in Cardeña, Etzel, Lynn, Steven, Jay and Krippner, Stanley (eds.) *Varieties of Anomalous Experience: Examining the Scientific Evidence*, Washington: American Psychological Association: 283–313.

Morley, David. (1986) *Family Television: Cultural Power and Domestic Leisure*, London: Routledge.

Murdoch, Graham. (2008) 'Re-enchantment and the Popular Imagination: Fate, Magic and Purity', in *Northern Lights, Vol 6, Issue 1: The Mediatisation of Religion: Enchantment, Media and Popular Culture*, London: Intellect.

Nead, Linda. (2008) *The Haunted Gallery*, New Haven, CT: Yale University Press.

Northcote, Jeremy. (2007) *The Paranormal and the Politics of Truth: A Sociological Account*, Charlottesville, VA: Imprint Academic.

O'Keefe, Ciaran and Wiseman, Richard. (2005) 'Testing Alleged Mediumship: Methods and Results', *British Journal of Psychology*, 96: 165–79.

O'Keefe, Daniel. (1982) *Stolen Lightening: the Social Theory of Magic*, New York: Continuum.

Pew Forum (2008) Report 'Religion and Public Life', London.

Picardie, Justine. (2001) *If the Spirit Moves you*, Oxford: Picador.

Pile, Steve. (2005) *Real Cities: Modernity, Space and the Phantasmagorias of City Life*, London: Sage.

Pringle, Trish. (2002) 'The Space of Stage Magic', *Space and Culture*, Vol 5, No 4: 333–45.

Redmond, Sean and Holmes, Su (eds.) (2007) *Stardom and Celebrity: a Reader*, London: Sage.

Ronson, Jon. (2004) *The Men Who Stare at Goats*, London and New York: Simon & Schuster.

Ruffles, Tom. (2004) *Ghost Images: Cinema of the Afterlife*, North Carolina and London: McFarland & Company.

Saler, Michael. (2006) 'Modernity and Enchantment: A Historiographic Review', *The American Historical Review*, June: 616–702.

Sancho, Jane. (2001) *'Beyond Entertainment?: Research into the Acceptability of Alternative Beliefs, Psychic and Occult Phenomena on Television'*, London: Independent Television Commission and Broadcasting Standards Commission publication.

Santino, Jack. (1988) 'Occupational Ghostlore: Social Context and the Expression of Belief', *The Journal of American Folklore*, Vol 101, No 400: 207–18.

Sassoon, Donald. (2006) *The Culture of the Europeans: From 1800 to Present*, London: Harper Press.

Scannell, Paddy. (2007) *Media and Communication*, London: Sage.

Schofield Clark, Lynn. (2003) *From Angels to Aliens: Teenagers, the Media, and the Supernatural*, New York: OUP.

Schofield Clark, Lynn. (2007) *Religion, Media, and the Marketplace*, Piscataway, NJ: Rutgers University Press.

Sconce, Jeffrey. (2000) *Haunted Media*, Durham: Duke University Press.

Sheller, Mimi and Urry, John. (2004) *Tourism Mobilities: Places to Play, Places in Play*, London, Routledge.

Sidis, Boris. (1899) *The Psychology of Suggestion*, New York: D. Appleton.

Silverstone, Roger (1994) *Television and Everyday Life*, London: Routledge.

Singer, Philip. (1990) 'Psychic Surgery: Close Observation of a Popular Healing Practice', *Medical Anthropology Quarterly*, New Series Vol 4, No 4: 443–51.

Sjöjin, Ulf. (2002) 'The Swedes and the Paranormal', *Journal of Contemporary Religion*, Vol 17, No 1: 75–85.

Smith, Gordon. (2007) *Life Changing Messages*, London and California: Hay Publishing.

Social Trends. (2008) *Annual Report*, National Statistics, published online at www.statistics.gov.uk/socialtrends38. Accessed 16 November 2008.

Spooner, Catherine. (2006) *Contemporary Gothic*, London: Reaktion Books.

Standage, Tom. (1998) *The Victorian Internet*, New York: Walker.

Steinmeyer, Jim. (2003) *Hiding the Elephant: How Magicians Invented the Impossible*, London: Arrow Books.

Stockwell, Tony. (2004) *Spirited*, London: Hodder and Stoughton.

Stockwell, Tony. (2007) *The Psychic Case Files*, London: Hodder and Stoughton.

Sutcliffe, Steven. (2003) *Children of the New Age: a History of Spiritual Practices*, London: Routledge.

Tanner, Amy. (1910) *Studies in Spiritism*, New York and London: D Appleton, reprint 2010, Nabu Press.

Targ, Elizabeth, Schlitz, Marilyn and Irwin, Harvey, J. (2000) 'Psi-related Experiences' in Cardeña, Etzel, Lynn, Steven, Jay and Krippner, Stanley (eds.) *Varieties of Anomalous Experience: Examining the Scientific Evidence*, Washington: American Psychological Association: 219–52.

Thomas, Keith. (1971) *Religion and the Decline of Magic: Studies in Popular Beliefs in Sixteenth and Seventeenth Century England*, Oxford: Oxford University Press.

Thussu, Daya. (2007) *News as Infotainment*, London: Routledge.

Treitel, Corinna. (2004) *A Science for the Soul: Occultism and the Genesis of the German Modern*, Baltimore, MD: John Hopkins University Press.

Turner, Graeme. (2004) *Understanding Celebrity*, London: Sage.

Turner, Victor. (1988) *The Anthropology of Performance*, New York: PAJ Publications.

Urry, John. (2002) *The Tourist Gaze*, second edition, London: Sage.

Warner, Marina. (2006) *Phantasmagoria: Spirit Visions, Metaphors, and Media into the Twenty-first Century*, Oxford: Oxford University Press.

Waterhouse, Rosie. (2008) 'Weird … or What', *Guardian Education*, Tuesday, 14 October 2008: 8.

Watt, Caroline and Wiseman, Richard. (2009) 'Forward' in Irwin, Jarvey, J. (ed.) *The Psychology of Paranormal Belief: A Researcher's Handbook*, Hertfordshire: University of Hertfordshire Press: vii–viii.

Weber, Max. (1922) 'The Nature of Charismatic Domination' reprinted in Redmond, S. and Holmes, S. (eds. 2007) *Stardom and Celebrity: a Reader*, London: Sage: 17–24.

Welchman, Jennifer. (2006) 'William James, the will to believe and the ethics of self experimentation', *Transactions of the Charles Pierce Society*, Vol 42, No 2: 229–41.

Williams, Carl. (1996) 'Metaphor, Parapsychology and Psi: an Examination of Metaphors Related to Paranormal Experience and Parapsychological Research', *Journal of the American Society for Psychical Research*, Vol 90: 174–201.

Williams, Raymond (Higgins, John, ed.) (2001) *The Raymond Williams Reader*, London: Wiley Blackwell.

Williams, Raymond. (1974) *Television, Technology and Cultural Form*, Technosphere series, London: Collins.

Williams, Raymond. (1977) *Marxism and Literature*, Oxford: Oxford University Press.

Winston, Brian. (1995) *Claiming the Real: the Documentary Film Revisited*, London: British Film Institute.

Winston, Brian. (2001) *Lies, Damn Lies and Documentaries*, London: British Film Institute.

Winston, Brian. (2005) *Messages: Free Expression, Media and the West from Gutenberg to Google*, London: Routledge.

Wiseman, Richard and Watt, Caroline. (2006) 'Belief in Psychic Ability and the Misattribution Hypothesis: a Qualitative Review', *The British Journal of Psychology*, 97: 323–38.

Wiseman, Richard, Watt, Caroline, Greening, Emma, Stevens, Paul and O'Keefe, Ciaran. (2002) 'An Investigation into the Alleged Haunting of Hampton Court

Palace: Psychological Variables and Magnetic Fields', *Journal of Parapsychology*, 66 (4): 387–408.

Wiseman, Richard. (1997) *Deception and Self-deception: Investigating Psychics*, New York: Prometheus Books.

Wiseman, Richard. (2007) *Quirkology: the Curious Science of Everyday Lives*, Oxford: Pan Books.

Wooffitt, R. and Allistone, S. (2005) 'Towards a Discursive Parapsychology: Language and the Laboratory Study of Anomalous Communication', *Theory and Psychology*, Vol 15, No 3: 325–55.

Wooffitt, Robin. (1992) *Telling Tales of the Unexpected: the Organisation of Factual Discourse*, Hemel Hempstead: Harvester Wheatsheaf.

Wooffitt, Robin. (2006) *The Language of Mediums and Psychics: The Social Organisation of Everyday* Miracles, Aldershot: Ashgate.

Woolfe, Richard. (2009) 1 September 2009, telephone interview.

Wulff, David, M. (2000) 'Mystical Experience' in Cardeña, Etzel, Lynn, Steven, Jay and Krippner, Stanley (eds.) *Varieties of Anomalous Experience: Examining the Scientific Evidence*, Washington: American Psychological Association: 397–440.

Ytreberg, Espen. (2004) 'Formatting Participation within Broadcast Media Production', *Media, Culture and Society*, Vol 26, No 5, 677–92.

Zelizer, Barbie. (2005) 'Finding Aids to the Past: Bearing Personal Witness to Traumatic Public Events' in Rothenbuhler, E. and Coman, M. (eds.) *Media Anthropology*, Thousand Oaks, CA: Sage.

Zelizer, Viviana. (2005) *The Purchase of Intimacy*, Princeton, NJ: Princeton University Press.

Index

053439874